SACRIFICE IN
JUDAISM, CHRISTIANITY, AND ISLAM

Sacrifice in
Judaism, Christianity, and Islam

David L. Weddle

NEW YORK UNIVERSITY PRESS

New York

NEW YORK UNIVERSITY PRESS
New York
www.nyupress.org

References to Internet websites (URLs) were accurate at the time of writing. Neither the author nor New York University Press is responsible for URLs that may have expired or changed since the manuscript was prepared.

Library of Congress Cataloging-in-Publication Data
Names: Weddle, David L. (David Leroy), 1942– author.
Title: Sacrifice in Judaism, Christianity, and Islam / David L. Weddle.
Description: New York : NYU Press, 2017. | Includes bibliographical references and index.
Identifiers: LCCN 2017003766| ISBN 9780814764916 (cl : alk. paper) | ISBN 9780814789315 (pb : alk. paper)
Subjects: LCSH: Sacrifice. | Sacrifice—Christianity. | Sacrifice—Islam. | Sacrifice—Judaism.
Classification: LCC BL570 .W43 2017 | DDC 203/.4—dc23
LC record available at https://lccn.loc.gov/2017003766

New York University Press books are printed on acid-free paper, and their binding materials are chosen for strength and durability. We strive to use environmentally responsible suppliers and materials to the greatest extent possible in publishing our books.

Manufactured in the United States of America

10 9 8 7 6 5 4 3 2 1

Also available as an ebook

For Ellyson Danielle Siebert and Nicolas Steven Siebert, our grandchildren, our hope for the future

CONTENTS

PREFACE AND ACKNOWLEDGMENTS

When someone asks me why I have spent my career reading, writing, and teaching about religion, my answer is, "It never ceases to amaze me what people will sell the farm for." That expression, of course, signifies giving up the security of productive land and family tradition to invest in a new and risky venture. In America's rural past "selling the farm" was the literal price paid by believers in western New York who skipped harvest in October 1844, awaiting the return of Christ. His advent had been predicted by William Miller (1782–1849), a farmer who spent his evenings studying prophecies in the Bible. Despite what became known among Adventists as the "Great Disappointment" when Christ failed to appear, the astounding fact is that recruitment to their new religious movement increased in the next few decades. Having sold their own farms to embrace an innovative form of Christian faith, the Adventists survived Miller's "failed prophecy" by convincing thousands of others that the problem was a minor interpretive miscalculation that did not cancel the value of their sacrifice. Perhaps to convince themselves that they were not dupes, the early Adventists eagerly sought to persuade others of the validity of their beliefs.[1]

The Adventists are one example; there are countless others. What I have come to think is that the demand for sacrifice is the most common theme in religion. After a half-century of studying religion, I am still fascinated by the cost religious people are willing to pay to confirm the meaning of their beliefs. The topic of sacrifice gets us as close to the heart of religion—to its passion and ecstasy, its nobility and degradation—as any academic investigation can. To get closer would require the violence of intimacy that practice of sacrifice entails, but this book is not intended to be a how-to manual.

At the outset, we should acknowledge that the topic raises skeptical questions. Why make sacrifice a way of life? Why must one give up possessions, time, energy, pleasures, even life itself, in pursuit of religious quests? Why must one deny natural desires in order to reach supernatural fulfillment? That critique of sacrifice finds expression in lines from the poem "Sunday Morning" by the American poet Wallace Stevens (1879–1955). Stevens pictures an insouciant lounger, skipping church to indulge the "complacencies of the peignoir." The young woman may be seen as sitting in for all those who no longer feel compelled to dedicate their time to worship. Why give up even an hour of the weekend in anachronistic gestures of self-denial, faint traces of ancient sacrifice? Perhaps her forbears once relinquished their ease, after a week of hard work, to extend their labor by performing "services" for God. Now, many people hardly see the point of weekly *liturgy*, literally "work," in voluntary servitude. At the very least, attendance at a church or synagogue, temple or mosque, requires forfeiture of time: a portion of one's history that can never be reclaimed and is, in that sense, priceless.

Stevens imagines a young woman unwilling to pay that price; she is confident that a Sunday morning is better spent enjoying sensual pleasures. Secure in quiet clarity and relative comfort, she remains indifferent to the mystery and pain of ancient sacrifice. Its "holy hush" drawn over the altar of unspeakable suffering does not move her to faithful imitation; it rather evanesces into the steam of late coffee and the bouquet of oranges. Why, after all, should she "give her bounty to the dead"? Why should she deny herself the satisfactions of bright colors and strong tastes and the delights of a body unrestrained and redolent of the boudoir? Why should these sensate riches of nature be denied or restricted or forbidden in return for an obscure intimation of divinity in shadows and dreams?

A conventional religious response to her indulgence might be to urge her to get off her couch, give up stimulating coffee and succulent fruit, and accept the disciplined self-denial that marks the path to transcendence. But she knows that she will eventually join the pigeons, gliding downward into final darkness. So why should she not recline in the sunshine and enjoy the cockatoo's song in the meanwhile? All of us who would like nothing better than to snuggle in with her for the morning also wonder, why not? Why sacrifice?

The skeptic, perhaps including the present reader, has reason to ask why demands of the spirit require denial of the body. Why is fidelity to the transcendent always tested by betrayal of the natural? These are questions that could disturb our Sunday lay-about unless, of course, she simply waved them off as distracting curiosities and took another sip of coffee, unmoved by the awe others feel in "the holy hush of ancient sacrifice." Her complacency exposes the fragility of religion. For the one who is content to lie in the morning sun, accepting her spacious dwelling, luxuriant clothes, juicy oranges, and exotic pet, and basking with no urgent awareness of the suffering of others, the call to sacrifice can be stifled by a yawn. Satisfaction is the disarming alternative to religious passion.

Why indeed should she "give her bounty to the dead"? That is the most compelling challenge to the religious demand for sacrifice—and it is the question that haunts this book. Sages, prophets, messiahs, lawgivers, and gods all require cost of admission to their company. But what if they also glide "downward into darkness," impotent to redeem their extravagant promises of salvation? To sacrifice is the ultimate gamble—and to many, on sunny Sunday mornings, it seems not worth the bother. In light of the high cost of religion and the risk of investing in its promises, one might well wonder: *Can I be religious if I am not willing to sacrifice?* That existential question is not the direct concern of this book, but perhaps this reflection on sacrifice will help to clarify what is at stake in choosing to live a consistently religious way of life.

This book takes a broad view of sacrifice, reflecting the wide range of acts and dispositions to which religious people apply the term. Accordingly, our examples of its usage will come from many different kinds of texts: ritual, devotional, mystical, ethical, and political. Within this varied collection of religious expression, the closest we come to a common meaning of *sacrifice* is that of *giving up natural and human goods for spiritual benefits.* In this most inclusive sense, sacrifice is the cost of religion. Other scholars find this approach naïve in accepting at face value the way religious folks refer to everything from donation and fasting to mystical ecstasy and animal slaughter as "sacrificial." Scholars prefer to confine the topic by specifying elements, some of which an act must exhibit in order to be called a sacrifice, and often by restricting the term to ritual performance. This method has produced many fine studies that we will note with appreciation, but the more unruly approach of this book respects the right of religious writers to use the word *sacrifice* as they see fit to describe their ideals and practices. For, while the reigning impulse of academics is to talk, our first duty as scholars is to listen.

The debts accrued in a work of this scope are many, and these acknowledgments are a meager attempt at repayment. First, to Sharon, companion and lover for more than half a century, then to Lisa, Chad, Elly, Nic, and all our family for support and encouragement over the years in which this book took shape. To my students at Westmont College, Cornell College, and Colorado College who inspired, challenged, and taught me for more than four decades. Thanks to members of the senior seminar on sacrifice at Colorado College who may detect traces of their own ideas on these pages—and would not be mistaken! Let me also acknowledge Andrew Osterman, Sierra Fleenor, and Jack Kat Teter, who provided invaluable assistance on theory, miracles, and sacrifice respectively with the support of student-faculty collaborative research grants from Colorado College. And I extend my gratitude to Rory Stadler, who has provided expert administrative support for the past fifteen years. Gratitude also goes to Steve Lawson, humanities librarian at Colorado College, who over the years has helped me, as well as our students, with research. Thanks to the David and Lucile Packard Foundation, which funded my participation in the 2014 Oxford Symposium on Religious Studies, where I enjoyed access to the Bodleian Library, and my travel to the University of Edinburgh, where Philippa Townsend was generous in sharing her work on Gnostic texts. Thanks to Helen Blatherwick and Ni'ma Burney at the *Journal of Qur'anic Studies* at the University of London for their invitation to review recent work on Islamic sacrifice. Colleagues in the Rocky Mountain-Great Plains region of the American Academy of Religion made helpful comments on my papers as the research progressed. My gratitude to good friends Rich Ball, Sam Bleicher, Clanton Dawson, Craig Nagel, Dan Shaw, and Zach Simpson, who reviewed various aspects of this project. Finally, my thanks to Jennifer Hammer of New York University Press for her patience and help throughout the editorial process, as well as to the anonymous readers for the Press, whose critical suggestions were very helpful. The remaining errors and eccentric readings are all mine.

Introduction

In the summer of 1986 Egypt was under the political control of Hosni Mubarak, at official peace with Israel, and enjoying the benefits of being a well-rewarded ally of the United States. Tourists happily traveled the length of the country, from the pyramids on the Giza plateau outside Cairo through the tomb of Tutankhamen and the temple of Karnak at Luxor to the monumental statues at Abu Simbel near Aswan. I had arrived in Egypt as a participant in a program that funded American academics to travel and study in the Middle East, sponsored by the National Council on US-Arab Relations. After my colleagues and I spent a few weeks learning faltering phrases of Arabic and traveling around Egypt, one of them, a Benedictine nun from Kansas named Frances, invited me to attend early morning Mass with her in Cairo. I am not a member of the Catholic Church, and I knew that intentionally receiving Eucharist from a Roman Catholic priest was against the rules; but the situation was compelling and the violation irresistible. In that unlikely setting I participated in the ritual reenactment of Christ's death in the drama of the Mass *as sacrifice*. The impression was indelible.

Frances and I met Father Shea in the lobby of the Cosmopolitan Hotel. He was accompanied by a young Egyptian, named Safwot, who had just taken vows as a Jesuit priest. Safwot drove us with joyful abandon to a nondescript neighborhood off Ramses Square and stopped next to a high wall with steel doors painted green on which hung a sign in Arabic and English: Missionaries of Charity. We had found the sisters from India extending the work of Mother Teresa among the poor of Cairo. The house was old and needed constant maintenance. Yet within its confines half a dozen nuns, including one Egyptian who had "taken the vocation," cared for twenty-five enfeebled men and women, aged Arabs who had been abandoned by their families. In this culture, they were as vulnerable as if they were the outcasts of India for whose care Teresa was known as "saint of the gutters." Here her sisters, daughters really, practiced her universal love in a very different location. They had given up family, home, language, food—all the markers of their personal identities in India—to live for the poor of Egypt. In the words of St. Paul, they "counted all as loss" in order to imitate Christ in self-sacrifice.

Father Shea was in his mid-eighties and his hands trembled slightly, but he moved with determination. He had served as an educator in Baghdad for thirty-one years before Americans were expelled, and had been at the Jesuit College (equivalent to an American high school) in Cairo since 1968. On our way to the second-floor chapel he stopped to inquire about the health of one of the men sitting outside the door. The old fellow's neck pain was better. They both said, "*L'hamdullilah*," thanking God in Arabic, Christian and Muslim together. Three sisters were waiting for us upstairs; one was just seventeen. Frances went into the room ahead of me, but when I had taken two steps on the rug spread out in front of the altar, I thought to look at Safwot's feet. Quickly backing out, I left my shoes outside also. I offered to take Frances's shoes and she blushed slightly while slipping out of them.

Father Shea reappeared, his brown outer robe replaced by a green decorated mantle over his white vestment. The sisters sat on the floor, leaving the chairs to the three guests. We sang from a hymnal, without instruments. The brown young women, swathed in white robes trimmed in blue, sang softly an old psalm in English: "I will never forget you, my people." Though forsaken by all, the orphaned in the world are reassured of providential care. How deeply I was aware that these women were keeping what they believed to be God's promise to the poor. Their sacrifice confirmed the authority of the biblical words by *enacting* its assurance. In Christian terms, they were the incarnation of the Word in the daily offering of their own bodies as the "real presence" of the crucified Jesus.

The moment of supreme mystery arrived. Twenty years after the liturgical reforms of Vatican II, Father Shea still knew the Latin formulae. The old man held the chalice aloft. He kissed the wafer. He invoked the miracle: Turn these ordinary elements of life into the living flesh and blood of Jesus Christ! One of the sisters rang a bell. Its single, pure tone filled the silence. I had read about Catholic belief in the "consecration of the Host," but never had the idea become palpable, even sensual. Crumbs flew in the air as the priest broke the wafer; wine splashed in the goblet. In that instant, Christ was broken again, the sacrifice of his torn body offered to God for the sins of the world. If it has ever happened, I thought, it just happened—in the midst, and for the sake of, these sisters from India. They revisit the crucifixion each day, serving as witnesses to its reality as the women of old, and draw from it the power to reenact Christ's self-sacrifice.

The Mass that morning was in honor of Mary Magdalene, described by Father Shea as "our Lord's favorite apostle." The service included a prayer for Kateri Tekakwitha (1656–1680), a member of the Mohawk tribe, who was declared "blessed" in 1980 and named the first Native American saint by Pope Benedict XVI in 2012. Her life was marked by heroic acts of penance in sacrificial self-denial. So there I stood, next to those praying for a Mohawk woman to be advanced in life after death: Mother Teresa's sisters from India, a nun sworn to the Rule of St. Benedict, and an Irish priest with an Egyptian Jesuit assistant. At one point, Frances squeezed my hand; her eyes were shining. She no doubt carried the story back to the sisters in Kansas and they shared her delight and wonder, with renewed commitment to their own vows of obedience, poverty, and celibacy.

None of their blessed hearts would brood over how faintly the flame of their self-sacrifice shone in the raging darkness. Nor would the sisters in Cairo be troubled by the profound spiritual desolation their foundress, Mother Teresa of Calcutta, was recording in letters to her confessor. Only after her death did their publication reveal the breadth of her sacrifice and the depth of her faith in its efficacy. Her private letters recount decades of spiritual destitution in which she felt abandoned by God. Teresa described her life as a "continual immolation for souls" and insisted that her Missionaries of Charity "must be living holocausts."[1]

Religion is costly. No matter how freely sacred texts speak of love or grace, there is always a price to pay to enter the path of salvation. This book argues that the high cost is one way religions signify the immense value of their benefits and the daunting difference between ordinary existence and life lived in relation to transcendent reality. The more demanding their devotional requirements, meditative practices, and ascetic disciplines, the more confidence their followers have that the sacrifices they exact will provide forgiveness, power, purification, or enlightenment. Some argue that it is precisely such high cost that attracts many believers. Call it the "Chivas Regal effect": Like that vaunted brand of blended Scotch whisky, the more expensive an item, the more valuable consumers consider it. The social scientists, Richard Sosis and Eric Bressler, describe this marketing strategy in the practice of religious communes as "costly signaling." They argue that the more stringent the restrictions placed upon members of a group, the greater their loyalty to the community's teachings and practices.[2] As a result, the members experience to a greater degree the benefits of the community's solidarity, in turn confirming their own investment. As a result, what began as perceived value because of the cost ends in real value created by individuals' commitment to the group's ideals.

We must acknowledge, however, that approaching a religious tradition through its sacrificial practices is an interpretive method that helps us limit the field of evidence we shall consider, but also runs the risk of giving the impression that all members of a tradition, in every one of its many and diverse branches, agree on the meaning of sacrifice. As we shall see, that is certainly *not* the case. The methodological problem of this text is similar to the one I faced in my book on miracles; and my resolution there is the same position I take here, namely, that the examples in each chapter "should not be taken as representative in some general sense of the traditions from which they are drawn."[3]

There is another connection between this work and the book on miracles that deserves mention. In that earlier work I was driven to understand the persistence of faith when miracles fail: How does anyone continue to believe in transcendent reality without some sign of its presence? I discovered that each tradition generated a sub-tradition of faithful dissent to belief in miracles that provided religious reasons for denying miracles. Yet, despite my sympathy with those objections, I found myself asking: *Is a religious tradition without miraculous signs worth the bother?* My strong hunch is that it is not. But I could only confirm that suspicion by looking carefully at just how great the bother is. Thus, I turned to the examination of sacrifice as the cost exacted by religions for access to their benefits. This book is the result of that study.

This comparative study is limited to three traditions associated with the patriarch Abraham. Each has a distinct interest in Abraham: Judaism reveres him as the head of the Jewish family; Christianity admires his heroic faith; Islam honors him as the first prophet of belief in one

God. These differences, elaborated over centuries, are great enough to raise questions about the designation "Abrahamic religions" because the adjective suggests greater commonality of belief and practice than the history of these traditions demonstrates. Nevertheless, some general designation of the three traditions is useful as an expression of the hope that a basis for common respect can be established in the claim of a shared history. In inter-faith conversations, reference to "Abrahamic religions" often indicates more a desire for unanimity than a literal claim of family relation, much less a common religion. In my experience, no religious people are more aware of their differences than Jews, Christians, and Muslims involved in honest discussions about each other's faiths. Still, scholars worry that the adjectival phrase obscures deep differences in theology, ritual, and scripture among the three traditions.

Carol Bakhos, scholar of Near Eastern languages, reviews objections to the category "Abrahamic," but accepts its practical value as indicating family resemblances shared by Judaism, Christianity, and Islam that are not found in Asian religions.[4] The influential biblical scholar Jon D. Levenson appreciates the intention behind the phrase "Abrahamic religions" to promote ecumenical good will, but provides detailed evidence for the sharp and significant differences in Jewish, Christian, and Muslim constructions of Abraham in their interpretive traditions. Arguing that there is no "neutral Abraham" who exists independently of those traditions, Levenson debunks popular claims that the three religions share in monotheism originated by Abraham (Christian belief in a God of three persons seems quite different from Jewish and Islamic insistence on divine unity) and that Abraham is the father of all humanity (Genesis designates the specific lineage of Abraham through Isaac and Jacob to the Jewish people). Levenson also details particular theological and institutional claims that are simply irreconcilable, such as Christian belief that faith in Jesus as the divine savior alone makes one a child of Abraham against the Muslim claim that Islam, which rejects the deity of Christ, is "the religion of Abraham" (Qur'an 3.68) against the Jewish insistence that only descendants of Abraham belong to his family and inherit the promise to him through obedience to Torah.[5]

In light of such deep and abiding differences, in this book we will use the designation "religions of Abraham" in order to keep the plurality of the three paramount and to avoid confusing their distinct identities with the common adjective "Abrahamic." Our interest is not in broad claims to the legacy of Abraham, but in ways the three traditions preserve and pass on the specific story of Abraham's near-sacrifice of his son. Versions of the story are recorded in the Bible (Genesis 22) and the Qur'an (surah 37) and have generated volumes of commentary in all three traditions. How that story and the history of its reception have shaped the meanings of sacrifice in religions of Abraham will be a unifying thread throughout this book.

Both miracle stories and practices of sacrifice are nearly universal. One is tempted to say that they constitute the foundation of any religious tradition: signs of the reality of the sacred and means of relating to, or participating in, that reality. Miracle and sacrifice, revelation and self-denial, transcendent power and human discipline: These are familiar conditions of a religious way of life. Together, they constitute a ground of confidence that there is a transcendent reality and a commitment to discovering the peace, wisdom, or salvation that reality offers—no matter what the cost and however uncertain the benefit. While the term miracle indicates an event of transcendent power, a sign of reality from "beyond" that disrupts ordinary experience, sacrifice is a human act, an attempt to participate in transcendent reality by relinquishing one's hold on, or holdings in, the conventional world. What the two have in common, as event and act, is that neither can be entirely determined by human initiative. Miracles cannot be summoned with confidence in their occurrence and sacrifices cannot be performed with assurance in their desired outcome.

The cost of sacrifice and the uncertainty of its efficacy add drama and suspense to its role in mediating a relationship to the transcendent. In contrast to views of religious sacrifice as payment offered to fulfill an economic contract, this book argues that in religious sacrifice one surrenders the gift as total loss with no guarantee of return. Only in that way can sacrifice retain its tragic and self-denying character as a marker of transcendent reality. In short, *sacrifice cannot guarantee its own success without canceling its religious value.* If I am right about this view of sacrifice, then my earlier question arises in a different form: *Is a religious faith without sacrifice worth bothering with?* Because religious traditions claim to bring participants into relation with the transcendent—reality "beyond" natural and human orders of being—the ways they trace to

that reality forsake ordinary calculation of self-interest and natural in-
clinations. As the goal of religious aspiration lies beyond nature, so the
path to the goal often requires sacrificing "what comes naturally," including sex, food, sleep, family, and possessions. Religious sacrifice is a
discipline of ordinary affections and dispositions in pursuit of extraordinary, but abstract, benefits. From ascetic rigors to mystical trances to
actual martyrdom, religions issue the "costly signal" that spiritual advancement requires leaving behind self-interest.

One may object at this point that some programs of spiritual formation include pleasures, such as music and dancing. Even in those
cases, however, the goal is to shape physical impulses by the restraint
of abstract ideals. For example, the gracefully whirling dervishes of the
order of the Islamic mystic, Jalal al-Dīn al-Rūmī (d. 1273), demonstrate
religious ideas translated into symbolic action; but their movements are
no more natural than the intricate choreography of a ballet. As with all
stylized dancing, the steps and leaps are learned and must be practiced
to train the body to execute them in order. That is, dancing mystics are
artificial creatures. To become religious is an act of self-making, a transformation from the "natural" to the "spiritual."

Along the way, the jeopardy of what Slovenian cultural critic Slavoj
Žižek calls "violent derailment of nature" by spirit is always present.[6]
What sacrifice reveals is that religion, like other cultural forms including morality, is unnatural; its ideals guide the construction of artificial
selves. As one writer comments on religious ritual: "Good is something
against which nature rebels. But nature has to be tamed. This is what
rites are for."[7] This observation, however, is not necessarily a criticism.
Human evolution proceeds by the impetus of imagined ideals that inspire us to experiment with new forms of individual and social identity. By imagination we created tools, planted crops, began to speak, and
formed communities. Sacrifice is also an imaginative way believers free
themselves from natural limits by resisting hunger, sex, and sleep, com-
forts of family and home, and security of possessions. In short, sacrifice
is one of the ways religious believers re-make themselves; therein lies its
creative power and its ethical danger.

While that danger drives many modern critiques of sacrifice as a barbaric enactment of discredited myths of redemptive violence, the demand for sacrifice increases as the tide of global religious fervor rises.

The current resurgence of religion in the world is a surprise that few saw coming. Believers have revived traditional practices, including ascetic discipline and sacrificial offerings, as the re-assertion of cultural identity. Voices from cultures that had been submerged under the symbols and institutions of Western societies began to be heard, as they peeled away the bindings over their own religious intuitions through the liberating power of postcolonial criticism. Among those intuitions is the power of voluntary sacrifice to affirm individual identity and to support communities of faith. Contrary to critics, not all those who sacrifice their goods and autonomy to charismatic religious leaders are dupes; at least some pay the cost in the hope of finding meaning in their lives.[8]

1

Common Features of Sacrifice

Sacrifice is pervasive in religions of Abraham. Instructions on sacrifice fill chapters of the Hebrew Bible read in synagogues. Christians celebrate the death of Jesus as a sacrifice for sins in the Roman Catholic Mass and in the passion plays of Protestant churches. Muslims put animals to death each year in obedience to divine command. Our broad view of sacrifice includes rituals of killing, imitative suffering, donation of possessions, ascetic discipline, loss of self in mystical states of consciousness, and martyrdom. We will consider each example in the larger context of the religious tradition in which it arises in the attempt to illumine similarities of practice and differences of meaning. In that sense, comparative analysis identifies ways in which religious people are alike without compromising ways in which they are different. The disparate forms of sacrifice arise as responses to a common demand across these traditions: to *give up* ordinary desires, to *give away* valuable goods, and to *give over* life itself. Every tradition requires its adherents to sacrifice as a condition of securing a relation with the sacred or transcendent.

Sacrifice as Signifier of Transcendence

Why is the way to salvation traced with suffering and loss? One answer is that *sacrifices mark the difference between ordinary and transcendent reality by denying or subverting natural desires and reversing conventional values.*

Now we should pause to explain what *transcendence* means as the goal of sacrifice. Beginning with etymology may be helpful. *Transcend* means to "move over or across," just as *ascend* means to "move up" and *descend* means to "move down." What transcends, then, is not necessarily "up there," but "over there." The shift in spatial metaphors is significant. Religious thinkers often describe the divine or absolute by the spatial metaphor "above" to indicate that it is greater than transitory events in nature and history which play out "below." That recognition of difference between above and below parallels other basic distinctions in religious discourse, as between sacred and profane, divine and human, eternal and temporal, reality and illusion.

The seminal expression of metaphysical dualism between the one absolute "up there" and everything else "down here" is in the writings of the Greek philosopher Plato (429–347 BCE). According to Plato, all that we know of ultimate truth, beauty, and goodness are only shadows of ideal forms, eternal abstractions that constitute the true nature of everything we experience. The forms are timeless in their immutable unity and are dimly reflected in imperfect and perishable beings on earth.[1] When religious thinkers adopted Platonism, they conceived of God as possessing the absolute perfection of Platonic forms: timeless, immutable, and infallible. By contrast, humans are transient, fragile, and limited in power and knowledge.

Absolute difference between divine and human beings, however, poses problems: How could we know or experience something that is utterly different from us? How could such reality create or enlighten or love or regulate—or even be conscious of—the world? The philosopher Leszek Kołakowski (1927–2009) was scandalized by the view of God as Absolute because it made God incapable of genuine relation to the world. For Kołakowski all forms of monotheism influenced by Plato entangle us in a "horrifying metaphysical snare." He asks, "How can the *Ultimum*, thus defined, be the creator whose fiat called the universe into being, and how can goodness, love or benevolence be attributed to it in any recognizable sense? How could it be a *person*?"[2] The problem is that if the Absolute cannot be affected by other beings, it cannot respond to attempts to relate to it, including sacrifices. No offering could move the Absolute to react to human need or desire.

In the face of such problems, some contemporary thinkers prefer to shift attention away from what is remotely "above" to what is "across," imagining transcendence as infinitely greater than us but not so utterly different that we cannot relate to it.[3] In fact, most religious people already think of the sacred in that way. Philosophical theologians may speak of God as "wholly other," but those offering gifts or undergoing fasts do so with the hope of becoming familiar with transcendence—as alternative reality different from, yet alongside, human existence that the sincere seeker may enter with training and discipline. For believers in religions of Abraham, the way to cross over into transcendence is through sacrifice.

Sacrifice may be thought of as a gift given "without strings." The metaphor suggests that a gift should not have a trailing cord by which the giver could retrieve it or pull the recipient into a reciprocal obligation. In an ideal sense of a sacrificial gift, the giver relinquishes all claim, with no expectation of return. In practice, however, a sacrifice may be given in loving generosity and also entail expectation of return—and, not surprisingly, the greater the deprivation the sacrifice requires, the more the gift costs, the greater the return expected. One gives up goods of this world in the hope of receiving benefit (personal, communal, or cosmic) this world cannot yield.

The intended exchange of what *is* for what one hopes *will become*, the concrete for the abstract, the actual for the imagined, can be offensive to non-believers. Among the most virulent critics of religious sacrifice was the philosopher Friedrich Nietzsche (1844–1900), who regarded the Christian ideal of self-denial as "hostile to life," an unhealthy suppression of natural impulses that "takes God for the *enemy* of life. . . . The saint in whom God takes pleasure is the ideal castrate."[4] Nietzsche may have had in mind the Church father Origen (c. 185–254), who reportedly emasculated himself in order to fulfill Jesus's words that "there are eunuchs who have made themselves eunuchs for the sake of the kingdom of heaven. Let anyone accept this who can" (Matthew 19:12). Such extreme renunciation led Nietzsche to declare that "hatred of the *senses*, of the joy of the senses, of joy in general is Christian."[5]

There is enough evidence of denigration of the body in Christian history to give the charge some force. But Nietzsche missed the point: Acts of sacrifice that deny, violate, or suspend natural desires are precisely the only gestures that could point to what is beyond nature. How else can one realize spiritual liberation except by cutting ties to the body and the world that sustains it? The clearest and most dramatic signifier of what lies across from human and natural orders of reality is what shatters both. The critical question is whether the transcendent benefit or purpose will be fulfilled—and that cannot be determined in the moment of sacrificial forfeiture. The one who sacrifices must leave the gift at the altar to be consumed, never again to be of use or profit, removed forever from one's personal inventory and never to be retrieved. The gift may evoke divine favor or communal gratitude, even cosmic transformation, but no specific outcome can be assured when the offering is utterly abandoned: "Nothing in sacrifice is put off until later."[6] All is invested in the moment and at great risk.

Sacrifice as Offering in Suspense

It is generally acknowledged that sacrifice poses a dilemma in both religious and psychological terms, linked to the reasons and motives for giving: If one offers a gift with the expectation of a benefit, then is the gift an authentic sacrifice or merely a token in an economy of exchange? A donation that is given with the purpose of receiving some return, whether material or spiritual, seems not to be a genuine gift but more like a bargaining chip or even a bribe. At the least, it is a gift with strings firmly attached. In psychological terms, the dilemma is the problem of altruism: Is any act of giving ever entirely free from self-interest? Granted, people do set aside self-interest in moments of crisis (by jumping into the path of a car to save a child, for example), but rarely do they manage to form an intention to donate without some sideward glance at potential return. Fortunately, for most of us most of the time it does not matter whether our gifts come from mixed motives; they still bestow benefits on recipients who appropriately offer gratitude. In these cases the value of the gift does not depend on the reason for giving it.

In religious terms, however, reasons for giving are extremely important because in most traditions motive affects virtue. In Islam, for example, one must approach all exercises of devotion with right intention (*niyya*). Jesus located moral value in "the heart" wherein lies the source of anger and lust. The commands to be undivided in mind or pure in heart, however, are particularly difficult to honor when it comes to offering sacrifice. St. Paul mused, "I may dole out all I possess, or even give my body to be burnt, but if I have no love, I am none the better" (1 Corinthians 13:3, *New English Bible*). But how is love for God to be measured if not by the ultimate act of giving oneself up? How can one be certain that even accepting martyrdom proceeds from selfless motive?

Ancient Romans, by contrast, rarely wasted time on torturous self-examination, preferring a practical approach to everything from road construction to religion. They addressed their gods in this straightforward fashion: *do ut des*, "I give so that you may give." In a similar way, most forms of sacrifice take place within a religious economy, a system of exchange of value between humans and divine beings or sacred powers. In his classic study of gift giving in pre-industrial cultures, the sociologist Marcel Mauss (1872–1950) argued that "contract sacrifice" obligates deities to reciprocate with benefits.[7] From the standpoint of the external observer, sacrificial actions seem to function within a system of mutual obligation, such that sacrifices properly offered yield remunerative benefits.

Yet we cannot avoid keeping open the question of whether, within the consciousness of the one offering the sacrifice there is a moment of uncertainty, in which one surrenders the gift as total loss with no expectation of return. Without such a moment, can the gift rightly be called a sacrifice? That is, if a sacrifice *necessarily* results in receiving paradise or forgiveness, then has human action compelled the transcendent benefit? Has the system of ritual exchange succeeded in containing the sacred within an order that reliably ensures reciprocity? For religions of Abraham, God commands respect precisely because the divine surpasses human control. The bestowal of God's grace cannot be entirely regulated by human piety or discipline. No matter how indispensable such preparations may be, they cannot determine their own success.

In every relation with the transcendent, humans are in a state of uncertainty—and that condition also prevails in the offering of sacrifices. Sacrifice requires a moment of suspense in the presence of the sacred, when the offering has been made or suffering endured or discipline practiced, and the goal is still unattained. While the logic of sacrifice plays out in different traditions with various intentions and expectations, the dialectic of exchange and suspense persists. The French mathematician and philosopher, Blaise Pascal (1623–1662), described his Christian faith as fraught with the same uncertainty as a wager. The question whether God exists or not, let alone whether God will reward those who believe with everlasting happiness, Pascal could not answer by reason alone. "A game is being played at the extremity of this infinite distance where heads or tails will turn up. What will you wager?"[8] For Pascal the gamble was to sacrifice a finite life of pleasure for the possible gain of infinite happiness.

As in every wager, there is uncertainty about the outcome; but Pascal insists that it is reasonable to put up a finite stake against the chance of winning an infinite prize. The wager requires one to give up self-interest and follow the way of religious discipline ("taking the holy water, having masses said, etc.") and moral virtue ("You will be faithful, honest, humble, grateful, generous, a sincere friend, truthful"). Pascal argues, however, that these acts of self-denial will confirm the wisdom of betting on faith by increasing one's confidence in winning the wager. He believes that "at each step you take on this road . . . you will at last recognize that you have wagered for something certain and infinite, for which you have given nothing." Our interest in Pascal's wager is not its persuasiveness as an argument for God's existence, but its acknowledgment of uncertainty that lies at the heart of religious faith, the impossibility of affirming its claims with rational certitude. Believers can never know in this life whether their sacrifices will "pay off." For many, that uncertainty is enough to convince them to pass on the bet that God is awaiting them at the end of a life of self-denial. They recognize that faith is inseparable from the sacrifices required to support religious communities and their institutions and rituals. So, as one commentator wrote, "To wager that God is not is to stop bothering about such things."[9]

The converse is that betting on God sets the believer on a way of great bother. "Did you suppose," Muhammad challenged his followers, "that you would go to Paradise untouched by the suffering which was endured by those before you? Affliction and adversity befell them; and so shaken were they that each apostle, and those who shared his faith, cried out: 'When will God's help come?' God's help is ever near" (Qur'an 2.214). This passage not only links suffering and faith, but also recognizes the uncertainty of divine deliverance in the anxious question: "When will God's help come?" While the Qur'an provides the assurance that "God's help is ever near," the question of those facing death in battle reveals their faith in suspense, intensified by the revelation that God "alternate[s] these vicissitudes among mankind so that God may know the true believers and choose martyrs from among you" (Qur'an 3.140). Suffering defeat, then, may be the sacrifice God requires to test faith. But if there is no guarantee of deliverance from enemies in this life, how can one be certain that Paradise awaits those who sacrifice? Every believer following Muhammad into armed conflict in the formative years of the

Islamic community proceeded on the basis of faith, wagering his life in this world against the promise of eternal life in Paradise.

The story of sacrifice offered in suspense that is honored in each of the traditions in this book is of Abraham obeying God's command to offer his son as a "burnt offering." The Danish philosopher Søren Kierkegaard (1813–1855) described Abraham's state of mind as one marked by simultaneous movements of infinite resignation of Isaac to death and infinite hope for his restoration.[10] There was no possibility of reconciling this opposition, but only the decision to risk all to obey the sacred command, the dangerous venture that Kierkegaard elsewhere called "the leap of faith." Abraham could launch into the religious stage of life only by crossing the boundary of moral restraint, literally stepping over the dead body of his son. Abraham gives (up) his son by giving (away) his moral integrity in order to gain what Kierkegaard calls "an absolute relation to the absolute." The Bible describes the deal in less abstract terms: God promises that Abraham will be the father of many nations and that his descendants will possess the land of Canaan forever. What interrupts either account of Abraham's action as an exchange, however, is that he has no assurance that once he sacrifices Isaac he will receive the promised benefits. Nevertheless, Abraham raised the knife, and has been called blessed by Jews, Christians, and Muslims for doing so.

These examples illustrate another common feature of sacrifice: *Access to the sacred requires sacrifice given in suspense.* While many instances of sacrifice can be understood as taking place within a religious economy, every sacrifice entails a moment of uncertainty, in which one surrenders the gift as total loss with no assurance of reciprocity.

Sacrifice as Conditional Event

The uncertainty of success, however, is not only in the mind of the sacrificer. After all, we cannot base our view of sacrifice solely on speculations about the motives of people who offer sacrifices.[11] While Kierkegaard was eloquent in giving poetic expression to what he imagined as Abraham's inner agony, the fact is that the nineteenth-century philosopher in cosmopolitan Copenhagen had little clue about what went on in the mind of the Semitic chieftain who lived two millennia earlier and half a world away in desert wilderness. The private dispositions and calculations of religious people—let alone their "religious experiences"—are inaccessible to us. The best we can do is to be relentlessly aware of our emotions as we project them on the stories we read. Indeed, the category of suspense may reflect modern skepticism about transcendent reality as much as it illumines a consistent state of mind among believers as they offer sacrifices. Still, there is reason to think that, regardless of the subjectivity of those who sacrifice, there is something about the action itself that entails risk and uncertainty.

We thus need to expand the meaning of suspense as an interpretive category from a description of subjective doubt about the outcome to include what we might call the objective *conditionality of the gift*. That phrase indicates (1) conditions attached to the type and value of what is offered and (2) the contingency of every sacrifice. First, a gift offered as a religious sacrifice must meet certain criteria. For example, the Hebrew Bible requires that animals brought for sacrificial slaughter must be "without blemish" (Leviticus 3). Contemporary regulations governing animal sacrifice during Islamic pilgrimage restrict the types of animals to sheep and goats (at least one year old), cows (two years old), and camels (at least five years old) and prohibit the sacrifice of sick, crippled, or wounded animals.[12]

Further, sacrificial gifts are acceptable only under certain conditions, including the high value to the giver of what is offered. In one famous story Jesus commended a woman for putting two small coins into the treasury box on the steps of the temple in Jerusalem: "Truly, I tell you, this poor widow has put in more than all of them; for all of them have contributed out of their abundance, but she out of her poverty has put in all she had to live on" (Luke 21:3–4). The value of the sacrifice here is reckoned in relation to the resources of the giver, not the recipient. For the writer of Luke—whose Gospel highlights the piety of the poor— the widow fulfills the condition of selfless generosity that makes her an exemplary worshipper of God. These few examples indicate some conditions for offering sacrificial gifts. But there is a second, more fundamental, meaning to the phrase *conditionality of the gift*.

In sacrifice the gift is forsaken, given up and given away. It may or may not be destroyed, and a portion may be reclaimed in communal consumption, but it must be abandoned, in the moment of offering, by the giver. What is sacrificed thereby reveals its contingent nature.

This disclosure is at the same time what many religions regard as the moment of insight into the truth of things, namely, that nothing in this world endures forever. Sacrifice is an enacted recognition of the transitory character of all things. Consider that any goods acquired will eventually be lost: That is the betrayal of matter. Physical realities seem so solid, even permanent, that some people have been seduced into thinking that material entities are the only things that exist: That is the illusion of matter. Yet every material thing hardly announces its arrival and it is out the door, doomed by its very solidity because what is fixed cannot adapt or defend itself against the wearing effect of time. Likewise, gifts brought to the altar of sacrifice, whether of animals, flowers, money, time, or pleasure, are dead on arrival; they are already forsaken. Sacrifice is the dramatic performance of the ephemerality of all material existence.

The contingency of sacrifice lies in part in the limits of what is offered; but there is another aspect of conditionality that is especially prominent in ritual sacrifice, where performance is subject to failures, mistakes, and interruptions. In ritual sacrifice, there are several points of risk besides wrong motives on the part of those offering the sacrifice, including procedural mistakes, unrecognized defects in the sacrificial gift, external disruptions of the ritual, and failure of the divine recipient to reciprocate. These are some of the ways rituals can "misfire" in the sense Ronald Grimes, the influential ritual studies scholar, uses the term to describe "infelicitous performance."[13] At the extreme, rituals may be so flawed as to constitute what Grimes calls "flops," in which the "appropriate mood" is not evoked and so the expected benefit is not derived from the ritual performance.[14]

Another telling indication of the contingency of ritual practice is provision for means of atoning for errors. The old saying that every law has a history applies here. The formulation of multiple ways of correcting ritual mistakes implies that such mistakes are frequently made, and that possibility increases anxiety among the participants about whether the ritual will work. General misgivings about human capacity to perform rituals correctly relate to the specific case of sacrifice as the recognition that both the subject and object of sacrifice are fragile: The subject may bring the offering with the wrong motive; the proffered gift may not be worthy; and the ritual procedure may be flawed.

Further, in sacrifices offered to the personal God of Abraham, there is an additional risk: The sacred recipient may not accept the gift and the implied transaction thus may fail to be honored. The anthropologist Raymond Firth (1901–2002) notes that "what distinguishes an offering from a gift . . . is that an offering implies an asymmetrical *status relationship*," specifically the dependence of the one making the offering on the reception of the one to whom it is offered. Further, "linked with the notion of status difference is that of *uncertainty*—decision as to the acceptability of the transfer of value may be thought to rest with the person designated as recipient, who may refuse it."[15] One example of non-cooperation by the divine recipient is found in the Hebrew prophet Hosea, who expresses God's refusal to accept animal sacrifices which he had earlier demanded: "Though they offer choice sacrifices . . . the LORD does not accept them. Now he will remember their iniquity, and punish their sins" (Hosea 7:13). In this case, the divine preference in offerings had shifted from the "sweet smoke" of burnt animals to a devout spirit: "For I desire steadfast love and not sacrifice, the knowledge of God rather than burnt offerings" (Hosea 6:6). Because their offerings were made from a position of inferiority, the Israelites had no choice but to bring the gifts currently required by God with no appeal of the changed conditions of their relationship. Nevertheless, priests continued to offer ritual sacrifices in the Temple, despite prophetic criticism.

When a sacrifice fails to secure the expected benefit, the one who offered it may reflect on personal failures and bring yet more offerings to compensate for guilt. But there is another possible response: frustration and resentment at the lack of divine reciprocity. Laments of unrequited sacrifice echo in the Hebrew Bible, particularly in the book of Job and the Psalms, where they form the basis for demands that God justify allowing the righteous to suffer and the wicked to prosper. Job daily offered sacrifices on behalf of his children, yet they were all crushed when a desert storm leveled the house in which they were gathered. "It is all one," Job charges, God "destroys both the blameless and the wicked . . . if it is not he, who then is it?" (Job 9:22, 24). If the recipient of the sacrificial gift does not give back proportionally, then human mistakes in ritual procedure seem trivial. How can those who sacrifice in good faith blame themselves for ritual failure, if the divine partner in the exchange fails to reward them? The primary problem is that what transcends human reality cannot be predicted, let alone controlled, by human actions. As the Qur'an states, "God does what he will" (2.253).

The relevance for our study of considering the various ways rituals can fail is to demonstrate the contingency of all performative gestures, including offering of sacrifices: "Rituals always bear some kind of risk."[16] Whether they are words in a healing ritual that leave the sick person no better or acts of self-denial that yield no insight, efforts to transform reality by what we say or do often prove ineffective. The problem is most acute in the case of sacrifice that involves killing. Humans kill to secure food, exact revenge, expand territory, offer gifts to the gods, or eliminate rivals. We execute murderers to uphold social order and we kill enemies in war to preserve the nation. Sometimes humans kill for no discernible reason and to no useful purpose, except perhaps the satisfaction of performing an act of ultimate finality.

Yet there is no act, to a reflective mind, that carries a greater burden of remorse than killing. Even if the desired end is attained, there remains lingering doubt about the legitimacy of the means. Thus, hunters, executioners, and warriors all develop elaborate rituals of preparation and expiation because the act of killing transforms the killer as well as the victim. No one who has killed intentionally can ever again entertain the illusion of innocence. Even when religious people are successful in offering a sacrifice, moral uncertainty about what they have done may linger. Despite the best intentions, then, reservations shadow the practice of sacrifice, whether in the death of another creature or in ascetic and mystical anticipation of one's own death in the embrace of the sacred.

Sacrifice as Self-Sacrifice

That consideration leads us to one other common feature of sacrifice: "the one who sacrifices is himself affected by the blow which he strikes—he succumbs and loses himself with his victim."[17] There is an element of self-sacrifice in every offering, not only in acts of killing but also in sacrifice of possessions. Sacrifice is the offering of what one owns, either through purchase from another or as the product of one's own labor. That is why, as Jonathan Z. Smith notes, humans generally do not sacrifice wild game, but only domesticated animals, creatures of their own making, in stylized action: sacrifice is *"the artificial (i.e. ritualized) killing of an artificial (i.e. domesticated) animal.*"[18] We, as the artificers of the sacrificial gift, offer the gift of our imagination and effort: in short, part of ourselves.

Sacrificing what is of value to oneself is a transparent instance of donation as a gift that enriches another by impoverishing oneself. What I give up of my possessions benefits another in direct proportion to the value they held, and perhaps continue to hold, for me; so the greater the cost to me, the greater is the sacrifice I make. As we noted earlier, the common assumption in various forms of discourse about sacrifice is that the cost of sacrifice must be high relative to the resources of the one making the sacrifice. In that spirit, some Christian churches and some mosques of Sunni Islam assign a minimal percentage to the donations required of members: 10% or *tithe* in the Christian case; 2.5% for Muslim *zakāt* (alms or poor tax). In theory, the numerical amount is less important than the relative size of the donation, for only that standard guarantees that the cost of giving is proportional and the degree of self-deprivation roughly equivalent.[19] The sacrifice becomes efficacious as the giver experiences significant personal loss.

These reflections on the dimension of self-sacrifice in every sacrifice are prompted by Marcel Mauss's comment that in the sacrificial exchange of presents there is an "intermingling" of emotions that indicates an intimate association of the giver with the gift: "Souls are mixed with things; things with souls. Lives are mingled together, and this is how, among persons and things so intermingled, each emerges from their own sphere and mixes together."[20] While there is understandable resistance to the reduction of persons to their material possessions, it is inescapable that we are, *in part*, constituted as physical bodies and the things that support, extend, and enhance our material presence in the world.

We also know that, under the hard conditions of an indifferent natural world of accident and disease and a competitive social order where the uneducated and unarmed are easy prey, what one *has* is crucial to who one *is* and what one may become. Wealth, influence, possessions: These sources of power cannot bestow the distinctive mark of humanity—whether designated as soul or spirit, reason or mind—nor can their absence cancel basic rights that humanity entails. But who can deny that the wealth one possesses beyond the demands of bare necessity strongly correlate with one's range of opportunities, breadth of experience and education, and horizon of possibilities? In short, resources determine what one is in the world.

While some idealists may lament this fact or try to pretend that they are above its vulgar reach, few can deny Aristotle's observation that happiness requires certain material conditions for its realization. The most free-spirited among us must have food (even if from a dumpster), clothing (anywhere but on a tropical island), and shelter (from natural elements and predators). We may be, in the privacy of our own thoughts, self-enclosed; but as social beings we are, *in part*, constituted by our relations to others based upon many scales of relative weight. None of us belongs to a single hierarchy of power or value (that claim is a rhetorical ploy of ideologues), but each of our social relations is arrayed on a scale that measures our material resources: clothing, food, cattle, shells, weapons, land, and cash. It cannot be otherwise; *who* we are, in the hidden sanctuary of our inmost being, is invisible, perhaps inviolable, preserved in secrecy and invulnerable to the reductive gaze of any other. But *what* one is, as a member of society, as a visible public actor, cannot finally be concealed. Further, that *persona* (face or mask) through which who-we-are appears to others is not ours alone to determine.

The language you speak, the gender you affirm, the clothing you wear, the foods you eat, the family you love or hate (but at any rate cannot entirely escape), the government under which your liberty is expanded or constricted—all of these elements, crucial to your identity, are not of your making. They are given as elements of your formative history. You are free to make of them what you will, but you are not free to deny that they *in part* constitute what you are. In addition, fierce loyalty to your personal identity includes commitment to certain possessions. Whenever we retain some thing or give it away or lose it or have it taken from us, our sense of who we are changes. This is a long way of explaining Mauss's strange language about the "intermingling" of persons and things in the form of gifts—and suggests that what I am is *in part* what I have. It follows that when I sacrifice a possession, I really am giving up something of myself. The more extravagant, unusual, and central to my role in society the sacrificial gift is, the more it represents, even identifies me. Every sacrifice is, to that extent, self-sacrifice.

In sum, we have identified three common elements in the practice of sacrifice: The offering is made in suspense, the gift is offered under conditions that allow for its failure as sacrifice, and what is offered constitutes in part a giving of oneself.

Definition of Sacrifice

In light of these preliminary considerations, we propose this working definition of our subject:

> Religious sacrifice is a costly act of self-giving, in denial of natural inclinations, that is offered in suspense, under conditions that threaten failure, for the purpose of establishing a relation with transcendent reality.

This definition is constructed for the purpose of guiding the selection of examples to come and directing our analysis of their religious meaning. It is not intended to be universal or normative or exclusive; indeed, it is widely inclusive. Like all definitions, it is meant to be faithful to common usage and to provide an arena of meaning within which we can conduct our study.

A definition, by definition, sets limits by assigning boundaries or ends (from Latin *definire*). In that role, a definition is problematic because it suggests a single universal meaning of a term that determines its "correct" usage. A definition implicitly claims authority over how a term is used and to what it "properly" refers. In that sense, a definition is a strategy of control over a given area of discourse and a means of identifying who has authority to direct discussion in the field: Definitions are the credentials of experts. But language is too elusively shape-shifting to be contained within the bounded roles assigned it by scholars. Academic definitions may seek to govern how words are used; but people use language in wildly imaginative ways, within ever-changing contexts, freely expanding and transforming the applications of familiar terms. That is why definitions in dictionaries are summaries of popular usage, always one step behind the evolution of language. How, then, can we decide what should be called a sacrifice?

Some scholars propose to resolve the problem by adopting Jonathan Z. Smith's mode of "polythetic" classification, adapted from biological taxonomy. As Smith explains, "In this new mode, a class is defined as consisting of a set of properties," rather than a single shared feature.

Each member of the class exhibits a greater or lesser number of these characteristics, which need not be consistent with each other, but no single property occurs in every member of the class.[21] This approach allows for the same term to apply to a wide range of phenomena, while distinguishing the set from other classificatory terms.

The religious studies scholar Kathryn McClymond uses the method in her study of ancient Hindu and Israelite ritual sacrifice, arguing that "religious phenomena should not be defined so much as characterized."[22] She identifies seven elements that provide the "building blocks" of sacrificial events: selection, association, identification, killing, heating, apportionment, and consumption. While no single element is necessary to classify an act as a sacrifice (not even killing), some combination of these elements serves as a sufficient condition to identify an act as sacrificial. The polythetic approach also explains why certain devotional acts, such as prayer, are called sacrifices: because they involve some of the properties of ritual sacrifices, such as apportionment (of time). Similarly, heroic death in defense of one's nation demonstrates properties that classify it as sacrifice.

McClymond sees these applications as secondary, however, employed in order to "appropriate some of the authority of traditional sacrifice."[23] She chooses to focus on the manipulation of substances offered in sacrifice, such as animal body parts, blood, and grains. Thus, her approach excludes from the primary category of sacrifice those acts in which there is no "substance" to manipulate. Yet believers routinely speak of sacrificing their thoughts, desires, and egos to the service of God. It seems somewhat arbitrary to assign these applications to derivative meanings of sacrifice in order to privilege its use in ritual settings. As stated earlier, the approach in this book is to observe how references to sacrifice resound over a wider range of religious expressions than ritual performance. While our range of examples is larger, however, we also identify sacrifice by common features and our "definition" is intended as no more than a general summary of those features.

Finally, it is important to bear in mind that "sacrifice" is an abstract category, an ideal that is never realized fully or consistently in practice, much like "truth" or "justice." We should not be surprised to find that—measured by the abstract ideal expressed in any definition or characterization—most sacrifices are compromised in some way or other. While sacrifice may be offered for the most exalted purpose, with the purest intention, and the highest approval of others, its result may be catastrophe. That possibility leads to our final common feature of sacrifice: moral ambivalence.

Sacrifice as Noble Gesture and Moral Danger

As a religious and moral ideal, sacrifice entails moral tension. On the one hand, forfeiting concrete goods and living beings for the sake of an ideal or abstract benefit can produce the carnage of war, the pain of self-deprivation, and the cruelty of inquisition. On the other hand, giving up private interests for the sake of the common good is the basis of social solidarity and provision for future generations. Without sacrifice, there would be no philanthropists, warriors, saints, or even parents. In that sense, from the standpoint of human evolution and social formation, it is "reasonable service," as St. Paul wrote.[24]

Nevertheless, sacrifice spawns monsters and saviors alike, and for that reason its demands and purposes must always be critically examined. The moral ambivalence of sacrifice is inevitable because humans can never be absolutely sure that the abstract ideal for which they give up concrete reality is worthy of their service. As the philosopher Alfred North Whitehead (1861–1947) warned, "Religion is by no means necessarily good. It may be very evil. . . . In your religious experience the God with whom you have made terms may be the God of destruction, the God who leaves in his wake the loss of the greater reality."[25]

In sum, sacrifice is a complex religious action, laden with suspense, shadowed by violence, and offered with a total dedication and wanton extravagance that exceeds narrow calculations of self-interest. Perhaps religious believers across the world are mistaken about reality "across from" and "other than" the one shaped by nature and history, but they are determined to experience its benefits no matter what degree of self-denial it takes. Religion is costly and risky. We next turn to some of the ways scholars have tried to understand the meaning religious people assign to that cost and the ways they assess and assume that risk.

Theories of Sacrifice

Jonathan Z. Smith notes, "Any explanation of sacrifice is, in fact, a theory of religion in miniature."[1] Why? Because if one could explain why religious people offer sacrifices, what cultural functions sacrifice performs, how sacrifice regulates relations to the transcendent, and where sacrifice occurs—that is, if a comprehensive theory of sacrifice were developed—then one may account for the why, what, how, and where of other activities we designate "religious." Inasmuch as sacrifice is a common practice in religious traditions as a principal means of connecting human life to transcendent reality, then its primary features may contain clues for a more general understanding of religion.[2] For now, however, we will be content to consider several attempts to explain sacrifice in sufficiently general terms to qualify as "theory."[3]

Even a sampling of influential theories of sacrifice constitutes a lengthy list: sacrifice as gift to the gods in exchange for favors; as evidence of devotion to one's deity; as means of communion with the sacred by sharing a meal of the sacrificial offering; as expiation for broken taboos; as condition of cosmic maintenance; as means of marking the presence and absence of the sacred; as collective violence sanctioned by myth with the effect of reconstituting social solidarity; and as means of confirming patrilineal descent by male blood-letting that supplants female blood-shedding in childbirth.[4] Most theories assume that sacrifice is a type of exchange, an arrangement in which human offerings evoke material or spiritual benefits. Thus, theories of sacrifice identify reasons why people sacrifice and, to that extent, make the practice intelligible. That is the role of theory; but it is important to remember that no theory is innocent. By establishing a rationale for sacrifice, theory is complicit in its practice.

On the other hand, philosopher Dennis Keegan argues, "Sacrifice is sacrifice only as the sacrifice of sacrifice. Sacrifice is (genuinely) sacrifice only as the sacrifice of (an economical understanding of) sacrifice. It is necessary for sacrifice to consume itself in an all-burning holocaust in order to be what it 'is.'"[5] A call for an "end to sacrifice" as exchange is common in religions of Abraham; but even when they give up animal sacrifices, they continue to exact offerings from their followers—thus indicating the value of their benefits by "costly signaling." Further, religions require sacrifice as the price of successful negotiation with the sacred. But should sacrifice itself be sacrificed in order to love the sacred without self-interest? Can sacrifice be an act from which one expects no benefit, an excessive giving with no hope of return?

There is no scholarly agreement on *why* people offer sacrifices or *how* sacrifices serve social, biological, or psychological needs. On the question of *why*, scholar of religion James Watts notes that among ancient records, there is practically no reflection on the motive of those who sacrifice. Explanations of sacrifice develop later: "In every case, the ritual action seems to be demonstrably older than the interpretations offered for it by the religious traditions in which it is practiced."[6] Theory always follows the data it attempts to explain, of course; but why do religious traditions choose *sacrifice* to designate actions they admire or regard as normative? To take Watts's example: "Jesus' crucifixion was obviously not a sacrifice to the soldiers who performed it. . . . Only religious reflection on this political execution transformed the evaluation of it by labeling it a 'sacrifice,' in fact the ultimate and final sacrifice."[7] But what prompted that line of reflection? The question of why some early Christians fixed on sacrifice as the key to understanding the death of Jesus applies, *mutatis mutandi*, to the use of sacrifice as an interpretive category in other traditions as well. Why is this term pervasive as the explanation for a wide range of religious practices? Theories of sacrifice address those questions.

One challenge theories of sacrifice face is to reconcile instrumental uses of sacrifice—to express thanks, seal vows, appeal for deliverance, or seek forgiveness—with wasteful expenditure of wealth and life. How can sacrifice serve the interests of a human collective by wasting a portion of what is of greatest value to it? Even under conditions of deprivation, religious people sacrifice vital resources: grains and animals, water and milk, precious possessions, personal vitality, and—most shocking of all—young men and women on whose lives the survival of the community depends. What accounts for this behavior? We begin with a theorist who explained sacrifice as symbolic expression, and ritual enforcement, of social values.

Sacrifice as Symbolic Enactment of Social Values: Émile Durkheim

The sociologist Émile Durkheim (1857–1917) placed sacrifice at the heart of his theory of religion as the symbolic "collective representation" of societal values. For example, by offering sacrifices to the totem plant or animal that signifies their ancestors, members of a tribe express their loyalty to a common origin and identity. By its power to evoke loyalty to the social group it represents, Durkheim claimed, "The totem is the clan's flag." By sharing a meal of the sacrificed totem, clan members "literally incorporate" the sacred power of the animal in a ceremony that also strengthens their social cohesion.[8] Further, individual sacrifices encourage the disposition to give up private interests for the sake of common good. Sacrificing to gods, then, enacts social values of altruism and mutuality both by requiring participants to donate to the ritual and also by imagining gods as models of reciprocity. Durkheim speculated that "the act of offering naturally awakens in people's minds the idea of a moral subject which this offering is meant to satisfy." He then concluded, "In its fully constituted form, sacrifice is composed of two essential elements: an act of communion and an act of offering. The worshipper communes with his god by ingesting a sacred food, and at the same time he makes an offering to this god."[9]

But therein lies a problem: Why does a god need an offering? What benefit could a divine being derive from a human gift? If gods are supreme and self-sufficient beings, why do they require humans to offer sacrifices to them? There seems to be a clear implication that gods who need human gifts are deficient in some way and thus dependent upon sacrifices to survive.

The problem can perhaps best be illustrated by reference to the oldest written story we know of, the *Epic of Gilgamesh*. Composed in Mesopotamia around 2500 BCE, the narrative was transcribed in cuneiform, a system of wedge-shaped symbols pressed into wet clay tablets. (The version we have is from a thousand years later.) The story is about a divine-human king, Gilgamesh, who sets off on a heroic journey in search of immortality under the protection of the sun god Shamash. At each stage of the adventure Gilgamesh digs a well facing the sun and offers a libation of flour on a mountain peak. It is striking how ritual sacrifice simply appears without explanation as the obvious way to relate to the divine being. But how did Gilgamesh know to present Shamash with just such a gift in just such a way? And why did Shamash need the flour that could have fed Gilgamesh?

What gods need from humans becomes clearer when Gilgamesh encounters the only man who ever achieved immortality, Utanapishtim, survivor of a great flood sent by the gods to annihilate humanity. In Utanapishtim's telling of the cataclysm, he was led by one of the gods to build an enormous boat and then, "I had all my kith and kin go up into the boat, all the beasts and animals of the field and the craftsmen I had go up." The deluge hit with such ferocity that the gods were terrified by their own destructive power: "The gods were frightened by the Flood, and retreated, ascending to the heaven of Anu." The goddess Ishtar "shrieked like a woman in childbirth" as the humans she had borne filled the sea "like so many fish." The assembled gods "humbly sat weeping, sobbing with grief," as the storm quieted and they saw that "all the human beings had turned to clay." Why were the gods dismayed? Because they realized they had lost the only beings who could offer them sacrifices. Thus they revived only when Utanapishtim emerged from the boat and "offered incense in front of the mountain-ziggurat." Immediately, "the gods smelled the sweet savor, and collected like flies over a (sheep) sacrifice."[10] The image is hardly flattering to the gods, but it conveys their buzzing hunger for the aroma of human worship. The gods are desperate for the smell of sacrifice, the odor that sustains them.

In this scene from an epic nearly five millennia old we see dramatic illustration of Durkheim's principle that "sacred beings exist only because they are imagined as such. If we cease to believe in them, they will cease to exist." Thus, "the gods would die if the cult were not celebrated." Sacrifice sustains the gods by acknowledging the supreme value of what they represent: social order. "What the worshipper really gives his god is not the food he places on the altar, or the blood he spills from his veins, but his thought . . . sacred beings, while superior to men, can live only in human consciousness." There the idea of social order arises and in ritual sacrifice it is enacted. Thus Durkheim concludes that "the cult really does periodically recreate a moral entity on which we depend, as it depends on us. And this entity does exist: it is society."[11] While Durkheim was careful to distinguish the two elements of sacrifice—gift and communion—in theory, he did not believe they were separate in practice. He was convinced that the ritual exchange of human gift and divine blessing was a symbolic representation of the way social reciprocity constituted religious ideals. That is, the blessings of the gods, secured by sacrifice, were nothing but the mutual altruism expressed in the giving and receiving of gifts.

To sacrifice is to participate in the subordination of private interests to common good that makes society possible, and at the same time to create the "obligation to reciprocate" that Durkheim's nephew and leading figure in the academic discipline of sociology, Marcel Mauss, highlighted in his classic study, *The Gift: The Form and Reason for Exchange in Archaic Societies* (1950). For Mauss, gift exchange is the premier "symbol of social life" because it denotes a relation between the giver, the gift, and the recipient that is not mystical in nature but grounded in economic interests and regulated by common law.[12] Inasmuch as religious sacrifice is a gift, then, it is offered under the general conditions that hold for the exchange of gifts among humans, including a system of reciprocity. As an example, he quotes from Muslim tradition—"If you make a generous loan to God, he will pay you back double" (Qur'an 64.17)—and then remarks, "Substitute for the name of Allah that of society and the occupational grouping, or put together all three names, if you are religious. Replace the concept of alms by that of co-operation, of a task done or service rendered for others."[13] That is, the sacrifice of private resources for the common good accomplishes the same social benefit whether offered in the name of God, one's cultural group, or fellow workers.

Mauss hoped that his reflections on the generosity and mutuality of gift giving would inspire a more just economy in which workers would receive financial security in return for their honest labor. He nourished nostalgia for the archaic disposition of generosity against the calculating self-interest of modern Western economies, believing that the "brutish pursuit of individual ends is harmful to the ends and the peace of all." But he also put his faith in rational pragmatism. Prudent sacrifice is the gift the individual offers in exchange for social communion and its benefits.[14] Theologian John Milbank connects sociological interpretations with the ancient Roman view of exchange, arguing that Mauss and Durkheim "still conceived of modern social sacrifice as a fulfilment of *do ut des*: individual *renunciation* sustains social forces, but the individual *gains back* social legitimation of his needs: material, erotic, spiritual."[15]

By insisting that gift exchange was a crucial element in sacrifice Durkheim departed from the earlier theory of the scholar of Semitic religions, William Robertson Smith (1846–1894), who argued that communion with the divine was the *sole* purpose of sacrifice. His model was the sacrificial system in the Hebrew Bible. Smith believed that the sharing of food offered on altars in ancient Israel indicated the divine interest in communing with human worshippers. By eating the meat of the burnt offerings together, God and the priests (representing the people of Israel) came to peace. The proof that God forgave the people's offenses against his commandments was his willingness to share the food they offered to him. In that reading, sacrifice is the sign of Yahweh's eternal mercy and the redeemed status of the people.

Smith's rejection of views of sacrifice as gift exchange was driven in part by his Calvinist theology of God as immutable and self-sufficient (he was an ordained minister in the Free Church of Scotland). On that view, sacrifice can neither benefit nor obligate God. Thus, explanations of sacrifice as gift exchange or offerings required to sustain the divine belittle the power and sovereignty of God. Still, sacrifices are offered for a purpose and, to that extent, with expectation that God can be persuaded to provide some return on investment. That brings us back to the problem noted at the outset of this section. If God is ultimately independent, beyond need or desire, then why would God require gifts, offerings, or sacrifices?

The problem was seen clearly by the second king of Israel, Solomon. When Solomon proposed to build a temple in which to worship God through sacrifices, he reflected on the dilemma of building a house on earth for the supreme deity who lives beyond this world. At the dedication of the temple, his solution was to ask God to hear the prayers offered there from God's true "dwelling place in heaven" (1 Kings 8:22–30). The gift of the temple, financed by an enthusiastic outpouring of gold and silver from the people, was offered with the full recognition that it was not needed by God. Nevertheless, the temple would express Israel's thanks for Yahweh's protection and guidance without presuming on his independence.

By contrast, Durkheim argued that, because sacrifice sustains the power of deities as the basis of social solidarity, it reveals the gods' dependence upon humans. "So, we can say that it is man who makes his gods, or at least makes them endure, but at the same time it is through them that he himself endures." That endurance is not of individuals, of course, but of the social and natural orders that nurture succeeding human generations. In religious symbolism sacred power upholds nature and society, but sacrifice represents the truth that deities require the vivifying force of human gifts for their endurance. From the sociological perspective, sacrifice indicates that gods live off human vitality. In one episode of an aboriginal ritual sacrifice Durkheim noted that the young men of an Australian clan cut their arms and let the blood fall on rocks near where their totem, a large grub worm, lived and reproduced. Durkheim remarks, "So that [man] may live, universal life must continue, and therefore the gods must not die. He tries to sustain them, to help them; for this reason, he puts at their service the forces available to him. . . . The blood that flows in his veins has fecundating powers: he will spill it." In this theory, sacrifices are the cost of cosmic and social maintenance paid in human currency. They are specific instances of Durkheim's general view that every religious ritual has the same role, namely, to act as "the means by which the social group periodically reaffirms itself."[16]

At such moments of heightened feeling the individual takes on the identity of the collective. The result is that within "a crowd moved by a common passion, we become susceptible to feelings and actions of which we are incapable on our own." At times of social crisis when "individuals seek each other out and assemble more often," the effect is more pronounced. "The result is a general effervescence characteristic of revolutionary or creative epochs. . . . People live differently and more intensely than in normal times . . . man himself becomes other. He is moved by passions so intense that they can be assuaged only by violent, extreme acts of superhuman heroism or bloody barbarism."[17]

In certain ritual settings among the Australian aborigines, "the effervescence often becomes so intense it leads to unpredictable behavior. . . . The ordinary conditions of life are set aside so definitively and so consciously that people feel the need to put themselves above and beyond customary morality," leading to sexual promiscuity in flickering firelight. Assuming in his readers a voyeuristic interest in exotic "primitives," Durkheim writes that "we can easily imagine" a scene of such erotic excess as to transport the participants into another world from that of ordinary life, the world of the sacred. "Therefore," Durkheim concludes, "it is in these effervescent social settings, and from this very effervescence, that the religious idea seems to be born. And this origin seems confirmed by the fact that in Australia, strictly religious activity is almost entirely concentrated in the times when these assemblies are held."[18] That blood sacrifice adds to the frenzy that evokes the sacred world would seem to go without saying.

At least that is how Durkheim understood sacrifice to be practiced by the Australian aboriginal tribes he took as his chief examples. Durkheim never set foot in the outback himself, but relied on ethnographic work conducted by others, particularly the British anthropologists, Baldwin Spencer and F. J. Gillen. They produced two ethnographies, published nearly thirty years apart; and Durkheim noted that their later work allowed for the generalized interpretation of ritual he favored, that is, as a means of drawing a social group together at periodic intervals to reestablish communal ties and shared interests. Ultimately, whether clan members believed their sacrifice supported the fertility of the totemic grub is irrelevant to the function of the ritual in gathering the clan together and renewing their common identity.

Jonathan Z. Smith astutely documented important differences between the two ethnographies by Spencer and Gillen (1899, 1927), arguing that even the renowned scholar Mircea Eliade was misled by their later report in his interpretation of an Australian myth. By 1927, for example, the earlier reference to a totemic ancestor had been changed to correspond to the celestial deity, "Lord God Eternal," invoked by local Christian missionaries in their prayers. The resulting account bears other evidence of "native-Christian syncretism" as well.[19] Durkheim was also aware of differences between the two ethnographies, but he was not as interested in indigenous interpretation as in the social function of ritual regardless of how its attendant myth is told. From his standpoint, sacrifice was an established practice among the aborigines long before

Western settlers made their way to Australia; and its theoretical significance remains the same despite changes in details. So Durkheim's theory of sacrifice stands as an application of his general view that "the sacred principle is nothing but society hypostasized and transfigured."[20]

The problem with Durkheim's theory is not that sacrifice fails to symbolize and enact central social values—it clearly does—but that sacrifice stretches the limits of functional explanation because of its heroic deviance and violent extravagance. To his credit, Durkheim did challenge his own theory by asking "if religion is a product of social causes, how do we explain the individual cult and the universalist character of certain religions?"[21] The question recognizes the difficulty of explaining social reformers and idealists. These individuals run against the grain of dominant social values and appeal to more general, allegedly universal, principles. For them, the sacred is not the emblem and guardian of their society, but the basis for criticizing and reforming social order. They use self-sacrifice as a persuasive power to change social conditions, not confirm them. They challenge theories of human behavior that reduce us to nothing but the formative power of cultural influences and limit our moral vision to our social horizon, as if individual imagination and courage counted for nothing. Views that social context determines everything we do are as drearily oppressive as theological schemes of predestination. But the challenge to societal determinism is not the most formidable one Durkheim's theory faces.

In an essay he called "The Politics of Theory," religious studies scholar Mark Taylor argues that modern thinkers and artists were fascinated by primitive cultures as exotic and erotic. Specifically, modernism tried to master the primitive in two contrasting representations: as harmonious ideal of a perfectly unified beginning and as savage counterpoint to civilization. We might say that modern people have imagined the primitive as either the original Garden of Paradise or the violent nightmare of Wilderness, Forest, or Desert. Taylor understands Durkheim and other modernists as driven by the search for primal unity represented by the primitive. "Unity, in turn, is associated with the origin from which everything derives and to what it longs to return." Such unity in human experience, however, almost always requires coercion of those who refuse to join the collective. "That which is effectively subjected to the gaze of theory is supposed to be mastered, controlled, disciplined, dominated, even colonized."[22] Thus, modernist theory found its counterpart in politics of domination. In the mid-twentieth century that meant fascism, but it could be any all-encompassing ("totalitarian") view of reality, including religion.

Specifically, Taylor argues that Durkheim's theory that social solidarity produces religious rituals does not sufficiently acknowledge the capacity for violence in collective behavior. Durkheim recognized that when social groups assemble in order to reinforce their shared interests, the passion aroused leads to behavior that transgresses conventional social prohibitions. But Taylor sees sinister potential in the erotic and deadly excesses during sacrifices and festivals. "Ostensibly an animal or a plant, the totem is actually the incarnation of violent and erotic passions unleashed during the ritual excesses of the festival."[23] Here Taylor finds that the effervescence of festivals may come to constitute a ferociously exclusive sense of collective identity and solidarity directed against a common threat. Taylor thinks of the spectacles of nationalistic hysteria produced by Adolph Hitler at Nuremberg. It is one of the tragic lessons of history that what brings a society together may be hatred of the stranger as much as love for the family. The effervescence fermented by national loyalty, religious purity, and ethnic cleansing has erupted into wars generated by politics of identity. Sacrifice itself has been transformed from a gesture of altruism and social cooperation into an instrument of tribal preservation, endured by its members as "martyrdom" and inflicted on its enemies as "justice."

What this analysis suggests is not that Durkheim was wrong about religious ritual *in general* serving as a means of reinforcing societal cohesion and sacrifice *in particular* representing the subordination of individual interests that makes community possible. To that extent, his insights help us understand the role of sacrifice in the religious traditions we will consider. What his theory cannot account for is the dark side of social solidarity: the violent exclusion of those outside the community. Their status is ambivalent, of course, since social identity is in part defined by one's difference from those belonging to other social groups. So could it be that sacrifice of one who is "outside" is what is required to preserve social unity on the "inside"? Our next theorist thought that was precisely the case.

Sacrifice as Basis of Social Solidarity: René Girard

The theorist who embraced moral ambivalence at the heart of his theory of sacrifice is the philosopher and literary critic, René Girard (1923–2015), who maintains, "Sacrifice is the primordial institution of human culture."[24] Girard spent forty years developing the view that ritual sacrifice is the replication of the collective murder of an innocent victim that provides temporary release from the tensions of competing desires among members of a society. He calls such jealous yearning for what others possess "mimetic desire" and locates it at the base of the human psyche. To resolve the vicious cycle of mutual aggression, members of a social order in crisis displace their antagonism on an anonymous victim, a stranger or outcast. In that way, after the victim has been killed, the persecutors can resume constructive relations without initiating a destructive cycle of retribution. That is, the poor devil or witch has no family demanding satisfaction for the murder, so everyone agrees on his or her guilt and goes back to business as usual with a clear conscience—until mimetic desire stirs the pot of animosity again and a new scapegoat must be identified and sacrificed.

Girard further speculates that the effect of this "scapegoat mechanism" is to re-establish social order in such an effective way that the victim comes to be regarded as a divine savior. Thus, sacrifice is the origin of religion. According to Girard, however, mythology disguises the killing at the basis of social solidarity by presenting the victim as guilty of crimes that justify the murder. In one of Girard's favorite examples, the Greek myth reads as if Oedipus *really* did kill his father and sleep with his mother, while Girard regards that account as an artful disguise for the unjust exile (and effective killing) of Oedipus.[25] Girard argues that narratives of sacrifice constructed by persecutors always mask the truth of their persecution. His argument is helped by the fact that myth and mystery are both related to the Greek verb *mustein*, to keep silent. For Girard, when it comes to sacrifice, myth is the original cover-up.

The founder of psychoanalysis, Sigmund Freud (1856–1939), read the Oedipus myth as the key to understanding primal urges of the human psyche, specifically a son's resentment of his father as competitor for the affection of his mother—a universal aspect of the human psyche that is famously called the "Oedipal complex." Freud extended his speculation to imagine that civilization originated in the murder of the tribal father by the horde of his progeny. These sons then assuaged their guilt by elevating the father, victim of their collective violence, into a divine figure; and, "in their reaction to that impious deed, they determined to respect his will thenceforward."[26] From this origin, religious beliefs and rituals arose as "neurotic relics" of the universal anxiety about the repressed memory of the murder of the primal father. Freud believed that psychoanalysis could overcome neurosis and rational "education to reality" could discredit the "system of wishful illusions" that sprang from it. Thus, religion would be abandoned when other childhood fears and obsessions fade away as we mature.

Inasmuch as Freud regarded the myth of Oedipus as the paradigm of the human condition, however, Girard claims that Freud did "no more than rejuvenate and universalize the eternal lie of mythology" that the victim is guilty as charged.[27] While Girard's claim may hold against Freud's interpretation of the myth of Oedipus, Freud understands the myth as a symbolic expression of the fraught relationship between any child and its parents. That is, he reads myths of primeval killing as coded expressions of *individual* psychological conflicts. In contrast, Girard reads such myths as suppressed accounts of *collective* violence against surrogate victims. With regard to the social function of sacrifices of scapegoats, Girard acknowledges in his later writing that his theory is more closely aligned with "what Durkheim called 'the volcanic origins of religion.' Mimetic theory is a radicalized Durkheimianism" in that it "seeks to make the violence it divines behind the myths reappear, even when the violence is considerably effaced."[28] For Girard the effervescence of religious festivals is the source of violent energy that the crowd directs toward a common sacrificial victim to reassert their social unity.

Girard moves his theory in a distinctly Christian direction by claiming that the story of Jesus's crucifixion exposes the "lie" of scapegoat mythology by insisting on the innocence of the victim. That is, Jesus's death reveals that killing innocent victims fails as the ground of social unity. While some Christian apologists employ Girard's theory to promote Christianity as the chief antidote to societal violence,[29] there is a more neutral and inclusive way to read Girard, namely, that the death of any victim who is transparently innocent calls into question the scapegoat mechanism of social formation.[30] Thus, we can generalize Girard's

theory to include all religious narratives that insist on the innocence of
victims killed in the service of social or nationalist ends. In stories, for
example, in which victims of injustice call for forgiveness rather than
retaliation, the violence of mimetic rivalry is defeated. Therefore, any
religion that builds unanimity on the basis of forgiveness, rather than
over the body of a victim, offers a non-violent means of achieving social
solidarity, exposing the murderous origin of the sacrificial system. Certainly, in religions of Abraham social conflicts are ideally resolved not
by the death of a scapegoat, but by the subordination of private interests
to the common good, a form of self-sacrifice.

Sacrifice as Marker of Patriarchy: Nancy Jay

An alternative interpretation of sacrifice as a means of creating social
order is the influential work of sociologist of religion Nancy Jay,
whose career was cut short by cancer in 1991. She locates the psychological basis of sacrificial ritual in the desire of males to control lines
of descent and inheritance. Through sacrifice, men displace women's
claims to the children they birth with men's claims to their offspring,
reborn by ritual sacrifice. Across a wide range of cultural sites, Jay finds
evidence that male blood-letting in sacrifice supplants female blood-
shedding in childbirth. In this way, men establish lines of paternity and
control transmission of property and wealth to favored sons in perpe-
tuity. "Sacrificially constituted descent, incorporating women's mortal
children into an 'eternal' (enduring through generations) kin group, in
which membership is recognized by participation in sacrificial ritual,
not merely by birth, enables a patrilineal group to transcend mortality
in the same process in which it transcends birth. In this sense, sacrifice
is doubly a remedy for having been born of woman."[31] She finds among
her disparate case studies a "common sacrificial principle," namely, that
sacrifice conserves an artificially (that is, ritually) constructed line of
descent from the father that surpasses in duration and authority natural
descent from the mother.[32]

By way of a familiar example, she recalls the story of Abraham's near-
sacrifice of Isaac, interrupted by an angel and completed in the death
of a ram. "By this act, Isaac, on the edge of death, received his life not
by birth from his mother but from the hand of his father as directed by

God and the granting of life was a deliberate, purposeful act rather than a mere natural process, a spiritual 'birth' accomplished without female assistance." She adds significantly, "Abraham received, at this sacrifice, assurance of countless descendants."[33] In the account in the Bible those chosen people are identified as offspring of Isaac, designated as the favored son (over Ishmael) by sacrifice. In this interpretation, Isaac is not "as good as dead" on Mount Moriah but is actually "brought to life" by the sacrifice that binds him to his father's covenant with God. That is, Isaac's natural birth is superseded by his spiritual rebirth through sacrifice. His birth mother, Sarah, is absent from the scene, just as women are generally excluded from sacrificial ritual. For Jay that exclusion is deliberate and consistent across religious communities that sustain patriarchal social order. Women generate mortal children from their bodies, while men create immortal spiritual sons through ritual. For that reason, in patriarchal societies women are excluded from priesthood. Their offspring are born as mortal creatures of nature who must be recreated by the artificial generation of blood sacrifice offered by men.

Jay's work is of interest here for several reasons. First, she illustrates that sacrifice is a cultural invention that can serve to confirm and sanctify hierarchical relations of power within a society. Second, she directs attention to the voices of women that are often muffled by layers of patriarchal tradition. Third, she challenges Girard's account of human culture as universally torn apart by reciprocal violence and thus always requiring sacrifice as the means of restoring order. To this bleak view, and its insistence on the imposition of male authority to resolve the problem of male violence, she notes that everything "that arises from the sociability of mothers and infants or from any other affectionate relationship is irrelevant."[34] Here is a point of primary importance for our study. The idea that human beings evolve as combative by nature and that their competition can be resolved only through violence is not a neutral observation but the expression of an ideology. Girard's theory that the mutual animosity of mimetic desire among males can be temporarily relieved through the persecution and sacrifice of a scapegoat derives from his conviction that humans are so threatened by any disruption of social order that we routinely turn to violence to restore stability.

Jay's study discloses the oppressive effect of that ideology on women and challenges its claim to be universally true. She is careful to limit the context of sacrifice as a legitimation of patriarchal order to "common conditions of life, such as the way agrarian and pastoral systems of production may lead to a concern for birth- and death-transcending male intergenerational continuity." That is, crops may fail and herds may die, but sons reborn through ritual sacrifice will continue the line of their fathers "forever." Jay understands sacrifice in these conditions as a putative remedy for the obsessive fear of death and social disorder. One question her study raises is, why make mortality the central focus of social construction? Why create rituals, institutions, and founding stories dedicated to averting death? Why not take the opposite tack and build social order for the purpose of sustaining and celebrating life?

That is the direction professor of religion and gender, Grace Jantzen (1948–2006), took in her groundbreaking work, *Becoming Divine: Towards a Feminist Philosophy of Religion*. She argued for displacing focus on death and morbidity with attention to birth and natality. Rather than ordering society into abstract categories, including gender and race, and restricting individuals within the roles assigned to those categories, Jantzen called for liberating personal creativity from social constructs (especially the ones enforcing male authority) and nurturing the natural vitality and beauty with which every human enters the world.[35] Her work also promotes an ethic of responsibility for the concrete other in whose company we pursue whatever ideal ends we imagine, but whose actual dignity and rights always take moral precedence over abstract visions of political or religious perfection. We may "become divine," but only through respect and appreciation for each other's human reality. In this view, sacrifice for other humans may be virtuous, but sacrificing humans (including oneself) for an imagined divine "other" may be the greatest transgression of all, the "original sin" of religion.

For both Jay and Jantzen religious sacrifice serves spiritual ideals at the expense of natural bonds. For Jay, sacrifice is a means of sustaining social arrangements that suppress women and mediate eternal life through male violence; for Jantzen, religion compensates for human fear of death by suppressing natural vitality and creativity within patriarchal social institutions that promise immortality to those who conform to their demands. These theories challenge the call for women and men to sacrifice themselves to maintain the very social order that oppresses them both. But what if religion, understood as an intimate relation with the divine, is opposed to social order of any sort—and what if sacrifice is the extravagant and decisive act that reunites humans with the order of nature rather than alienating us from it? These are the startling and radical views of sacrifice developed by the last theorist we shall consider.

Sacrifice as Liberation from Economies of Value: Georges Bataille

The controversial philosopher of surrealism, Georges Bataille (1897–1962), is best known for his celebration of excess and his obsession with sex, pain, and death—in all the ecstatic and degrading combinations those primal human drives are capable of forming. It is his focus on extremity that makes him a promising guide into the subject of sacrifice. The most provocative of his proposals is that any form of sacrifice that occurs within a system of exchange or "economy" is a covert attempt to serve self-interest, whether it is the sacrifice of a sheep to secure atonement for sins or the death of a warrior in battle to prove his valor and win honor in defense of his homeland. For Bataille, every sacrificial act that functions as the condition of a benefit is tainted with self-interest.

The problem is fundamental to all religious systems that require giving (up) self to gain liberation, enlightenment, salvation, immortality, or whatever is on offer as the ultimate possibility for human experience. How can I shut both eyes to my private interests and still keep one open, focused on my spiritual advancement? For the theorists we have considered so far, that is a false worry since sacrifice always serves some social purpose: from promoting altruism to conserving established political order. Even those who sacrifice to achieve a relation with transcendent reality have a goal in mind, some benefit the sacrifice promises to produce. For Bataille, on the contrary, "Sacrifice is the antithesis of production."[36] Religious sacrifice has nothing to do with maintaining society or even communing with gods; it is the means of escape from every economy of exchange. By sacrifice alone can we return to the state of being prior to the rise of human self-consciousness—the pure immanence of animal existence, free from all distinctions based on economic value. That, for Bataille, is the sacred.

Bataille opens up the disruptive power of religion by emphasizing the way the sacred stands against social order, rather than sanctioning and representing it. His theory contradicts Durkheim's view that religion serves the function of establishing and maintaining social solidarity. For Bataille religion signifies the transcendent precisely by overthrowing all systems constructed by humans, systems that reduce individuals to cogs in a machine, whether industrial, military, or religious. Where sacrifice contributes to sustaining any system of exploitation and alienation of the individual, it fails to reach transcendence. Only sacrifice that is offered as total loss, with no interest in future return or benefit, can free individuals from systems of production that measure their worth in terms of economic contribution. Only by returning to an original state of nature can we find the sacred that is prior to religious institutions that mediate access to it and apart from theological ideas that designate it in objective terms. In the realm of immanence there are no selves or gods or "others" of any kind.

For Bataille, a return to "lost intimacy" with the sacred requires subverting every system of mediation, whether political, economic, or religious. Intimacy violates the isolation of the individual by transgressing personal boundaries, disclosing secrets, and dissolving identity. What is true of human relationships is also true of the relation to the sacred, whether established in mystic ecstasy or in the excess of sacrifice and festival. True religion, then, enables periodic return to the state of immanence through rituals of sacrifice by which we remove the offering and ourselves from the economy of production and through celebrative festivals in which moral order is suspended in transgressive orgy. The return can never be permanent, however, because human consciousness requires an awareness of the objectified other. Yearning for lost intimacy with the divine in the state that precedes the rise of self-consciousness, and grasping that intimacy only in rare and fleeting moments of total loss, religious persons exist in "sacred anguish."[37]

In his most lengthy work, *The Accursed Share*, Bataille argues that economy should be based on consumption rather than production. His evidence is that no system of production (from the organism to the cosmos) can expand indefinitely by investing the energy it produces into new growth. Inevitably, the system accumulates an excess of energy that must be expended without purpose or profit. The surplus energy, in whatever form, must be given up or given away as sheer loss, squandered as the "accursed share" of the exuberance of life. At the cosmic level, the sun exemplifies this law of economy by supplying earth with light and warmth that nourishes life by an operation of self-destruction with no possibility of receiving reciprocal benefit: "Solar energy is the source of life's exuberant development. The origin and essence of our wealth are given in the radiation of the sun, which dispenses energy— wealth—without any return. The sun gives without ever receiving."[38]

Bataille believes that, in pre-industrial societies, this law was understood and honored in economies that encouraged consumption rather than production and valued giving over hoarding. While he offers several examples, we will consider one that urgently poses the question whether humans can ever give as the sun does, that is, without interest in reciprocal benefit: human sacrifice by Aztecs. Bataille notes that Aztecs followed an economy unlike that of European nations influenced by Christianity. "Their world view is singularly and diametrically opposed to the activity-oriented perspective that we have. Consumption loomed just as large in their thinking as production does in ours. They were just as concerned about *sacrificing* as we are about *working*. The sun himself was in their eyes the expression of sacrifice."[39]

Aztec human sacrifice was astonishingly cruel. Priests tore the still-beating hearts from the flayed chests of victims atop pyramids constructed for the purpose and then flung their lifeless bodies down the stairs.[40] Bataille notes that most victims were prisoners of war and infers that for the Aztecs "wars meant consumption, not conquest" and then adds, they "thought that if they ceased [to offer sacrifices] the sun would cease to give light."[41] This comment suggests, however, that Aztec sacrifice was also a form of production achieved by exchange and thus not different from the Roman bargain, "I give that you may give." The exchange of the lives of slaves for solar energy occurs in what Bataille calls the "order of things" in which individuals are valued for their utility. Thus, slaves are reduced to property before their lives are squandered.

For Bataille, however, the act of being sacrificed has the paradoxical effect of liberating the victim from the status of an object by destroying its value *as a commodity*. "Once chosen, he is the *accursed share*, destined for violent consumption. But the curse tears him away from the *order of things*." At the same time, through identification with the victim, those who sacrifice also withdraw from the economy of production by their wastrel consumption. Sacrifice suspends the "order of things" and returns every participant in the stylized drama to what Bataille calls the "order of intimacy." This state of consciousness is not divided by awareness of the other and is uninterested in production of wealth and obsession with growth and accumulation that wealth generates. Rather, in the condition of intimacy there are no projects, no achievements, and no investment in future outcomes—only intense awareness of the present. "If I am no longer concerned about 'what will be' but about 'what is,' what reason do I have to hold anything in reserve? I can at once, in disorder, make an instantaneous consumption of all that I possess."[42] To be free from the future is to escape from bondage to things so that all can now be consumed, donated, or wasted. All three gestures of intimacy are performed in sacrifice and create a bond between the sacrificed and the one who sacrifices.

In that way both the victim and the sacrificer are removed from economy of exchange. "The thing—only the thing—is what sacrifice means to destroy in the victim." Putting words into the mouth of an ancient priest addressing his victim, Bataille gives dramatic expression to the intention of religious sacrifice: "I withdraw you, victim, from the world in which you were and could only be reduced to the condition of a thing, having a meaning that was foreign to your intimate nature. I call you back to the *intimacy* of the divine world, of the profound immanence of all that is." While death also releases the individual from the "society of labor," death is not necessary for sacrifice.[43] What is essential is freedom from value based on future consumption. "Sacrifice is the antithesis of production, which is accomplished with a view to the future; it is consumption that is concerned only with the moment. This is the sense in which it is gift and relinquishment . . . in sacrifice the offering is rescued from all utility."[44]

When morality and reason attain the status of transcendence as attributes of God, then the religious quest is reduced to a business in which one "achieves salvation in the same way that one spins wool."[45] This thought leads Bataille to his clearest statement that the significance of sacrifice lies not so much in the destruction of the victim but in the disruption of systems of value that alienate us from the intimate or sacred order. For example, conventional morality cannot sanction violence, but intimacy requires its transformative power as exercised in sacrifice. What makes the violence "divine" is precisely that it disrupts human systems of morality, revealing "that the sacred and the forbidden are one, that the sacred can be reached through the violence of a broken taboo."[46] The challenge Bataille poses is whether the transcendent character of the sacred *must* be experienced through violent disruption of systems of mediation. How can we know that the sacred is "other" than an artifact of human construction unless it razes every site we erect?

The means of that undoing is sacrifice, practiced as a form of *via negativa* (the way of negation that refuses to identify God with any known object in the world). That is the inner connection between sacrifice and mysticism. Bataille writes that "mystical experience seems to me to stem from the universal experience of religious sacrifice." As sacrifice destroys its object as a useful thing, so "mystical experience reveals an absence of any object."[47] In short, Bataille's view is "the heir to a fabulous mystical theology, but missing a God and wiping the slate clean."[48] By sacrificing traditional views of God as a supernatural agent capable of intervening in nature and history, Bataille accepts that each individual is alone in the world, bereft of divine assistance, concluding that "the sole truth of man . . . is to be a supplication without response."[49]

Bataille poses the most radical interpretation of sacrifice as total relinquishment, as a mystic erases personal identity in union with the divine without thought of future benefit. "Our desire to consume, to annihilate, to make a bonfire of our resources, and the joy we find in the burning, the fire and the ruin are what seem to us divine, sacred. They alone control sovereign attitudes in ourselves, attitudes that is to say which are gratuitous and purposeless, only useful for being what they are and never subordinated to ulterior ends." Thus, Bataille can say, "God—for me—means the lightning flash which exalts the creature above the concern to protect or increase his wealth in the dimension of time."[50]

If, then, incessant sacrifice is necessary for freedom, does Bataille propose we live in constant ascetic denial? By no means. Rather than recommending self-sacrifice as a form of humanist altruism, Bataille takes the opposite position, rejecting all asceticism. "One attains the extreme limit in the fullness of means: it demands fulfilled beings, ignoring no audacity. My principle against ascesis is that the extreme limit is accessible through excess, not through want." Over against the religious ideal of self-denial, Bataille insists that only by releasing erotic energy in full indulgence can we experience the depth of inner freedom. That is, our love for other beings in the intimacy that dissolves our separation is also key to our access to the sacred. He writes that "eroticism around us is so violent, it intoxicates hearts with so much force—to conclude, its abyss is so deep within us—that there is no celestial opening which does not take its form and its fever from it."[51] It is not by restraining natural vitality that we reach the divine, but by throwing off political, religious, and moral systems that seek to suppress and control erotic energy and individual freedom. Rather than sacrificing the concrete to the abstract, Bataille counsels the opposite. In this sense, his theory is the critique that shadows the analysis to follow.

If humans are to achieve "sovereign self-consciousness," they must sacrifice every other claimant to authority over them, including the sacred. The final twist in Bataille's theory of sacrifice is that the loss of the subject who sacrifices also signals the loss of the object to which one sacrifices. "The gods to whom we sacrifice are themselves sacrifice, tears wept to the point of dying."[52] To sacrifice the gods is also to accept the anguish of living without stable world order under divine control. Bataille calls for unending sacrifice of every security and for clear-eyed acceptance that human life itself finally ends as irretrievable loss. Bataille is as much a non-theist as Durkheim; but, unlike social scientific theorists of religion, Bataille believes there is a sacred realm, even if it is unknowable and beyond moral or rational control. Mystics might agree with him; but he would press them to acknowledge also that to achieve intimacy with the sacred, they must do violence to themselves, if not to others.

Bataille notoriously embraced sacrificial violence as the only act that can destroy the very status of the victim *as object*, so that what is offered no longer retains a place in the world of social and economic relations. Only from that ecstatic position, "standing outside" the world of useful transactions and mediated orders, can one glimpse the divine in the dark intimacy where the self is ravished. In the moment when interiority and thus alienation dissolve, when the one who offers becomes the gift that is offered, the sacrificer disappears in the sacred order of immanence. But no exchange is possible where there is no agent to initiate it and no economy to regulate it. Thus, the end of sacrifice as self-erasure also signaled for Bataille the death of God as the being who demands and accepts sacrifices.

This selective survey of theories of sacrifice presents us with a variety of functional explanations for sacrifice: gift exchange, expression of social values, communion with deity, displacement of cultural aggression, maintenance of patriarchal order, and freedom from economic systems of value. From these various reflections we may identify a common use of sacrifice to mark the difference between human and transcendent orders of reality. Sacrifice demonstrates the utter alterity of God in comparison to whom all human possessions, achievements, and identities are transient and disposable.

3

Sacrifice in Jewish Tradition

You shall lay your hand on the head of the burnt offering,
and it shall be acceptable in your behalf as atonement for
   you . . .
an offering by fire of pleasing odor to the Lord.
—Leviticus 1:4, 9

For I desire steadfast love and not sacrifice,
the knowledge of God rather than burnt offerings.
—Hosea 6:6

The destruction of the Second Jewish Temple in Jerusalem by Roman forces in 70 CE ended animal sacrifice that had been performed there for centuries. That loss simultaneously opened the way for reimagining devotional acts, such as prayer, good deeds, and Torah study, as offerings to God. Jewish tradition appropriated *sacrifice*, originally denoting ritual offerings, to describe and sanction ascetic and altruistic actions. Scholar of comparative religion Guy Stroumsa argues that the survival of Judaism depended on its transformation of sacrifice through finding in itself "an implicit medium of change, the leaven of interiorization."[1] Jewish teachers reinterpreted sacrifice as moral discipline and religious devotion in obedience to Torah (divine "instruction"). The sacrificial transaction is internal, but still carries potential for violence.

Legal scholar Moshe Halbertal notes that sacrifice as an act of self-transcendence, far from sublimating violence, may increase it. Having abandoned self-love for the sake of a higher cause, one may be more willing to compromise love for others in "self-transcendent actions, which might provide the basis for horrible crimes."[2] Denying self-interest cannot by itself insure moral conduct because the transcendent ideal one serves may itself prove to be evil. In that case, the determination to "lay all on the altar" in sacrifice may prove catastrophic to oneself and to others. Sacrifice is a fraught basis for morality. Nothing makes that fact clearer than the story in the Bible of Abraham's near-sacrifice of his son.

Sacrifice in Absolute Obedience: Abraham and Isaac

The best known story of sacrifice in Jewish tradition is one in which the sacrifice was not completed: Abraham's offering of Isaac, known as the *Akedah* or "binding."[3] God spoke to Abraham, "Take your son, your only son Isaac, whom you love, and go to the land of Moriah, and offer him there as a burnt offering on one of the mountains that I shall show you."[4] The command is introduced by the inside information that "God tested Abraham." As Abraham "took the knife to kill his son," an angel stayed his hand with the words, "now I know that you fear God, since you have not withheld your son, your only son, from me." When Abraham looked up, he "saw a ram, caught in a thicket by its horns. Abraham went and took the ram and offered it up as a burnt offering instead of his son" (Genesis 22:1, 9–13). Then the angel spoke a second time:

> By myself I have sworn, says the LORD: Because you have done this, and have not withheld your son, your only son, I will indeed bless you, and I will make your offspring as numerous as the stars of heaven and as the sand that is on the seashore. And your offspring shall possess the gate of their enemies, and by your offspring shall all the nations of the earth gain blessing for themselves, because you have obeyed my voice. (Genesis 22:15–18)

As a result of offering his son as a sacrifice, and accepting the provision of an animal as the proper substitute, Abraham received assurance that he would have countless progeny and that God would help them defeat their enemies and would make them the means of blessing the rest of humanity. Levenson notes that this second speech by the angel reads like an interpretive supplement to the story, grounding God's earlier call of Abraham in his "heroic act of obedience."[5] While the extravagant pledge of countless descendants is evoked by Abraham's obedience, it was not the condition for it. Abraham bound Isaac as a sacrifice with no indication that he expected to be rewarded—yet from that singular act issued not only Abraham's progeny, but also the basis of their divine protection and calling as a channel of blessing to the world. Abraham was blessed by his obedience to God's command, so the Jewish people came to believe that they would be blessed by obeying all God's commandments as a witness to virtue and faithfulness in the world.

That neat summary of the story is the version most readers learn in religious school; it sets the shocking narrative of an intended child sacrifice within the morally soothing framework of test and reward, faith and vindication. For Jewish children it is important to be assured that God did not desire the deaths of children; that even in that distant time, killing animals sufficed to atone for sins and that now obedience to God's commandments, following the example of Abraham, brings divine forgiveness. Their teachers shield their consciences by linking the offensive story to a later prophetic reversal. To the rhetorical questions, "Will the LORD be pleased with thousands of rams? . . . Shall I give my firstborn for my transgression?" the answer comes that the Lord requires you "to do justice, and to love kindness, and to walk humbly with your God" (Micah 6:7–8).

Christians also protect the moral sensitivity of their children by reading the story through a lens finely ground by apologetic interest. Christian teachers defend the moral character of both God and Abraham by focusing on the patriarch's heroic faith and not on his murderous intent. They instruct their charges to read Genesis 22 alongside the New Testament Epistle of James: "Was not our ancestor Abraham justified by works when he offered his son Isaac on the altar? You see that faith was active along with his works and faith was brought to completion by the works" (James 2:21–22). Thus they gently lead the young away from the scandal of the story and its potential to disrupt trust in the moral authority of scripture and to dampen enthusiasm for sacrificial self-giving.

Muslims soften the moral offense of the story in the Qur'an by emphasizing the obedience of the son to the divine command to his father. While the son is not named in the Qur'an, most Muslims believe it is Ishmael and not Isaac who accompanied Abraham. Islamic teachers assure their students that Ishmael was no passive victim of violent intent, but an exemplary *Muslim*, one utterly submitted to the will of God. In this version God tested both father and son and they were together declared faithful and given an animal to offer in the son's place. For that merciful substitution, Muslims continue to give thanks by offering animal sacrifices during the time of the annual pilgrimage to Mecca. In this way the moral problem of the story is dissolved, while its religious meaning as an occasion to thank God is crystallized.

All three religions of Abraham have ways of muting the ethical outrage of the story for their children—and, to be frank, for their adult members who prefer not to disturb their childhood faith with troubling questions. Nevertheless, serious thinkers in all these traditions have been profoundly disquieted by the spectacle of Abraham engaged in child sacrifice that they all denounce as despicable and barbaric, the very mark of pagan religion. We shall consider later Christian and Muslim interpretations of the story. For now, we are interested in the long and complex history of commentary developed within Jewish tradition and what we might learn from it about Jewish understanding of sacrifice as a paradigm, or normative model, of virtue—and also Jewish misgivings about sacrifice as religious ideal.

The story of Abraham tying his son and laying him on top of a pile of wood, ready to slit his throat and set him on fire as a "burnt offering" to Yahweh certainly sets an ominous scene. But just as Abraham raises the knife, an angel calls the whole thing off. Over the centuries, rabbis underscored the happy ending and insisted the whole point of the story was to demonstrate that God did *not* want Israelites to sacrifice their children to Yahweh as Canaanites did to gods such as Molech.[6] Their restraint was to be a mark of distinction between them and other people and their God and other gods. That is the "moral" Talmudic scholar and philosopher Emmanuel Levinas (1906–1995) also draws from the story: "Abraham's attentiveness to the voice that led him back to the ethical order, in forbidding him to perform a human sacrifice, is the highest point in the drama."[7] Levinas resolves the paradox of the sacrifice by denying it was required at all. In his reading, nature and religion are harmonized; faith lies down in peace with ethics. But that proposal merely transfers the moral scandal of the Akedah from Abraham to God who issued the horrible command in the first place.

A similar attempt to modify the moral scandal of God's requirement can be found in an annotation to Genesis 22:1 in the HarperCollins Study Bible, where we are complacently assured that God's "command is not in earnest, but Abraham does not know this."[8] But how does the commentator know what divine commands are "in earnest"? Abraham at least thought he knew with terrible clarity exactly what God demanded. Levenson argues that child sacrifice was practiced frequently enough in ancient Israel that the narrator of Genesis 22 would have good reason to believe that God was altogether serious and to expect his readers to acknowledge that fact.[9]

Certainly the unsparing law of Exodus 22:29—"The firstborn of your sons you shall give to me"—seems clear enough. Yet a straightforward reading of the command stands in sharp contrast to God's words in Leviticus 18:21: "You shall not give any of your offspring to sacrifice them to Molech, and so profane the name of your God." Prophets later offered interpretations of child sacrifice that sought to maintain the consistency of divine will, while providing guidance for how to obey that will. Jeremiah simply denies that God ever issued such a commandment (Jeremiah 7:31, 19:5) or that it even entered his mind.[10] Ezekiel affirms that Yahweh made the demand, but only as a form of punishment for the Israelites' failure to obey his laws: "I defiled them through their very gifts, in their offering up all their firstborn, in order that I might horrify them, so that they might know that I am the LORD" (Ezekiel 20:26). This solution, however, only makes the problem worse. God deceives the people and uses the death of their children to shock them into compliance. Ezekiel's explanation of why God required child sacrifice succeeds only in presenting Yahweh as a moral monster.

It is the word of *this* God that comes to Abraham—and it is precisely Abraham's willingness to kill his innocent son that calls forth divine approval.[11] Is the purpose to horrify Abraham so that he will acknowledge God as Lord? But God does not accuse Abraham of disloyalty and Abraham performs no more great deeds that this trial might have prepared him for. There is no evident precipitating occasion for God's command, and God never again speaks directly to Abraham in the Bible. The "angel of the LORD" declares the whole episode a "test" and commends Abraham for his "fear" of God. But what was the point? Was the sacrifice a *test* to be passed by performing it or was the call to sacrifice a *temptation* to be resisted in order to illustrate the true divine character? In either case, Abraham is caught in a dilemma. But is the conflict simply between divine demand and natural desire? Could the call to sacrifice come to Abraham *from within*? That is the sort of disturbing question that religious school teachers avoid; but it may open another avenue for exploring the allure of sacrifice, namely, the cathartic power of decisive and irreversible action.

Could it be that the choice facing Abraham is between two sides of his own disposition: Should he offer the innocent to seal the covenant and complete the exchange of boy for land or spare his child and risk the wrath of the divine partner? Were there other unresolved tensions that led him to bind his son and ready him for the fire? What uncertainty required the drastic resolution of sacrifice? Such questions evoke the psychoanalytic reading of the event that the commentator on Torah, Avivah Gottlieb Zornberg, offers in her reflections on interpretive traditions about the Akedah. Zornberg locates a thread running through the cycle of stories about Abraham that serves as a prologue to the climactic binding of Isaac: Abraham's misgivings about his relation to God. In support of her reading, Zornberg cites interpretations of Genesis in the form of *midrash*, rabbinic commentary on biblical narratives. She notes that in Genesis Abraham is never said directly to have offered animal sacrifices to God; as a result, the rabbis speculated that Abraham may have been unsure of his dedication to Yahweh.

Zornberg quotes midrash which interprets the opening phrase of Genesis 22—"After these things"—as referring to Abraham's qualms about his failure to sacrifice "a single bullock or ram for God."[12] God reassures him with the foreboding words, "In the end you will be told to sacrifice your only son to me, and you will not refuse." One rabbi modified this reading by imagining a dialogue in the heavenly court, much like the one in the prologue to the book of Job. The angels challenge whether Abraham is truly faithful if he has never offered a sacrifice and God answers, "If we tell him to offer his own son, he will not refuse." This account is immediately followed by an argument between Ishmael and Isaac over who is more beloved. Ishmael claims the honor because he consented to circumcision as an adult, while Isaac was circumcised as an infant. When Isaac declares himself willing to be slaughtered if God asked, God responded, "This is the moment!"—and immediately, "God tested Abraham."

Here it is the angels with misgivings, not Abraham, and it is Isaac who volunteers to be sacrificed; in these subtle ways the rabbinic commentator sought to brighten the shadow that otherwise falls over the intent to kill an innocent child. But Zornberg insists on the original midrash in which Abraham worries about his own identity and requires the sacrifice as a means of "coming close" (literal meaning of one Hebrew term for sacrifice, *korban*) to God. In her reading, sacrifice addresses "the human need for intensified experience, in which . . . the cloudy ambiguities of life in time are violently charged with apocalyptic clarity."[13] In his quest for intimacy with Yahweh, Abraham desires the irrevocable and decisive act of sacrifice to resolve his inner uncertainty.

Further, it is the only way to enact his understanding of God's command which "comes to him clouded with possible meanings."[14] Zornberg reconstructs from various *midrashim* (the Hebrew plural of midrash) a pre-history for Abraham in which he is nearly murdered by his own father for smashing his father's idols; an angry crowd throws him into a furnace from which God miraculously rescues him (a tradition that also figures in the Qur'an). Thus, Abraham comes to the place of sacrifice as a fatherless child, perhaps the odor of the smoke in which he might have died lingering in his memory, carrying the knife with which he plans to become a childless father and the fire in which he will immolate his son's body. Driven by misgivings about his relation to God, Abraham resolves to act in a way that will leave no question about his absolute allegiance to God.

With Zornberg's exploration into the "unconscious" of Abraham we have intruded more deeply into the patriarch's subjectivity than we should perhaps dare to tread. Yet Zornberg makes the ambitious claim that through her analysis, "a theory of sacrifice emerges," namely, that humans desire sacrifice "as a clarification, as a simplification, a showing-forth, in a world of moral ambiguity. At the heart of all symbolic and hypothetical rhetoric about commitment waits the possibility, even the necessity, of literal enactment."[15] According to the old proverb, talk is cheap; and its unspoken counterpoint is, actions are costly. So Abraham proceeds to sacrifice his beloved son to prove his loyalty to God.

Or does Abraham obey the divine command because he regards his privileged relation to God as canceling the obligation to protect his son? That is the way Kierkegaard read the story, reflecting his obsessive worry about Abraham's subjectivity. Given the intertextual relations between later Jewish thinkers and Kierkegaard's Protestant Christian commentary on the Akedah, we reintroduce the latter here. Kierkegaard emphasized that Abraham loved his son, even as he raised the dagger over

Isaac's bound body. Abraham's state of mind was marked by simultaneous movements of resignation of Isaac to death and hope for his restoration to life. There was no possibility of reconciling these opposed states of mind and no miraculous benefit Abraham could count on as a reward for passing the test. There was only the unrelieved strain of risking all by killing his son as an unconditional offering in obedience to divine command. Abraham could enter the religious realm only by transgressing ethical boundaries, by literally stepping over the body of his dead son.

Extending Kierkegaard's analysis, philosopher Jacques Derrida (1930–2004) renders Abraham's choice utterly exclusive. Since "every other is entirely other (*tout autre est tout autre*)," Derrida argues, Abraham cannot attend to God with full loyalty and care for his son at the same time.[16] To obey God he must abandon Isaac and in doing so give up his own rationality. "Paradox, scandal, and aporia are themselves nothing other than sacrifice," Derrida writes, "the exposure of conceptual thinking to its limit, to its death and finitude. As soon as I enter into a relation with the other . . . I know that I can respond only by sacrificing ethics, that is to say by sacrificing whatever obliges me to also respond, in the same way, in the same instant, to all the others." Derrida ends this remarkable passage with the claim that Abraham "would not be able to opt for fidelity to his own, or to his son, unless he were to betray the absolute other: God, if you wish." But that is an odd way to think about God, as a limited being in competition with other finite objects for human loyalty. It is also a very odd way to think about human relationships, as if love for one person requires betrayal of all others. In what intelligible sense could one's child be "every bit other (*tout autre*)" to oneself? Here is a dramatic example of the truth that a pun does not constitute an argument; it remains a joke—and not all that funny.

Further, Derrida supposes that we are incapable of making discriminating choices among the urgency and legitimacy of multiple ethical demands. "I will never be able to justify the fact that I prefer or sacrifice any one (any other) to the other," he continues. "I will always be in secret."[17] Secrecy may preserve the mysterious freedom of individual choice, but it can hardly serve as a basis for ethical conduct. Most of our decisions are a matter of sorting out prima facie duties, competing obligations that we must decide among, and then acting out that choice in public where we are held accountable.

Finally, Derrida's interpretation undercuts the possibility of ethical reflection on sacrifice. He insists that "there is no language, no reason, no generality or mediation to justify this ultimate responsibility which leads us to absolute sacrifice."[18] At the same time, his intention is to increase our obligation to every human by making every individual as transcendent to the other as each is to God. The choice to help one person rather than another cannot be justified if each lays an absolute claim upon one's time and resources. As one scholar astutely observes, "the Kierkegaardian sphere of absolute duty to God is reconstructed as the sphere of the absolute duty that any human being has to every other. . . . we cannot distinguish between the infinite alterity of God and the otherness of every human being anymore."[19] In a reversal of the Enlightenment move to demystify religious claims as exaggerated moral prescriptions, Derrida intensifies ethical duty to the point that facing the call of any other human is the functional equivalent of encountering the sacred, "God if you wish."

By this provocative re-inscription of religious language on to ethical duty, Derrida cannot avoid also imprinting the mystery and ambiguity of the sacred on human relations—with the result of removing Abraham's sacrifice from moral judgment or constraint, as well as from the coherence of theoretical understanding. In this view sacrifice is unconditional and unintelligible. Abraham cannot even exercise deliberate choice. What considerations of piety or prudence or duty could he consult? Just as anything may follow logically from a paradox, so nothing follows morally from an utterly unique action hidden from view by secrecy, particularly if Abraham is hearing only the echoes of his own concealed trauma in the chamber of his mind.

That consideration brings us to another element of uncertainty in sacrifice that the Akedah illustrates: How does Abraham know that it is God who speaks to him? Commentators often take the biblical text at face value—"God said"—and move immediately to ponder the moral scandal of the divine command. But the Jewish philosopher Martin Buber (1878–1965) raises the prior question posed "by the problematics of the hearing itself. Who is it whose voice one hears?" Buber points out that elsewhere in the Bible the "voice of God" is not clearly identifiable. That uncertainty makes Buber very cautious about agreeing that religious faith requires suspending moral duty. He insists that "the question of questions which takes precedence over every other is: Are you really addressed by the Absolute or by one of his apes? . . . Ever and ever again men are commanded from out of the darkness to sacrifice their Isaac." For Buber, when it is unclear whether the call to sacrifice comes from God or an imitator of divine authority, one should be guided by clear and agreed-upon ethical restraint. Otherwise, we may offer our children and our integrity on the altars of false gods. "In the realm of Moloch, honest men lie and compassionate men torture. And they really and truly believe that brother-murder will prepare the way for brotherhood. There appears to be no escape from the most evil of all idolatry."[20]

Buber is famous for his mystical prose, but here his critique is soundly pragmatic. In considering calls to sacrifice we should be deeply suspicious of those who claim to speak with absolute right. In our age, when divine presence is so evanescent as to be nearly invisible (that is, when it approaches absence) and when divine voice is a thin whisper all but inaudible (that is, when it approaches silence)—in this time of the "eclipse of God"—now is precisely *not* the time to claim religious authority for suspending moral constraint. Now is *not* the time to sacrifice our children and our virtue in the name of absolute value, regardless of whether we call that compelling abstraction "God." For Derrida, absolute responsibility to every person makes sacrifice a paradoxical necessity, while Buber argues that the very idea of "absolute duty" is as vague as the "voice of God." There is not enough clarity about divine revelation to justify abandoning the moral guidance that forbids "brother-murder." *Sacrifice* may be one way of talking about killing and dying as sacred, but it is a rhetorical mask worn by false gods. Buber would have little patience with Derrida's exemption of sacrifice from rational analysis and ethical critique.

Yet Derrida indicates another way of approaching the story that may move us beyond paradox when he notes "the absence of woman" in the story of the binding of Isaac. This void startles him into speculating whether sacrifice entails "an exclusion or sacrifice of woman," but he is content to "leave the question in suspense."[21] We can correct that omission by attending to the voice of Sarah, wife of Abraham, whose presence in the rabbinic tradition is registered as a scream. In that tradition Sarah tells us something about the cost of sacrifice that the Bible does not include.

According to one midrash, Abraham persuaded Sarah to let Isaac leave home, but when he returned, she was horrified by his story. When she heard what nearly happened to her son, she wailed six times and died. Her cries provide the tones of the *shofar*, a ram's horn representing the animal substituted for Isaac blown as a trumpet on High Holy Days.[22] Why does Sarah die? Zornberg attributes Sarah's death to the shock of the fragility of human life, the "unbearable lightness of being" that spins her downward into the "vertigo of Nothingness."[23] Sarah's wailing (*ululation* or howling in grief) gave voice to the truth of a scream; for her, the near sacrifice of Isaac was apocalyptic, revealing the end of her world.

But what did she learn that she had not known before? Could it have come as news to a woman in the ancient Mideast that life is precarious? Levinas argued that the Akedah is a story of restoration of moral order, the foundation of the ancient Israelite social world, not its destruction. If so, that insight escaped Sarah. Perhaps what the midrash indicates is that she died of horror at Abraham's ferocious loyalty to Yahweh by which he overcame his natural inclination and moral responsibility as a father; he ceased to be human for love of the divine. Abraham acts as if he were God, deciding who lives and who dies, under the spell of the illusion of absolute authority that fuels all religious violence. Perhaps Sarah foresaw the horror of human will, unconstrained by natural sympathy, sacrificing children for God or Land or Nation.

From this perspective, Abraham's binding of Isaac signifies the triumph of religion over nature achieved in every bloody offering, every ascetic torture, and every hermetic isolation from human companionship; in short, every sacrifice. Spiritual heroes often violate the moral code of their traditions. That conflict with social ethics is inevitable insofar as sacrifice is a means of establishing a relation with transcendent reality; to go beyond the human requires surpassing cultural obligations. The spectacle can evoke a gasp of admiration or a scream of protest.

At this point, though, we must pause to consider Levenson's strong objection to this line of moral criticism, placing the story "exclusively within the domain of ethics."[24] He regards this approach as grounded in Enlightenment rationalism and characteristic of modern use of the story to condemn Abraham and, by implication, the religious traditions that continue to revere him. For Levenson the historical record is clear that

Jews, Christians, and Muslims never understood the story as an example to be followed literally. All three traditions forbid child sacrifice; indeed, their ethical teachings require the care and nurture of children. He insists that the meaning of the story in Jewish tradition lies in its religious significance as a demonstration of "Abraham's absolute commitment to God—his obedience to God, his faith in God, his love of God." Thus, "Jews can still reenact the profound message of the Aqedah in their self-surrender to the will of God in the form of observance of the mitsvot, the commandments of Torah."[25]

After that eloquent benediction, with which Levenson concludes his discussion of the Akedah, it may seem insensitive to persist in moral critique of the story. As Buber demonstrates, however, one need not be a secular humanist to question the wisdom of "absolute commitment" to anything. The adjective itself indicates an unqualified certainty and total absence of doubt no reflective human being could responsibly claim—except perhaps the Abraham of Kierkegaard's heated imagination who dared to believe he was in an "absolute relation to the Absolute" that transformed his murderous intent into religious faith. Surely, though, Levenson is not using "absolute" in Kierkegaard's sense of "unconditional" because he reads Abraham through Jewish tradition that teaches love of God is exercised by obedience to his commandments, including the prohibition of murder. Thus, Abraham's "absolute commitment" to God cannot be reenacted by Jews precisely because their relation to God is conditioned by Torah and by traditional mediation of its instruction. That is, between Abraham and his children stand Moses and the rabbis.

That's a good thing, too, because Abraham by himself in Genesis is still scary. The spectacle that evoked Sarah's scream has required centuries of ingenious exegesis and ritual domestication to become suitable as a story to tell children. Yet after all the effort to contain the scandal of the story, the salient feature, even in the revisions, is that God provoked Abraham to form the intention to sacrifice his son. Even Levenson, in an earlier work, placed that fact in the foreground to be taken with utmost seriousness—and we will continue to do so in this book.

We have devoted a great deal of attention to the story of the binding of Isaac in Jewish tradition because it illumines elements of the practice of sacrifice that contribute to comparative study. Without question, Abraham's act is risky: He offers his son with no guarantee that the sacrifice will be accepted or that his performance of the irrevocable act will quiet his indecisive mind or that he will perform it impeccably.[26] In short, as Zornberg notes, the Akedah is "an event haunted by misgivings."[27]

Yet this near sacrifice is recalled in temples and synagogues each year during Rosh Hashanah (New Year) services as an occasion for reflecting on transgression and forgiveness when the sound of a ram's horn represents God's compassion in substituting the animal for the child. Even though God's demand of the sacrifice from Abraham was not because the patriarch had sinned, the function of sacrifice to atone for violations of divine law is deeply embedded in Jewish tradition. Further, while scholars dispute the interpretation of the Akedah as a polemic against human sacrifice, the story lives on in popular Jewish piety in precisely that way, namely, as evidence that God showed mercy in response to Abraham's faith by ransoming Isaac through the death of a ram. In similar fashion, those who offer their will to the guidance of Torah have grounds for asking forgiveness of their sins on High Holy Days.

Ritual Sacrifice in Ancient Israel

While the best known parts of the Pentateuch (first five books of the Hebrew Bible, also called Torah) are stories of Adam and Eve, Noah, Abraham, and Moses, much of Torah is devoted to instructions in sacrificial rites. During the time the Temple stood, ritual slaughter and disposition of animals was the chief enterprise of Israelite priests. It is important to distinguish between these later rituals, performed by priests in designated areas for purposes of community formation, and stories of sacrifice by exemplary figures, such as Abraham, for emulation (if not duplication) by individuals within those communities. In the preceding section we dealt with the story of the Akedah and its troubling example of loyal obedience to God. Now we turn to rituals of animal sacrifice in ancient Israel as represented in the books of Leviticus and Deuteronomy.[28] But first we return to Genesis for the story that reveals God's preference for animal victims.

The first sacrifice in the Bible by the sons of Adam and Eve was a partial failure: Cain brought an offering of "fruit from the ground" of his field but the Lord "had no regard" for it and instead accepted Abel's gift of "the firstlings of his flock, their fat portions" (Genesis 4:4–5). God's preference for succulent lamb over grain is not explained, even though Yahweh reprimands Cain, implying that he should have known better. But how did either of the brothers know that they were expected to sacrifice to God, much less what offerings were acceptable? Each brought choice products of his work, emblems of his success as a productive agent—but we are not told *why* they should do so. There is no record of Adam and Eve offering a sacrifice. How did it come into the heads of their sons to make these strange, destructive gestures? Were they driven by a sense of duty by which they owed gifts in exchange for God's providing the fecund earth and fertile flocks? Or perhaps their labor had produced a surplus they could neither use nor preserve and so could only waste as what Bataille called the "accursed share."

Either as gift exchange or as useless consumption, Cain and Abel brought their offerings with the expectation that they would be accepted. Yet without warning or explanation, Yahweh turned up his nose at Cain's leafy stalks and smacked his lips at Abel's roasted meat. Cain is angry and turns his jealous wrath on Abel, killing him.[29] The deed cannot be concealed from God who declares, "your brother's blood is crying out to me from the ground" (Genesis 4:10). In punishment God makes the ground infertile for Cain and exiles him to wander as a fugitive, cursed and banished from the presence of Yahweh but given a mark of protection.

Yet the story in Genesis does not end with the divine curse on Cain, nor does it consign him to endless wandering. On the contrary, we read something more promising. Unable to raise crops, Cain "knew his wife, and she conceived and bore Enoch; and he built a city." Then, to make it utterly clear that Cain was making the most of the creative power left to him, he named the city after his son. Child and city, progeny and settlement, became Cain's mature response to his failed sacrifice. He replaced his violent outburst of jealousy with constructive actions that do not, notably, include offering sacrifices to God. Instead, his offspring domesticated animals, created music, and were the first to make bronze and iron tools.

What can we make of this curious story? If we read this text against its standard interpretation, we might suppose this is not a story of failed sacrifice at all but a tale of sacrifice as failure.[30] Suppose the point is not the curse of Cain but the blessing of his wisely displacing violence by natural and cultural creation—a celebration of human civilization free from sacrifice. Cain's culture, like Sarah's scream, is a "counter-tradition" that challenges traditional readings of the stories. We shall see that other accounts of sacrifice also contain seeds of their own undoing. For now we return to the risk in sacrifice.

The scholar of Jewish thought, Moshe Halbertal, notes that "the risk of rejection is inherent in the act of sacrifice." He explains that the Hebrew term used for these first offerings in the Bible is *minchah*, designating a gift offered by an inferior to a superior which is laid before the receiver, "who will decide whether to take it or not." It is this risk of rejection that led to the development of ritual procedures to protect priests offering sacrifices. The danger, as Halbertal sees it, is that such ritual can easily be viewed as having magical efficacy, "introducing a causal dimension that closes the gap between giving and receiving, thereby ensuring acceptance of the gift and leaving nothing voluntary to the recipient."[31] It is in protest against a magical reading of ritual that Hebrew prophets brought their thundering denunciations against sacrifices, reasserting the sovereign right of Yahweh to reject offerings that displease him. Anxiety about provoking divine wrath may well account for the obsessively detailed regulations of sacrifice in ancient Israel.[32] The excessive attention to detail reminds us of the uncertainty surrounding the offering of every sacrifice, but specifically the sacrifice performed on Yom Kippur, Day of Atonement.

The high priest performed the sacrifice, carrying the animals alone into the holiest place of the Temple. He was clothed in jewel-encrusted vestments, including a lower hem on his robe adorned with pomegranates fashioned of yarn alternating with golden bells.[33] The purpose of the bells is explained: "Aaron shall wear it when he ministers, and its sound shall be heard when he goes into the holy place, before the LORD, and when he comes out, so that he may not die" (Exodus 28:35). Other priests listened closely for the reassuring tinkle of the bells, proof that God had not struck the high priest dead for improper ritual performance that in turn might lead to rejection of the sacrifice (a possibility noted in Leviticus 16:2, 13).

A passage in the Talmud comments on a description in the *Mishnah* ("repetition" or "teaching," commentary compiled at the end of the second century) of the high priest's action in the Holy Place where he places a fire pan in front of the ark of the covenant "between the two bars" by which it was carried, piling incense on the coals, "so that the whole house was filled with smoke." Then these details are enumerated:

> He came out, going along by the way by which he had gone in.
> And he said a short prayer in the outer area.
> He did not prolong his prayer, so as not to frighten the Israelites.

Talmudic scholars read the first line as indicating that the high priest departed from the Holy of Holies in a respectful manner, not turning his back to the divine presence on the ark, but turning his face to the side and edging carefully out of the curtained area. They debate about the content of the prayer, but agree on the importance of its brevity so that the people awaiting the result of the atoning sacrifice would not be left in anxiety. They recall the case of a high priest who lingered in the Holy Place until the other priests decided to come in after him. He met them coming out and explained he had been praying for a long time to ensure their safety from divine wrath. But they admonished him, "Don't get in the habit of doing things that way. For lo, we have learned in the Mishnah: He did not prolong his prayer, so as not to frighten the Israelites."[34] Their fear was well-founded, given the precarious conditionality of ritual sacrifice.

The extent and complexity of ritual instructions in Leviticus and their elaboration by authorities in the first century are another source of performance anxiety in offering the various sacrifices associated with Yom Kippur. "As to every rite concerning the Day of Atonement that is set forth in a fixed order, if a deed was done out of order and prior to its fellow, the priest has done nothing of consequence" (Yoma 5:7). In Grimes's phrase, there are many opportunities for the ritual to "misfire" through inadvertent violation of the broad and ambiguous instructions in Torah. For example, rabbis devote much discussion to the timing of the Passover meal and the procedures for selecting and preparing the sacrificial lamb. They debate at length such questions as whether the lamb should be roasted over coals or an open flame, whether it is permissible to retrieve gravy that spilled onto an earthenware oven (if it was hot when spilled, no; if cold, the mixture is permissible), whether the blood of the offering should be sprinkled on the ground to secure atonement (if there is an "olive's bulk" of meat remaining after the sacrifice, yes; if not, no), and whether one may eat the gristle of the lamb but not its sinews.[35]

Further, throughout the entire ritual the priest must maintain the proper intentionality for, even "if all the rites are correctly carried out, if the priest does not do them with the right attitude, the sacrificer [the one on whose behalf the sacrifice is made] loses out."[36] Jewish law (*halakha*) governing ritual sacrifice requires meticulous attention to details of performance, intention, location, and timing. Ritual in general, Jonathan Z. Smith wrote, is "first and foremost, a mode of paying attention."[37] That attention is often so intense that Sigmund Freud likened ritual action to obsessional neurosis, the sort marked by compulsive hand-washing.

Certainly there are many commands in Torah about the hygiene of priests. But in the passages from the Talmud cited above, the rabbis seem anxious to develop standard procedures for sacrifice along the lines of a faculty handbook of a contemporary university, spelling out exactly what must be done in all areas of potential conflict, from tenure review and discrimination grievance to parking permits and library privileges. Is such attention to detail pathological? It can surely become exhausting, but the moral justification for such detailed legislation is far from trivial. The rule of civil law is the consistent application of judicial procedures to everyone equally. As dull as they may be at times, regulatory manuals serve justice by spelling out what each party in a dispute or transaction may expect from the other. The procedures, once agreed upon and confirmed by relevant authorities, protect all parties from further jeopardy by the law.

Sacrificial procedures as refined and extended by the rabbis appear to constitute just such a handbook, defining the what, where, when, and how of fulfilling the covenant with God—and thereby doing everything they could to insure God's acceptance of sacrifices. The curious fact, however, is that at the time they were composing the Mishnah (around 200 CE), the Temple in Jerusalem was long gone and animal sacrifices were no longer being offered! As historian of religion Kathryn McClymond argues, the elaborate discussion of how to avoid errors in rituals that were no longer performed is primarily "a display of rabbinic ritual mastery" designed to establish the authority of rabbinic discourse over cultic order: The Mishnah "unseats the priest as the central agent . . . and replaces him with the rabbi." Rabbinic ritual discourse, then, displaces sacrificial practice in the Temple with its own exercise in the academy as a "constant renegotiation" of the relationship between the people of Israel and the divine lawgiver.[38] While the rabbis created a complex and fluid language of sacrifice, reimagined as prayer and Torah study, not even they could eliminate the risk of rejection of their discursive offerings. That God exercises sovereign judgment in transcendent secrecy is a point of belief that places every sacrifice in suspense and finds ritual expression in the celebration of High Holy Days.

Sacrifice on High Holy Days

Despite its conditionality, however, sacrificial ritual is also intended to provide participants with a sense of confidence in divine acceptance. For examples, we turn to references to sacrifice in rituals of High Holy Days. The holiday of Rosh Hashanah falls on the first two days of the Hebrew month *Tishrei* (meaning "beginning") and marks the start of the Jewish ritual year, usually occurring during September–October. Yom Kippur (Day of Atonement) follows after an interval of ten "Days of Awe," and the celebration of Sukkoth (Feast of Booths) completes the season. The fall is a busy time for observant Jews, calling for special preparations in homes and synagogues. We are interested in the first two festivals because each focuses on passages from Torah about sacrifices: the birth of Ishmael and offering of Isaac (Genesis 21–22) on Rosh Hashanah and the sacrifice of a scapegoat by the high priest (Leviticus 16) on Yom Kippur. Both texts pose disturbing interpretive challenges: the moral offense of Abraham binding Isaac for slaughter and the religious anomaly that the sacrificial goat is offered to a mysterious demon named Azazel, not to Yahweh.

Rosh Hashanah is not mentioned by name in the Bible, but its date and manner of observance are specified in Leviticus 23:23–25: "In the seventh month, on the first day of the month, you shall observe a day of complete rest, a holy convocation commemorated with trumpet blasts. You shall not work at your occupations; and you shall present the LORD's offering by fire." It is one of the festivals of ancient Israel that required rest, as a Sabbath, and called for a communal gathering marked by the sound of a horn and burnt offerings of ten sacrificial animals, as prescribed in Numbers 29:1–6, and that provided "a pleasing odor to the

LORD." Since the destruction of the Second Temple, Jews cannot offer animal sacrifices; nevertheless, the rituals of Rosh Hashanah remain steeped in sacrificial symbolism.

In the month preceding Rosh Hashanah, Jews offer penitential prayers called *Selichot* (meaning "forgiveness") to prepare for Yom Kippur and its reminder of the coming Day of Judgment. Sephardim (Jews from the Mediterranean basin, North Africa, and the Middle East) recite Selichot for the entire month (except on Sabbaths), while Ashkenazim (Jews from Eastern Europe) recite the prayers for a minimum of four days preceding Rosh Hashanah. Ashkenazim base their practice on the biblical law requiring sacrificial animals to be quarantined for four days to preserve their ritual purity before they were killed. In this way, Ashkenazim offer their prayers, and themselves, as living sacrifices in devotion to God. Echoes of sacrifice are heard in the weekly observance of the Sabbath as well. "On Shabbat, after saying *Ha-Motzi* (the blessing recited over bread before a meal is eaten), we dip the challah [braided bread] in salt to create a parallel between the salted sacrifices on the Temple altar and the food on our own table."[39]

The most prominent symbol of sacrifice during Rosh Hashanah is the shofar made from the horn of a ram and recalling the animal that was offered in place of Isaac. According to one early rabbinic source, God created the ram in the twilight of the Sabbath on the last day of the week of creation and from that time prepared it to be the burnt offering instead of Isaac.[40] In this text the symbolism of the ram reflected the political oppression of the Jews after a failed revolt against Roman rule in the mid-second century and inspired their hope because the horns of the ram signify both the history of Israel in thickets of foreign occupation and the messianic future of final deliverance. In another reading, the two horns of the ram represent one blown at the giving of the Law on Sinai, marking the basis of Jewish identity as loyalty to Torah, and the other whose sound will announce "the ingathering of the exiles in the time to come." In this interpretation of the ram, the binding of Isaac illumines the calling of the Jewish people to live in constricted and imperiled circumstances in this world with the hope of reunion in the land of Israel in the messianic age. For those with ears to hear its political overtones, the ram's horn can summon resistance and determination to realize its promise.

More conventional interpretations emphasize that the piercing tones of the ram's horn are meant to awaken the believer not only to the dissonance of the world, but also to the disorder in one's own moral conduct. While issuing a call to repentance, the sound of the horn is, at the same time, an assurance of divine mercy. According to one midrash, "the blowing of the shofar has its roots with the Binding of Isaac, when God told Abraham that it would be the sound of the ram's horn that will stir God's compassion toward the Jewish people on Rosh Hashanah." Rabbi Will Berkovitz, an executive director of Hillel, comments that "the voice of the shofar is a challenge to look within our souls. It is a call to godliness, to redouble our efforts toward humility, justice, and mercy and recall that the Day of Judgment has arrived."[41] In another instance of interpretive creativity the ram's horn, synecdoche for the animal's sacrificial role in the Akedah, is associated with sublimated sacrifices of prayer and good deeds.

In this way, emphasis is shifted from horror at Abraham's intention to kill Isaac to gratitude for moral substitutes for sacrifice. Sarah's scream of protest is muted, and what is left is transferred to general anxiety about failure to honor the divine commandments. Yet in one prayer during the New Year service, the scandal of Abraham's act against nature is acknowledged—"Remember in our favor . . . how Abraham suppressed his fatherly love in order to do Your will." But Sarah's scream will also echo throughout this book—and we will not forget that her terror was aroused by the man who was willing to betray the life of their son in a test of his faith. Every sacrifice we will consider in religions of Abraham, in one way or another, requires an analogous exchange of human value for transcendent benefit.

Rosh Hashanah and Yom Kippur are separated by the ten Days of Awe in which Jews await divine judgment on their lives during the preceding year. While these two holy days are not connected in the Bible, later sages integrated them in this way: "All are judged on Rosh Hashanah and the verdict is issued on Yom Kippur."[42] In effect, these ten days are a time of extended suspense, during which believers engage in rigorous self-examination, prayer, and fasting, with the hope that God will judge in one's favor. In rabbinic analysis, there are three sorts of people: righteous, wicked, and those in between (*beinoni*)—the category that includes most of us. During the Days of Awe, believers are in a state of indeterminate identity, neither in nor out of the Book of Life. This condition of ritual uncertainty is what the anthropologist Victor Turner famously called "liminality," when an initiate exists on the boundary between two states of being while fully participating in neither. During this period, Jews cannot presume to know whether their prayers and good deeds will outweigh their human failings and persuade God to forgive their sins. The efficacy of sacrificial repentance depends upon the sovereign will of God; but the ritual is meant to focus attention on self-scrutiny with an intensity that will demonstrate sincerity and increase one's likelihood of securing divine approval.

Another aspect of ancient ritual assimilated to modern practice is the fasting required on Yom Kippur. In the Mishnah the rabbis specify the general prescription of self-denial as not only refraining from food, but also from bathing, anointing with oil or perfume, wearing leather shoes, and engaging in marital intimacy (Yoma 8:1). In his commentary on Torah, Moses Maimonides (1138–1204) also associated repentance with atoning sacrifices that could no longer be offered in the Temple. "At this time, when the Temple no longer exists, and we have no atonement altar, there is nothing left but repentance. . . . Yom Kippur itself atones for those who repent, as it is written: 'Atonement shall be made for you this day' (Leviticus 16:30)."[43] Maimonides emphasizes that sins forgiven in this way are offenses against God; but for transgressions against other humans, "as when a person either injured or cursed or robbed his neighbor, he is never pardoned unless he compensates his neighbor and makes an apology."

In Leviticus 16 the sacrifice required to atone for the sins of the people on Yom Kippur was of two goats. The high priest offered one to Yahweh as a purification offering; the other he sent into the wilderness for Azazel, after transferring the sins of Israel to it by laying his hands on it. In later apocalyptic writing, Azazel is identified as one of the "fallen angels" (nephilim) who cohabited with women and produced giants, monstrous hybrids who transgressed the boundary between heaven and earth. They are cited in Genesis 6 as one reason God devastated the earth in the Great Flood. From this legend, coupled with Azazel's association with the goat, may have grown the idea of Azazel as a "goat demon." While the meaning of Azazel is unclear, later tradition refers to the sacrificial animal as "scapegoat."

"The goat shall bear on itself all their iniquities to a barren region; and the goat shall be set free in the wilderness" (Leviticus 16:22). In this case the purpose of sacrifice to "atone" (*kipper*) is accomplished without killing the animal.[44] One rabbi speculated that a crimson string was tied to the goat so that when it reached the wilderness the thread would have been blanched white "so they knew that the religious duty connected with the goat had been carried out, as it is said, 'If your sins be as scarlet, they shall be as white wool' (Isaiah 1:18)" (Yoma 67A). Accordingly, for some who observe Yom Kippur, the story of the sacrifice of the scapegoat is a reminder of the need to recompense for sins through repentance and prayer.

In these ways, Jews translated the literal terms of animal sacrifice into sublimated forms of self-denial, according to the biblical principle, "The sacrifices of God are a broken spirit; a broken and contrite heart" (Psalm 51:19). By extension the suffering caused by fasting during Yom Kippur came to be understood as redemptive. The scholar of ancient history, Veronika Grimm, notes that by the time of the Babylonian Talmud, "fasting as a substitute for the sacrificial sin-offering is explicitly acknowledged." She cites a passage that records the prayer of a rabbi at the end of a fast, who recalled that, when the Temple was standing, "if a man sinned he used to bring a sacrifice, and though all that was offered of it was its fat and blood, atonement was made for him. Now I have kept a fast and my fat and blood have diminished. May it be Thy will to account my fat and blood . . . as if I had offered them before Thee on the altar."[45]

Since sins could no longer be forgiven through sacrifices in the Temple or punished by the authority of religious courts after the destruction of both institutions, the rabbis taught that the suffering of a sincere penitent atoned for sins. The suffering of fasting, while not as severe as might be prescribed by legal judgment, is a symbolic substitute for the punishment—just as the sacrificial animal was a symbolic substitute for the sinner. As sacrifice was no longer possible in a literal sense, the rabbis transferred its meaning as redemptive suffering to "the materials of life itself, its pains and end, and transforms them into components of atonement."[46] But it must be kept in mind that Jewish tradition places a high value on the body and never developed a tradition of extreme asceticism. While a few pious rabbis are reported to have fasted "until their teeth turned black," in general the Talmud advises moderate fasting to prevent becoming too weak to defend and support the community, the primary beneficiary of sacrificial virtue.

Sacrifice as Moral Discipline in Rabbinic Judaism

The disastrous loss of the Temple in Jerusalem brought an end to a millennium of sacrifices, displaced the hereditary priesthood, and stripped political authority from Jewish leaders. Jewish teachers (known as Pharisees, who were precursors of the rabbis) translated the anachronistic laws of animal sacrifice into moral and religious requirements of prayer, fasting, charity, good works, and Torah study. The change required reforming personal identity through "above all a moral reform, starting with the recognition of sins and repentance."[47]

Stroumsa proposes that the Mishnah is an interpretation of ancient Jewish scriptures in competition with the New Testament which was beginning to take the form of canon. "In both cases, it is a matter of a secondary text, 'new' or 'a repetition.' This text has no meaning unless read in parallel with the Scriptures, which, for their part, only find their real significance through the prism of the new text."[48] The relation of Torah to Mishnah is no mere intertextuality, but a revision of the meaning of the original text, so that Hebrew Scriptures would henceforth be read through the lens ground by rabbinic exegetes. The hope was to work out in searching detail the normative reading of the "word of God." While the rabbis never claimed Mishnah superseded Torah, they did work tirelessly to make their "repetition" so thorough and consistent that no Jewish reader would feel the need to look beyond their commentary for the meaning of Torah. In the process of appropriating Jewish scriptures in which sacrifice is a central theme, rabbinic interpreters faced the problem of retaining the significance of sacrifice in its absence. Animal sacrifice could not be performed as prescribed by Torah without temple, priesthood, or victims. So either large sections of Torah must be regarded as rendered irrelevant by the destruction of the Temple or they must be assigned a religious meaning beyond their literal enactment.

The first alternative carried the unthinkable implication that history could abrogate divine revelation or, in more specific terms, that a Roman emperor could cancel the word of God. Jews could not entertain such a possibility, so they turned to the only other path open to them: reinterpretation. Their reimagined version of the ancient text managed to retrieve every detail of the sacrificial system and to integrate it into a comprehensive way of life. Rabbis transformed directions for offering animals and plants in the Temple into instructions for how to live in accordance with God's will. Jews transformed sacrifice into daily offering of the self in service to God. The rabbis employed the strategy of re-reading Torah to preserve the sacred text, and the people who based their identity on it, from extinction by accidents of history.

Their re-reading required what Stroumsa calls the "turn inward" that was common in the Mediterranean world of late antiquity following the abolition of animal sacrifice by the Roman Emperor Constantius II.[49] One ironic consequence of that turn is that the sacrificial blade was turned on the self, if not literally in ascetic mutilation, then figuratively in flaying the conscience with guilt that could be assuaged only by renewed self-denial: The end of animal sacrifice marks the beginning of self-sacrifice. It would seem that the religious mind cannot escape the conviction that to "become sacred" one must sacrifice what is given in the concrete for what is promised in the abstract. Since historical events had destroyed the actual site of ritual sacrifice, the rabbis constructed a new location for offering gifts, turning the human heart into an altar.

The prolific scholar of rabbinic Judaism, Jacob Neusner (1932–2016), posed the problem facing Jews this way: God allowed Rome to destroy the Temple because of our sins, but in so doing God removed the only means of atoning for our sins. So where do we go from here? That is the dilemma a formative figure in the rabbinic movement, renowned teacher Yohanan ben Zakkai, addressed in his well-known response to a bewildered disciple lamenting the disaster:

> Once as Rabban Yohanan ben Zakkai was coming out of Jerusalem, Rabbi Joshua followed him, and beheld the Temple in ruins.
>
> "Woe unto us," Rabbi Joshua cried, "that this place, the place where the iniquities of Israel were atoned for, is laid waste."
>
> "My son," Rabban Yohanan said to him, "be not grieved. We have another atonement as effective as this. And what is it? It is acts of loving kindness, as it is said, *For I desire mercy, not sacrifice* (Hosea 6:6)."[50]

Yohanan draws on an extensive prophetic tradition according to which God was more pleased by a humble spirit and a charitable will than by the blood of animals.[51] As the leader of the early rabbinic school at Yavneh, Yohanan began a program of transforming Judaism from a religion centered on animal sacrifices offered in Jerusalem into a religion that could be practiced anywhere through prayer, fasting, good deeds, and study of Torah. Neusner paraphrases his goal: "If one were to make an offering to God in a time when the Temple was no more, it must be the gift of selfless compassion. The holy altar must be the streets and marketplaces of the world."[52]

Yohanan claimed the authority of Torah scholars to interpret Levitical laws of purity and their application to the everyday life of Jews, in competition with the few surviving Sadducees who were the primary custodians of Temple ritual. He could draw upon precedent in the prophets for reinterpreting the sacrifice of animals as discipline of human passions and thus forged what Neusner calls "a middle way between the spontaneous religion of Galilee which looked for daily miracles, signs, and wonders, and the loyal literalism of the Jerusalem priesthood which held fast to Scripture's commandments concerning the sacrificial cult."[53] This compromise assigned to the study of Scripture the same religious value as performance of Temple rituals. The compromise eventually led to the replacement of sacrifice by Torah study, as in this couplet in later literature, composed to be easily memorized and taken to heart:

> Whoever busies himself in Torah needs neither burnt-offering nor sin offering.
> Whoever busies himself in Torah—it is as if he offered a burnt-offering.[54]

Henceforth, rabbis would function as priests and the sacrifices would be of mind, will, time—and eyesight. Even though the Temple lay in ruins, Yohanan and his disciples "affirmed their faith that the Torah remained the will of their unvanquished God. Their duty to obey him endured." Further, what the rabbis did full-time would provide a model for all Jews to occupy themselves with most of the time, namely, reading Torah and obeying its precepts. From the study of Torah, the Pharisees devised "a comprehensive program for the religious life to replace the sacrificial system."[55] As Stroumsa puts it, "The religion of intention invented by the prophets is adopted by the sages, who make it the foundation of their orthodoxy."[56]

Sacrifice did not end, only the victim changed. Now every Israelite became a lamb in the flock of the Lord to be consumed in daily offerings of time, desire, and freedom. Neusner notes, "What Yohanan demanded was that Israel now see, in its humble day-to-day conduct, deeds of so grand a dimension as to rival the sacred actions, rites, and gestures of the Temple.... Man must now see in himself, in his selfish motives to be immolated, the noblest sacrifice of all."[57] The rabbis stood ready to dive enthusiastically into the composition of a new handbook, interpreting even biblical narratives as yielding regulations governing every aspect of Jewish life, particularly the primal human activities of eating, sexuality, commerce, fashion, and death. In this way the early rabbis resolved the crisis precipitated by the destruction of the Temple. Recalling the prophetic tradition that God is more pleased by a humble spirit and a charitable will than by the blood of animals, they transformed the meaning of sacrifice from a literal burnt offering (*holocaust*) to good deeds (*mitzvoth*) in obedience to divine commands. One scholar of the history of religious sacrifice notes that, after 70, charity (*zedekah*) "quickly rose to a position of dominance in the repertoire of giving of Jewish communities."[58]

The renowned teacher of Jewish ethics and mysticism, Abraham Heschel (1907–1972), confirmed the connection between self-giving for the good of others and religious piety by defining a *mitzvah* as "a prayer in the form of a deed." He continued, "Prayer is not a substitute for sacrifice. Prayer *is* sacrifice. What has changed is the substance of sacrifice: the self took the place of the thing. . . . We do not sacrifice. We are the sacrifice." Further, like all sacrifices, prayer is attended by risk. "To the saints, prayer is a hazard, a venture full of peril. . . . 'It is a miracle that a man survives the hour of worship,' the [seventeenth-century Jewish mystic] Baal Shem said."[59] Heschel was concerned that an exchange of animal sacrifice for altruistic actions would erode worship of the transcendent God, the one in whose presence the believer bows in suspense, as the high priest entered the darkened sanctuary in ancient Israel. Heschel understood the appeal of secular humanism as a substitute for religious observance, particularly after the Holocaust. But he insisted on a fundamental difference between worship of the One God and observing Jewish customs as a form of cultural identity. For him prayer marked that difference as an inward act of devotion to God that informed every good deed with religious value.

Heschel emphasized that mitzvoth derive their significance, not as symbols, but as personal sacrifices in submission to divine will by posing the question, "who would be willing to sacrifice his dearest interests observing the Sabbath just because it symbolizes creation or the redemption from Egypt? If the Jews were ever ready for such a sacrifice, it was not because of a symbolic idea but because of God. The ideal of Judaism is to serve for the sake of God."[60] Unlike Buber, Heschel was confident that "God has made known His will to His people. To us, the will of God *is neither a metaphor nor a euphemism*," but the literal command to sacrifice one's "dearest interests" to redeem humanity. For Heschel, the alternative is the horror of world wars, such as he lived through. "We have failed to offer sacrifices on the altar of peace; thus we offered sacrifices on the altar of war." The only salvation, in his view, lies in more sacrifice. He wrote that "we will survive if we shall be as fine and sacrificial in our homes and offices, in our Congress and clubs as our soldiers are on the fields of battle."

Heschel's final challenge is daunting: "God is waiting for us to redeem the world." In that project Jews should be inspired by examples of sacrifice in the Holocaust: "The martyrdom of millions demands that we consecrate ourselves to the fulfillment of God's dream of salvation."[61] For Heschel, the "quest for God" proceeds along the path of sacrifice in pursuit of the divine ideal for humanity, "God's dream of salvation." In Heschel's reflections we find leading themes of the discourse of religious sacrifice: Good deeds are offered in suspense as enacted prayers; sacrifices mark a relation with the transcendent; and self-giving for others fulfills the divine will for the redemption of the world.

To someone with a less mystical disposition, however, promoting human welfare through self-sacrifice may be seen as civic virtue devoid of religious significance. For many in the Jewish community, the Holocaust shattered faith in a personal deity with special interest in the fate of his "chosen people." For them the old question of whether Judaism can be maintained as a cultural system without belief in God became urgent again—as it had been under conditions of exile and persecution of Jews in early modern Europe. Could a Jew live as a responsible citizen of the world, committed to acting virtuously toward other humans, even giving one's life in their defense, without being "religious"? That is, can self-sacrifice be a Jewish moral ideal, allowing for assimilation into Western societies, apart from its religious significance as mitzvah in obedience to divine command? For Jews influenced by the European Enlightenment and the Reform movement, the answer was *yes*. But for medieval Jewish mystics and continuing through religious Zionists today, the answer is a resounding *no*.

Through centuries of diaspora as Jews migrated from the land of Israel throughout Europe, the Mideast, and Russia, rabbis taught that faith in God required sacrifice in the form of inward offerings of prayer and public acts of charity. Contemplative sages among them also sought guidance beyond the written text of Torah through lives of self-denial and ecstatic meditation. Their sacrificial devotion fulfilled the earlier motto: "Whoever busies himself in Torah—it is as if he offered a burnt-offering." From daily giving themselves to meticulous scrutiny of Torah, the rabbis sought to discern not only the will of God, but the divine mind as well. Their goal was to know not only *what* God said, but *why* God said it. Their ambition was breath-taking as they sought to understand how every thought and action could fulfill divine will. If successful, they could transform every human act into a sacrifice of individual desire to divine intention.

The earliest teachers flourished in Palestine in the first two centuries CE and are known as the *Tannaim*. Rabbi Judah the Prince edited their commentaries on Torah in the Mishnah, a digest arranged in six tractates. The fifth tractate is devoted to laws of sacrifice, perhaps reflecting a strong hope that the messianic age was close at hand and the Temple in Jerusalem would soon be restored. The teachings of the Tannaim are considered so authoritative that they are called Oral Torah. Their reflections in turn were explicated by teachers living during the third to fifth centuries CE, who are called the *Amoraim* or "expounders." The Amoraim gathered their commentaries on the Mishnah and other Tannaitic writings in massive volumes known as *Talmud*: One set compiled in Palestine is identified with Jerusalem; the other took form in Babylon. These works aimed at producing systematic application of Torah to every aspect of Jewish life. (Jewish scholars study Talmud today, searching its complex dialectic style and rehearsing debates among early rabbis for clues to the contemporary relevance of Torah.)

Thus, what would continue for the next two millennia as the dominant form of Jewish life and faith was the creation of scholars and teachers: an agenda of mundane moral conduct and domestic ritual to replace the drama of blood and mystery performed by priests in the Temple. What we now call "rabbinic Judaism" was born in a time of war and violence but has nurtured a tradition of ethical idealism, religious tolerance, and rational integrity. Not even the rabbis, however, dispensed with the call for sacrifice, even when they turned it inward and confined the violence to humbling the self before God. While the call to self-giving did not lead to formal asceticism in rabbinic practice, it did suggest a subordination of private interests to divine will that some scholars call "de-centering of the self."[62]

Throughout the first millennium of Jewish diaspora, rabbinic leadership emphasized the importance of sacrificial obedience to Torah. Their project was reasonable and practical. Its aim was to maintain Jewish identity under conditions of exile and persecution until God inaugurates the messianic age by re-gathering the people of Israel in the Promised Land. In the meanwhile, rabbis counseled patience in suffering, following the prophet Isaiah, who spoke of Israel in captivity in Babylon as the "suffering servant" of Yahweh who served God by remaining faithful in exile. Jewish loyalty to the God of Sinai and acceptance of the "yoke of his commandments" would offer an example of faith in the true God that would shine in the world as "a light unto the Gentiles."[63] When the Persian ruler Cyrus decreed that Jews return to Palestine and rebuild their Temple, Isaiah hailed him as God's "anointed one" (or "messiah") whom God led to emancipate his long-suffering people (Isaiah 45:1–4). The rabbis shared the prophet's confidence that God would vindicate the suffering of faithful Jews in diaspora under foreign rule.

But a millennium is a long time to wait for deliverance—all the while continuing to offer sacrifices of prayer and good deeds in obedience to Torah. Parents and rabbis faced the enormous challenge of training each generation anew in disciplines of personal piety and ritual practices. Jewish immigrants formed communities within cities and villages where they took refuge—spaces in which to maintain their distinctive religious identity apart from lures of assimilation. Whatever the language of their neighbors, they also taught their children Hebrew so they could read Torah and recite communal prayers. In these "ghettoes" even time could be made holy, each day ordered by the rhythm of prayer in anticipation of the seventh day of the week. The Sabbath, on which work and most play were strictly forbidden, was devoted to prayer and study; and the evening meal, however meager, was sanctified by elaborate ritual that transformed the family table into an altar. The persistence of Jews in maintaining "the way of Torah" after the destruction of Jerusalem is one of the most impressive cases of cultural survival on record.

They "waited on the Lord," yet their exile, and often persecution, continued. They offered daily sacrifices of prayer, contrition, and charity. They studied Talmudic instructions for offering sacrifices in hope of a restored Temple. They remained faithful as the "suffering servant" of the Lord, but the day of redemption seemed no nearer. Some argued for observing Torah even more closely, working harder, sacrificing more. Others wondered, could there be a deeper reason for the delay? Are there clues hidden in Torah that legal scholars have missed, insights that cast the exile of the Jews in a different light? Perhaps, these mystics thought, our exile is not merely an accident of history we must bear with grace and faith. Perhaps exile is a cosmic condition: not a tragedy that God directs from inaccessible heights but a reality God directly experiences. Perhaps the cost of creation is divine sacrifice by which God gives up infinite singularity to form a world of variety, diversity, and conflict. If so, then human efforts to create harmony could contribute to the restoration of divine unity and the "healing of the world" (*tikkun olam*).

Divine and Human Sacrifice in Jewish Mysticism

From the tenth century, such speculation began to form a body of secret doctrine known only to a community of initiates and designated by the term *Kabbalah* ("tradition"). This broad range of esoteric wisdom took definitive form in the thirteenth-century mystical text, known as the *Zohar* ("radiance") or *The Book of Splendor*. Attributed to a wandering teacher in Spain, Moses de Leon, the Zohar transforms study of Torah from the rabbis' sober attempts to regulate Jewish life in every mundane detail into a wildly imaginative discernment of coded meaning in the biblical text. While composed a thousand years later, the Zohar claims that its teachings are from a second-century authority, Rabbi Simeon ben Yohai. The scholar of Jewish mysticism, Arthur Green, argues that the early kabbalists saw themselves as defending older Jewish teaching regarding human characteristics of God, the agency of demons and angels, and the magic power of divine names. They were particularly interested in the efficacy of ecstatic prayer, as substitute for animal sacrifice, capable of affecting divine reality and human destiny.

The teaching of the Zohar was intended to defend its reading of tradition against the rationalism of medieval philosophers, particularly Moses Maimonides. Maimonides rejected anthropomorphism in theology in favor of abstract views of divine perfection drawn from Greek philosophy. The problem with that approach, as Green notes, was a familiar one: "If perfect and unchanging, this God was necessarily self-sufficient and in no need of human actions of any sort. Why then would such a God care about performance of the commandments?"[64] Indeed, once one understands God in that way, why should anyone continue to observe mitzvoth, to offer even the spiritual sacrifices of daily prayer? To put it bluntly, why should one persist in being a Jew? For kabbalists that question required a more compelling answer than the rabbis offered.

Masters of Kabbalah believed that Jewish obedience to the directives of Torah had a direct effect on God, restoring divine harmony disrupted by exile in the material world and by human transgression. In the Zohar, creation emerges from the infinite divine reality, hidden from human knowledge, called *En Sof* ("the endless"). The source of all being reveals itself in the form of ten manifestations or *sefiroth*. These emanations appear in pairs, corresponding to male and female. While the sefiroth represent aspects of God, to the mystics they were "divine life itself . . . this hidden root and the divine emanations are one."[65] Thus, God who appears in the sefiroth is the true God, but in divided forms. Beginning with the first emanation, called *Keter* or "crown," each *sefirah* reveals a creative latency within God by which God is known and through which God interacts with the world. By identifying En Sof with its manifestations, the kabbalists both maintained the essential unity of divine reality and also affirmed multiple forms of God's relation to the world, including the compassion and judgment of the personal Lord of the biblical narrative. In this way, they resolved the theological problem of reconciling the infinite and hidden divine essence with its unfolding presence in nature and history.

Kabbalists detected signs of sefiroth everywhere. The first letter in the sacred name of God, *yod* (ʾ), is the smallest in the Hebrew alphabet; yet its position points up on the page toward Keter. For kabbalists, that orthographic form signified divine transcendence by directing prayers upward, as the smoke of ancient sacrifices ascended to God. Drawing from rabbinic lore, the kabbalists "adapted an ancient myth . . . of the daily coronation of God by a diadem of words and letters fashioned out of the prayers of Israel. That crown reaches over the head of God, the highest 'place' imaginable."[66] Thus, prayers are sacrifices of the spirit that enhance the glory of God and evoke divine blessing, as effectively as the slaughter of animals in the Temple. Far from passive acknowledgment of divine blessing or quiescent adoration of divine majesty, prayers in this view are powerful evocations of divine action and instruments of cosmic integration. The kabbalist is a priest whose prayers and study of Torah mediate between the complex unity of the manifest God and the fragmented world of human cultures.

In the process of creative emanation, Keter is joined in a triad by *Hokhmah* ("wisdom") and *Binah* ("intelligence"), from which flow sefiroth that manifest divine love, judgment, beauty, everlastingness, and majesty. Finally, the sefirah of male potency (*Yesod*) combines with the female *Shekinah*, the tenth and final emanation, in a sacred marriage that brings forth the world. In sexual imagery typical of the Zohar, Shekinah is "impregnated with the fullness of divine energy and in turn gives birth to the lower worlds, including both angelic beings and human souls."[67] Shekinah was the term for the presence of God on the ark in the inner sanctum of the Temple, both inviting and threatening as the high priest entered to offer atoning sacrifices. Shekinah is used in Kabbalah to represent the divine presence with the people of Israel in exile and persecution. Inasmuch as their exile in foreign lands required sacrifice, both literal and symbolic, the kabbalists believed that Shekinah not only received their offerings but also was restored by them from her own exile in the world.

Isaac Luria (1534–1572) constructed the version of Kabbalah that emphasized the sacrifices of the Jewish people as not only redeeming the world but also restoring the lost unity of divine being. His work was in response to the expulsion of Jews and Muslims from Spain by Christian monarchs in 1492. Luria attracted a school of disciples in Safed in northern Israel who referred to him as "the Ari" ("holy lion") and continue to honor his "ascent" into the higher world by gathering each year at his grave on the anniversary of his death. While Luria creatively modified many aspects of the teaching of the Zohar, we will focus on his astonishing doctrine that En Sof created a space for the world to exist through a rupture within the divine being itself. Then God reorganized the sefiroth into "faces," symbolizing the healing of the inner divisions created by their fragmentation into ten emanations. From this recasting of Kabbalah, Luria drew the insight that God chose the people of Israel, scattered throughout the Gentile world like sparks of the divine being, to assist in the process of re-forming God by re-membering Torah.

To be specific, Luria taught that at the time of creation God made space for the world by withdrawing or constricting his being, an act the master of Jewish mysticism Gershom Scholem (1897–1982) called God's "primordial exile or self-banishment" which "makes possible the existence of something other than God and His pure essence."[68] In more dramatic terms, creation requires opening a wound in the divine body in order to birth the world. Luria described this primordial sacrifice as *tsimtsum*, meaning "contraction," but Scholem notes that kabbalists use it in the sense of "withdrawal" or "retreat." Luria cited a midrashic teaching that God concentrated his presence in the Holy of Holies in the Temple, but he reversed that reading to signify not "the concentration of God at *a* point, but his retreat *away* from a point."[69]

There are two comparative parallels to note here briefly. First, the image of creation as divine sacrifice can be found throughout religious myths. In most, primordial victims provide their bodies as material from which the cosmos is crafted, so that from its genesis the world is made sacred by their sacrifice. In the creation myth of ancient Babylon, called *Enuma elish*, the god Marduk defeats the marine monster Tiamat by inflating her body with strong winds and sending an arrow through her gaping mouth into her heart. He splits her body, forming heaven and earth from the two halves. Marduk sacrifices her demon-commander, Kingu, and creates from his blood the "black-haired men of Mesopotamia." Henceforth, as the other gods agreed to serve Marduk, so human beings would serve his representative on earth, their king. In Hindu myth, the primordial person known as Purusha is laid on an altar and the gods divide him into four parts, corresponding to the constituent regions of the cosmos and to the four traditional castes in Indian culture. Thus, the sacrifice of Purusha and those in the *Enuma elish* not only establish cosmic structure, but also install political and social orders as sacred and inviolable. What distinguishes Luria's notion of tsimtsum from these myths is that the divine sacrifice of self-withdrawal does not provide the material condition for the construction of the world, but the silent void in which the world is free to produce itself.

That consideration leads to the second point of comparison with divine sacrifice in other traditions, namely, tsimtsum does not sanctify any political or social hierarchy but opens a space in which humans can exercise freedom and take responsibility. God remains the Lord of creation, the Crown whose Wisdom and Intelligence combined to produce a stable and intelligible world; and God is the one who revealed his will for human life in Torah. But it is up to humans to work at caring for the world and directing their individual and corporate lives by divine revelation. What the idea of tsimtsum adds to traditional Jewish emphasis on human responsibility is the dramatic damage the self-withdrawal caused *to God* and the role humans play in repairing it.

In Luria's account, the primal space resulting from God's "self-banishment" contained forms prepared to receive the light of creation. But the power of divine light shattered them, an event Luria called the "breaking of the vessels." In that conflagration sparks were struck off that fell to earth and lodged in human bodies. The displacement continued throughout subsequent emanations of the sefiroth. As a result, "everything is in some way broken, everything has a flaw, everything is unfinished."[70] Further, the crisis purged En Sof of evil, but concentrated the form of divine judgment (*Din*) in isolation from compassion and love; subsequently, all the sefiroth became alienated from their counterparts. Most calamitously, demonic forces, called the "other side," drew strength from the concentration of negative energy in Din. For Luria it was necessary to restore proper relations among the sefiroth by balancing them in five pairs he called the "countenances of God." It was especially important that the male Yahweh be reconciled with the female Shekinah, the complementary aspects of the personal God of the Bible.

While the divine tsimtsum was necessary for the creation of the world, its consequences were a disaster, reflecting the circumstances of the Jewish people, separated from their land and temple, flung abroad, and isolated. Luria declared that Israel's exile was not a test or punishment, but a mission: "In the course of its exile Israel must go everywhere, to every corner of the world, for everywhere a spark of the *Shekinah* is waiting to be found, gathered, and restored by a religious act." Kabbalah took shape in diaspora and defines the Jewish people by vocation, not location. Just as sacrifices in the Temple once restored the broken covenant with God, now human deeds of mercy and justice re-establish the soul's union with God and bring about the healing of the world (tikkun olam). "In submitting to the guidance of the Law, Israel works toward the restitution of all things."[71] As God sacrificed to create the world, the Jewish people must sacrifice to redeem the world—and to restore divine unity. An early work of Kabbalah notes sacrifice is called *korban* in Hebrew because "it draws the inner divine forces near to one another."[72] Thus, prayer and study of Torah are acts of worship that contribute to "the birth of God's personality."[73]

In that process Kabbalah teaches that sacrifice must also acknowledge and appease the demonic forces that emerge from the "other side" of divine judgment. In this light the story of the Akedah reveals the necessity of reconciling divine love, represented by Abraham, with divine judgment, represented by the bound Isaac. According to the Zohar, Abraham fulfilled his own being by combining his love for Isaac with his willingness to sacrifice his son to satisfy divine command. Abraham's test was that "water [free-flowing love] was embraced by fire [judgment]. Abraham had been incomplete until now, when he was crowned to execute judgment, arraying it in its realm. His whole life long he had been incomplete until now when water was completed by fire, fire by water."[74] Abraham's action contributed to reconciling aspects of the divine being that were separated in the primordial "shattering of the vessels." Similarly, the sacrificial acts of observant Jews continue the process of resisting evil and healing the disruption within the divine being. As Arthur Green observes, "every good deed they do, every commandment they fulfill or prayer they offer with the proper mystical intent, serves to awaken the *Shekhinah*. She unites with her spouse, is energized by Him, and they together become mighty warriors in the battle against evil."[75] That battle will continue until the dawn of the messianic age.

With stakes that high, it is no wonder that Jewish mystics like Rabbi Moshe of Kobryn (d. 1858) regarded every moment as a call to sacrifice. Martin Buber cited three sayings at the heart of his teaching: "You shall become an altar before God"; "There is nothing in the world which does not contain a commandment"; and "Just as God is limitless, so his service is limitless."[76] These mottos constitute a sacrificial trifecta: the faithful believer is the altar whose every act and thought are regulated by divine law and whose offerings have no end. The rabbi once fainted dead away in the synagogue while reciting the prayer "which is a substitution for the offerings of Sabbaths and feast days." Only later, while at table, did his disciples understand when he cried out, "Lord of the world, we, we, we ourselves shall bring ourselves to you in place of the offering!" Rabbi Moshe followed the logic of substitution: In place of sheep and goats, he sacrificed not only prayers and good works but his entire being. The one who offers becomes the offering, every moment willing to be consumed in the service of God. Rabbi Moshe explained that "the ultimate significance of the Kabbalah is to accept the yoke of the Kingdom of God. . . . When a man says: 'The Lord is my God,' meaning: 'He is mine and I am His,' must not his soul go forth from his body?' The moment the rabbi said this he fell into a deep faint."[77]

Rabbi Moshe demonstrated the meaning of dedicating one's life to God by entering into a state of symbolic death, a sacrificial victim who is then revived to repeat the self-giving in an endless cycle of obedience to Torah. Changing the metaphor from loss of consciousness, one contemporary kabbalist describes the experience of entering the divine presence as "dreams of being eaten alive."[78] The mystic disappears into the maw of the deity who accepts the gift of the self by consuming it, as in every sacrifice. The contemporary teacher of Kabbalah, Yitzchak Ginsburg, makes the analogy explicit in his interpretation: "In the *Zohar* we find, 'Israel sustains her Father in heaven' (Zohar 111:7). The effect of the Jew's loving performance of Torah and *mitzvot* on G-d is compared to the effect of food on the body."[79] In this remarkable analogy, Ginsburg interprets obedience to Torah as an offering of the believer's will and spirit that God feeds on. As Rabbi Moshe taught by example and Abraham Heschel expressed unambiguously, "We do not sacrifice. We are the sacrifice."

Mystics are often gentle and diffident persons, but their spiritual discipline serves the triumph of divine violence. What is human disappears in sacred fire, not as a gift to be exchanged for heavenly reward, but as total annihilation in which giver and gift are destroyed together along with any future interest. The mystic quest for absorption into divine reality demonstrates Bataille's point that the only way to enter the sacred realm is to abandon human subjectivity altogether. Thus, the intimacy that sacrifice restores is only possible through violence: by breaking through, *violating*, every boundary we construct around our personal spheres of privacy. In Kabbalistic terminology, reflection on the divine Nothingness from which all things emerge leads to the recognition of the "nothingness" (*ayin*) of an independent self. The logic is straightforward: "If you think of yourself as something, then God cannot clothe himself in you, for God is infinite. . . . You are simply a channel for the divine attributes."[80]

Gershom Scholem argues, however, that ecstatic loss of self is not characteristic of Jewish mysticism where a sense of distance between creature and Creator is paramount. He notes that the "ultimate goal of religious perfection" is "adhesion" (*devekuth*) rather than union. He defines devekuth as "a perpetual being-with-God, an intimate union and conformity of the human and the divine will."[81] But surrender of individual autonomy to divine rule *is* a self-sacrifice that is even more intentional than ecstatic trance. If what defines an individual is independence of will—and the story of Adam and Eve in the Bible suggests that exercise of will is the origin of self-consciousness—then submitting one's will unconditionally to another, even the divine other, is tantamount to self-erasure.

My encounter with Luria's form of mystical Judaism took place in 2000, as part of a seminar on "Conversion and Religious Identity" in Jerusalem, sponsored by the Elijah School for the Study of Wisdom in World Religions. The school is the creation of a visionary and academic entrepreneur by the name of Alon Goshen-Gottstein. Born in Alsace, Alon speaks German and French, Hebrew, English, and some Russian. His dream is to bring members of all the world's religions together for serious dialogue. He states his purpose on the website: "The Elijah School is a UNESCO sponsored interfaith academic institution, bridging the academic study of religion and interfaith dialogue, in the heart of conflicted Jerusalem." It is the sort of enterprise—noble in intention and gauzy in concept—that attracts idealists from around the world.

One Sabbath, well after sundown at 9:30, we participants in the seminar boarded a bus for a four-hour trip to the city of Tzfat (Safed) in

northern Israel. There we joined a group of Hasidic pilgrims to celebrate
Isaac Luria's "ascent," the final stage of his spiritual journey achieved at
the moment of his death. The pilgrims believe that on this night of the
year, at the very spot of his burial, the master's spiritual energy is available to those who light fires at his grave and recite psalms and prayers.
They come to participate in the recurrence of the Ari's moment of illumination. We mingled among the tombstones, most painted blue to
ward off the evil eye. One woman was speaking on a cell phone while
standing near Luria's headstone. She urged her pregnant daughter on
the other end to put her own phone on her stomach so that the unborn
child could receive spiritual energy from the master. All around, dressed
in the dark formal clothes of Hasidic Jews, followers of Rabbi Nachman
of Breslav recited prayers with loud enthusiasm.

Our observation was disturbed only by an impromptu debate between Alon and Barry Levy, our rabbinic expert from the University of
Toronto, over whether the veneration of the graves of saints is "main-
stream" Judaism. Alon insisted that such acts of devotion were the very
heart of Jewish tradition. "Nonsense!" Barry huffed, "My father wouldn't
even visit his own father's grave!" Barry is a Talmudic scholar, impatient
with what he regards as superstitious accretions and spurious claims to
hidden meaning in the Torah beyond the reach of disciplined human
reason. He was in for a long weekend.

After five hours of sleep in a hostel, we were up at 9:00 to begin a
tour of Sephardic synagogues in Tzfat, ending at the office of Ascent of
Safed, an organization dedicated to the promotion of Jewish mysticism
and the cultivation of "Jewish inner life." Rabbi Shaul Laiter, director of
Ascent, provided an explanation of the veneration of the anniversary
of the death of Luria. He then launched with gleeful enthusiasm into
speculative interpretation of the shape of Hebrew letters as conveying
messages of special relevance as the messianic age draws nearer. Given
6,000 years of creation, we were then in the year 5760, Friday afternoon,
the time of preparation for Shabbat. "When everyone in the world focuses on Shabbas as the moment of the unity of man, Messiah comes,"
he declared. The Sabbath bride will be the savior of the world when she
is finally re-united with her heavenly bridegroom, Yahweh: a reunifica-
tion achieved through the faithful sacrifices of the Jewish people.

At that point, we left for Galilee in order to hear a lecture in English by Rabbi Yitzchak Ginsburgh, a leading exponent of Kabbalah in Israel and president of a Yeshivah (or school for the study of Torah) in a Jewish settlement. As cited earlier, Ginsburgh regards mystic devotion as sacrifice that nourishes God. He spoke solemnly to an audience of attentive disciples on the occasion of *Tish'a be'Av*, the ninth day of the month Av on the Hebrew calendar. He explained that this time of mourning for the loss of the two Temples (one built by Solomon and one rebuilt after the return from captivity in Babylon) symbolizes exile from our righteous nature. Perhaps because he resides on the West Bank, Ginsburg interpreted Jewish experience as internal exile, a division analogous to the separation of the sefiroth in God. This message he deduced from the form of the letters of the Hebrew alphabet by matching the shapes of the twenty-two letters into eleven pairs and then analyzing the numerical value of the pair assigned to the present ritual period. In that way, Ginsburgh created an interpretive scheme that yielded the fairly simple admonition to examine our own actions for any trace of oppressiveness toward others.

What was hidden in this esoteric caution against injustice was a concrete political agenda. Ginsburgh had been recently released from prison for having incited his followers to occupy the Temple Mount in preparation for reclaiming the sacred space from Muslim control, rebuilding the Temple, and thus setting the conditions for Messiah's return. His mysticism gave birth to politics. To fulfill the messianic vocation of the Jewish people that Kabbalah teaches Ginsburgh requires their re-gathering in Jerusalem, on the traditional site of Abraham's binding of Isaac, where Messiah will rebuild the Temple and offering animal sacrifices will resume. Only then can the entire Torah be obeyed and the exile of God in the scattered people of Israel be ended.

For some contemporary Orthodox Jews the hope of the messianic age is so compelling that they prepare for the restoration of sacrifices in a rebuilt Temple by preserving and handing down the necessary ritual knowledge. Some trace their ancestry to the Levites of ancient Israel through the family line of Cohen (*Kohanim*), and they train males in each generation to perform sacrifices. Founded by Rabbi Yisrael Ariel, who was among the first paratroopers to reach the Temple Mount in the

Six Day War of 1967, the Temple Institute in the Jewish Quarter of the Old City of Jerusalem states that its "ultimate goal is to see Israel rebuild the Holy Temple of Mount Moriah in Jerusalem, in accord with the Biblical commandments."[82] To that end, it sponsors the crafting of ritual vessels and garments according to biblical specifications in preparation for the time when a ritually purified priesthood, sanctified by the ashes of a red heifer and clothed in proper vestments, will again offer animal sacrifices in the temple.[83] In anticipation of that time, some rabbis are calling for the offering of the Passover sacrifice, involving the slaughter of a lamb, on the Temple Mount now. The chief rabbi of Safed, Shmuel Eliyahu regards the Passover sacrifice as one of two "active *mitzvoth* (along with circumcision)" and warns that those who fail to offer it risk supernatural punishment and "cause great damage to themselves and to the entire world."[84] As the leading rabbi in the venerable center of Jewish mysticism, Eliyahu advocates animal sacrifice as literal obedience to Torah that sanctifies faithful Jews and brings blessings to the whole world. Several groups in Jerusalem continue to seek legal permission to perform the sacrifice on the Temple Mount, despite potential conflict with Muslim authorities.

Israel captured the Old City of Jerusalem in 1967, but Israel recognized the right of Muslim authorities to administer the site where the First and Second Temples had stood. The Temple Mount now contains the al-Aqsa mosque and the Dome of the Rock, a shrine that covers the spot from which Muslims believe Muhammad ascended into heaven. It is the third holiest place in Islam (after Mecca and Medina), and Jews and Christians are not allowed to pray publicly there. Still, the desire to fulfill the biblical command to offer sacrifices is strong enough for supporters of the restoration of the Temple, like Ginsburgh, to stage periodic demonstrations by bringing building blocks onto the Temple Mount in a symbolic gesture of reconstruction. Citing rabbinic teaching that the Messiah will announce the day of redemption *from the temple*, some Orthodox rabbis conclude that the Third Temple must be built *before* the messianic age arrives (and they are supported in this view by some evangelical Protestants). While offering Passover sacrifices on the Temple Mount would violate the political agreement to restrict the space to Muslim prayer, actual rebuilding of the Temple in its original dimensions would require the destruction of Islamic holy places—a prospect that would surely bring more bloodshed to that sacred space. Rabbi Eliyahu has raised the stakes in this dangerous confrontation by insisting that failure to offer animal sacrifices threatens divine judgment on Jews, even if performing them would result in humans sacrificing themselves to defend or prevent the practice.

For enthusiasts at the Temple Institute such sacrifice would be the cost exacted for re-establishing the Temple in Jerusalem as the spiritual center, not only of Judaism but of the world, where all of humanity could enter into daily contact with their Creator. In this cosmic vision, characteristic of Jewish piety from Kabbalah through Hasidic masters and still guiding some Orthodox believers today, the Temple is the site of universal sacrifice. "This is the role of the Holy Temple in the life of man: to enable one to realign himself, to dedicate one's whole self to G-d, to elevate every aspect of the human experience to holiness and return the energy which He gives us to His service."[85] Here total surrender to divine will through continual sacrifice of word, thought, and deed, as well as in ritual, is presented as supreme Jewish duty. Because Orthodox Jews believe that sacrifices in the restored Temple will bring about the redemption of the world, they call upon God to restore the Temple in daily prayer ('amidah): "May it be Thy will that the Temple be speedily rebuilt in our days." The prayer is recited three times daily to correspond to the schedule of sacrifices in ancient Israel.

Reform and Conservative Jews do not share the interest some Orthodox have in rebuilding the temple. In fact, Reform Jews name their places of worship "temple" rather than "synagogue" (from Greek for "gathering place") in order to declare their belief that sacrifices of the heart can be offered anywhere and, indirectly, to indicate that they do not believe Messiah will return to rebuild the Temple in Jerusalem. Nevertheless, Reform and Conservative Jews often express fervent loyalty to the State of Israel and its right to the sacred space of Jerusalem. That loyalty can find expression in calls for personal sacrifices to defend Jewish possession of the land of Palestine, including the expansion of Jewish settlements in areas occupied since 1967. Even for those who reject Orthodox literalism, the Temple remains the imagined sacred center of Jewish devotion and identity, whose central activity is the offering of sacrifices.

The celebrated Romanian scholar Mircea Eliade (1907–1986) described sacred space as the center of a religious cosmos, the *axis mundi* at which the world was created. Thus, to revisit the center is to renew relations with the transcendent and participate in the power that originally formed the cosmos. The purpose of ritual, in Eliade's view, is to reenact myths of creation and so to return to "that time" (*illo tempore*) when all was perfect. Eliade identified sacred centers everywhere in the history of religions and concluded that humans could not live without a central orientation for their lives. He often cited the temple in Jerusalem as a prime example. Its construction in concentric circles—leading from the outer court to the holy place, open only to priests, to the inner sanctuary, "the holy of holies" entered annually only by the high priest—corresponded to the three cosmic regions of sea, earth, and heaven, and thus served as an image of the world (*imago mundi*).[86] Sacrifices offered in the Temple according to the ritual schedule harmonized earth and heaven and reconciled humanity with God. Temple service sanctified both space and time. For Orthodox Jews restoring those ancient sacrifices is thus essential not only for the atonement of the people of Israel but for the recreation of the world.

Insistence on literal restoration of the Temple, however, seems at odds with the purpose of the early reformulation of Jewish ritual in the Mishnah after the destruction of the Second Temple. According to noted Talmudic scholar Baruch M. Bokser (1946–1990), "In response to the Temple's loss, mishnaic rabbis made the *seder* [Passover meal] independent of the sacrifice and, by reaching back to biblical accounts that predate the centralization of the cult, turned the celebration into a kinship gathering in the home instead of in the capitol city." What is important to note here is that these early authoritative interpreters of Torah focused on its meaning before the establishment of the "sacred center" of the temple. That is, the celebration of deliverance from bondage in Egypt remains at the heart of Passover while the ritual act of sacrificing a lamb and daubing its blood on the doorpost of the home is discontinued. The ritual re-focusing allows for "a liturgical overcoming of the 'space' of the Temple and Passover offering."[87]

Bokser follows Jonathan Z. Smith in rejecting Eliade's view of ritual as integrally bound to a particular location, the sacred center. While Smith acknowledges that Eliade's theory applies to some religious rituals, he notes that "symbolism of the 'Center' is, above all, a complex ideology of building—a matter of temples, palaces, and the like," and thus does not help us very much in understanding itinerant or displaced people, such as the Jewish nation after the destruction of the temple. Under conditions of itinerancy or exile, ritual is primarily a means of recollection or remembrance. What Smith concludes applies potentially to the attachment of Jews, Christians, and Muslims alike to sacred property in Jerusalem when their faiths have been thoroughly internalized: "All that remains of Jerusalem is an image, the historical narrative, and a temporal sequence."[88] Once the "holy of holies" is located in the individual heart and sacrifices become offerings of prayer, Torah study, good works, and table ritual, cannot the actual ground be left to the shifting possessions of political history?

Sacrifice or Disaster: Jewish Response to Nazi Genocide

Sacrifice is a recurrent theme in the religious and political history of Judaism. Yet the unthinkable horror of Nazi genocide in the mid-twentieth century has shaken Jewish faith in suffering as a sacred vocation and in sacrifice as required by God to redeem the world. In the late 1940s, as the full magnitude of the killing became known, Jewish thinkers used the term *shoah* ("catastrophe") to refer to it. A decade later holocaust ("burnt offering") came into general use, but many Jews have returned to the original term to avoid the suggestion that the engineered destruction of one-third of the Jews in Europe was somehow a redemptive sacrifice. For them, the murder of six million people did not establish a relation with the transcendent; it did not achieve some mysterious divine purpose; and it did not sanction the Nazis as God's agents, much less priests, offering up Jews to the sacrificial furnaces to atone for guilt.

The latter view did, however, become the interpretation of some Orthodox rabbis: That the Holocaust was another instance of divine judgment on Jews who assimilated into Gentile culture and neglected Torah. Their view seemed to be confirmed when European powers established the Jewish state in Palestine. The creation of Israel signified divine vindication, as when Cyrus freed their ancestors from captivity in Babylon and they returned from exile. The state of Israel was, in this view, dreadful compensation for the sacrifices made in the Holocaust. In a rerun of the book of Job, the gift of a Jewish homeland is divine reciprocity for the suffering of faithful Jews.

For many other Jews, however, this view is morally reprehensible, putting God in the role of an abusive parent who tries to placate his child for injuries by offering gifts. For them, the Nazi genocide was a horror conceived and executed by human imagination and ingenuity in pursuit of an abstract vision, a fascist utopia. There was nothing mysterious or inscrutable about Adolph Hitler's program of extermination of Jews. His plan was clear and consistent; it promised rational order, imposed without pity—crystal clear and cold as the point of a bayonet. All who did not fit the ideal form were eliminated, ruthlessly and efficiently. Their deaths were horrific, but not beyond understanding. They died in order to serve an abstract ideal: the Third Reich, the final Aryan kingdom rendered *Judenrein* ("free of Jews") by mass death. In this light, the furnaces of Auschwitz did not serve as altars; their burning bodies were not holocausts. The entire matter was tragic, signifying nothing beyond its own ghastly spectacle: A catastrophe to be condemned and never to be repeated. In giving up the term *sacrifice* for the loss of Jewish lives, what is lost is the consolation of redemptive meaning and purpose. What is gained is clarity of moral judgment. Replacing holocaust with shoah represents the "end of sacrifice" as an explanation for Jewish suffering and as the primary duty of Jewish devotion.

But if not sacrifice, what meaning can be assigned to the central horror of the twentieth century? In each of four traumatic moments in the history of the Jewish people, interpreters have found significance that rendered the suffering intelligible and, therefore, endurable. When the ancient Israelites were led into captivity in Babylon, the prophet Isaiah declared their suffering to be the vocation God had assigned them. By their faithful resistance to assimilation and their steadfast trust in Yahweh, they would serve as "a light to the Gentiles." Their redemptive witness was then vindicated by their return to the land and rebuilding the Temple in Jerusalem. When the Romans destroyed the Temple and the people were scattered in diaspora, the Pharisees explained that prayer, Torah study, and obedience of mitzvoth were of greater spiritual meaning than animal sacrifices. After the expulsion of Jews from Spain in 1492, teachers turned to Kabbalah to discover cosmic significance in God's presence with the people in exile. In these afflictions, the suffering of Jews was given the meaning of sacrifices, offerings of faith and obedience, even to the point of martyrdom, that played a role in the redemption of the world. But the Nazi genocide of 1933–1945 strains the explanatory power of sacrifice to the breaking point.

Responses to evil in the Hebrew Bible have in common two assumptions: (1) *that God is the single sovereign ruler of nature and history*, and (2) *that nothing happens in the world apart from God's power*. On the basis of those convictions each traditional view of suffering leads to a response that is appropriate for a specific kind of evil. First, if suffering is *punishment*, the response is to *repent* of sin and bear its consequences—as in the story of Adam and Eve. If suffering is a *test*, the proper response is to develop stronger *faith*—as in the story of Abraham and Isaac. Third, if suffering is a *mystery*, the response is to accept one's limited status as a creature, expressed either in *worship* or *protest*—as in the story of Job. Finally, if endurance of suffering is *witness*, the response is to set an *example* of loyalty to the will of God in Torah that will influence others to lead righteous lives. In each of these views of suffering, the point is not to understand why evil befalls us, but to respond to it in a creative and redemptive way. That is, to see suffering as sacrifice and, thus, meaningful.

The Nazi genocide seems to shatter all of these traditional theodicies and the meanings they assign to Jewish suffering. Despite Orthodox condemnation of the failure of European Jews to honor Torah, what sin of negligence or even disobedience could warrant the indiscriminate slaughter of millions, including children? Further, what is the point of a "test" if the suffering it inflicts is so severe that it overwhelms one's spirit to live?[89] How can one learn anything from a test that one does not survive? Finally, if deaths of the innocent serve some dark, mysterious, divine purpose, what can we conclude about the character of God?

In his dense work, *The Tremendum*, Jewish scholar Arthur Cohen (1928–1986) argued that the Holocaust revealed only the impenetrable mystery of evil: The camps "represent the presence of an enormity of terror, an 'unparalleled and unfathomable' celebration of murder, awful, chilling, overwhelming. It is a caesura, 'the discontinuity of the abyss,' of the negative." Still, the undeniable historical reality of Jewish destruction calls for theological interpretation. Cohen "invokes the Lurianic notion of the divine as *ein sof*, nothingness, and creation as *tsimtsum*, contraction, executed through logos, divine speech."[90] It is that withdrawal of God in the gift of creation that opens the space for human freedom, even if exercised in unprecedented scope and ferocity. For Cohen, the immensity of Nazi evil is utterly incommensurate with human reason or moral judgment.[91] We are reduced in its presence, as Job was in his encounter with the divine Whirlwind, to "dust and ashes" (Job 42:6).

Cohen draws his central category, *tremendum*, from the work of the Lutheran theologian, Rudolf Otto (1869–1937), called *Das Heilige*—a title misleadingly translated as *The Idea of the Holy* since Otto argued that no adequate concept of transcendent reality could be formulated. Rather, Otto focuses on the "non-rational factor in the idea of the divine." That factor is the experience of the sheer otherness of the holy as tremor-inducing mystery that both terrifies and attracts at the same time (*mysterium tremendum fascinans*), like the consuming fire to which the sacred is often compared. Otto took great pains to distinguish religious experience from moral judgment or aesthetic wonder or sheer horror for that matter. Religion, he claimed, is an "original faculty" of human consciousness that is awakened in the overwhelming presence of the divine.[92] Accordingly, that unique experience required a form of analysis peculiar to itself.

For that analysis, Otto extended the critical method of Immanuel Kant to religious experience by arguing that reason comprehends the holy in a way analogous to the way reason understands empirical data, acknowledges moral obligation, and makes aesthetic judgments (the topics of Kant's three famous critiques). Just as Kant deduced a priori categories required for the operation of reason in its theoretical and practical modes, so Otto constructed a priori categories necessary for reason in what he called its numinous mode, that is, in thinking about the sacred. Otto argued that reason organizes the primal divination of the numinous into the schematized experience of the Holy, complete with moral attributes. Thus, what begins as raw experience ends in fully elaborated theology. To take the example closest to Cohen's appropriation: The dread aroused by the sacred as "wholly other" evokes the symbol of divine wrath. The "ideogram of a moment whose singularly *daunting* and awe-inspiring character must be gravely disturbing to those persons who will recognize nothing in the divine nature but goodness, gentleness, love, and a sort of confidential intimacy."[93] Like

Luria, for whom the divine sefirah of judgment, unreconciled with its counterpart of mercy, was the origin of evil, so for Otto wrath expresses a dimension of the tremendum that can be overcome only by other qualities, such as love.

Luria and Otto both honestly acknowledge that if God is one, then all things, including evil and the suffering it causes, have their ultimate source in the holy. Cohen fails to match the theological courage of his sources by shifting the category of tremendum from God to the immensity of evil created by the Third Reich and declaring the horror incomprehensible. But if all the Holocaust represents is a greater extent of human perversion, then it tells us nothing new. If it reveals anything about God, however, then it must be that the holy manifests itself as wrath, as well as grace. Despite his insistence that Jews must recover a sense of transcendence, Cohen does not acknowledge this ambiguity in the moral character of the divine. For example, can God be trusted to remain in covenant with the children of Abraham? The problem with Cohen's project of theodicy is that to remove the Nazi program of genocide from rational analysis is to make effective ethical condemnation impossible and to defeat the understanding necessary to prevent its recurrence. To call such actions "demonic" or tremendum is to abandon what Jonathan Z. Smith insists is the scholar's vocation: "the quest for intelligibility."[94]

Finally, there is the interpretation of evil as a test of faithfulness and suffering as a vocation of witness. But are there instances in which a faithful people suffer beyond the limits of punishment or testing, yet their example is ignored by the world? If the murder of Jews had no influence on the rest of humanity, elicited no sympathy, and failed to arouse compassion—if they disappeared into the flames without a trace except for their own thin voices chanting the *Kaddish*, the prayer for the dead, because there was no one to offer it on their behalf—then their witness went unheeded and whatever meaning can be assigned their murders, it cannot be *sacrifice*. It must be accepted as *catastrophe*.

Elie Wiesel (1928–2016), Holocaust survivor and winner of the Nobel Peace Prize, dedicated his life as a witness to the memory of those who died and as an advocate for persecuted people everywhere. Wiesel used his gift as a writer to achieve what rituals of his tradition were intended to accomplish, namely, preservation of Jewish memory. He honored those who died by preventing their murderers from erasing the memory

of their crimes. In his haunting memoir of survival in Nazi concentration camps, Wiesel recalled first entering Auschwitz and seeing infants
thrown into an open fire. In horror, he asked his father how humanity
could allow burning people to death and received this reply: "The world
is not interested in us. Today, everything is possible, even the crema-
toria." Wiesel would witness and suffer many other acts of murderous
cruelty, but that night already changed him: "Never shall I forget those
flames that consumed my faith forever. . . . Never shall I forget those
moments that murdered my God and my soul and turned my dreams
to ashes."[95]

What God died for Wiesel that night? Precisely the God of Kabbalah.
In his original Yiddish version of *Night* Wiesel began this way: "We believed in God, trusted in man, and lived with the illusion that every one
of us has been entrusted with a sacred spark from the Shekinah's flame:
that every one of us carries in his eyes and in his soul a reflection of
God's image."[96] For Wiesel the very theology that had been created centuries before to assure and comfort Jews in exile went up in the smoke
of the fires of Auschwitz. No sacred vocation here; holocaust is not in
this sense a metaphor for moral conduct or mystical ecstasy. Real Jewish men, women, and children were given as coal to the furnace and the
world was largely indifferent.

A sense of common humanity was the first thing Nazi command-
ers knew must be suppressed in their troops and the first thing to be
ground out of the souls of their prisoners. Many have written about the
dehumanizing effect of the camps, perhaps none as unsparingly as Jewish psychiatrist Victor Frankl (1905–1997) in his reflection on who survived the atrocities and who did not, *Man's Search for Meaning* (1946).
As he saw it, what determined whether a prisoner succumbed to death
or clung to life was the ability to affirm significance in continuing to
struggle, despite every impulse to surrender. In our terms, Frankl saw
that submitting to "God's will" as a sacrificial victim was tantamount
to assenting to one's own murder. Whatever it might mean in religious
terms, such capitulation to the killers was the final gesture of despair. In
the nightmare of the Nazi camps, all that was left to the individual was
the existential decision to find meaning in the chaos, even if by a heroic
venture of imagination. For Frankl, the challenge of the camps was to
find a reason to affirm the significance of one's own survival. But what

of the Jewish people as a whole? If the Nazi genocide was not a sacrifice (holocaust) offered in fulfillment of their divine vocation, what did it mean?

Jewish thinkers have offered a number of possible answers. Richard Rubenstein argued that the appropriate response to the indifference of the God of heaven to Jewish suffering was to repudiate him and return to deities of the earth, to affirm an ethic of responsibility for other human beings through "a mystical paganism which utilizes the historic forms of Jewish religion."[97] One of those forms is sacrifice. Rubenstein recognizes that ritual sacrifice is not a magic palliative, but he believes it is necessary to retain at least its verbal form, as created by early rabbis and elaborated in mystical literature, in order to satisfy the human need for psychic catharsis through violence. He criticizes the Reform substitution of moral exhortations from Deuteronomy in place of traditional passages on sacrifice from Leviticus in Torah reading for Yom Kippur. Rubenstein finds the command to pour out the blood of the animal on the ground before its meat may be consumed to be a powerful symbol of human connection to our "cannibal Earth-Mother" and of specific Jewish attachment to the land of Israel. After having "tasted the bitterest and the most degrading of deaths," Jews know that they are "insubstantial nothingness before the awesome and terrible majesty" of the Holy Abyss. "We have lost all hope and faith. We have also lost all possibility of disappointment. Expecting absolutely nothing from God or man, we rejoice in whatever we receive."[98] For Rubenstein the Holocaust dispels finally the illusion of a personal God guiding the destiny of the Jewish people and requiring sacrifices from them to satisfy their part of a covenant.

Yet if Torah is valuable only as a reminder of the faceless source of our absurd existence—the mystery, wonder, and grace of our brief time from birth to death—where can one hear a guiding word from the God of Israel? One Jewish theologian offered an answer. Emil Fackenheim (1916–2003) was a philosopher and Reform rabbi, who spent three months in a Nazi camp before escaping to Scotland and from there to Canada, where he eventually became a renowned professor at the University of Toronto. In 1984 he moved to Hebrew University in Jerusalem and became involved in political defense of the state of Israel. While his intellectual interests ranged across the works of European Enlightenment thinkers, some of his work recast philosophical insights in traditional forms of midrash, informed by the Kabbalistic ideal of tikkun olam, mending the world.

That goal was even more urgent in the aftermath of the shattering disaster of the Nazi genocide. In the brief work that directly addresses the question of God's absence in the Shoah, Fackenheim offered reflections on the radical theology of the 1960s, including the "death of God" movement and Rubenstein's call for a new paganism. He argued, however, that abandoning Jewish identity now would hand Hitler a posthumous victory. He wrote, "Hitler failed to murder all Jews, for he lost the war. *Has he succeeded in destroying the Jewish faith for us who have escaped?*" He noted that one million Jewish children were killed because their great-grandparents were Jews, then offered this dramatic commentary: "Like Abraham of old, European Jews some time in the mid-nineteenth century offered a human sacrifice, by the mere minimal commitment to the Jewish faith of bringing up Jewish children. But unlike Abraham, they did not know what they were doing, and there was no reprieve."[99] For Jews to abandon Judaism now would render that sacrifice meaningless.

By traditional count the divine Voice of Sinai issued 613 commandments to the people of Israel. In stark contrast Fackenheim announced that the Voice of Auschwitz sounded only one, the 614th commandment, which can be expressed simply as "Thou shalt survive!" In Talmudic fashion, Fackenheim went on to elaborate the mitzvah from Auschwitz in this way:

> . . . we are, first, commanded to survive as Jews, lest the Jewish people perish. We are commanded, second to remember in our very guts and bones the martyrs of the Holocaust, lest their memory perish. We are forbidden, thirdly, to deny or despair of God, however much we may have to contend with him or with belief in him, lest Judaism perish. We are forbidden, finally, to despair of the world as the place which is to become the kingdom of God, lest we help make it a meaningless place in which God is dead or irrelevant and everything is permitted. To abandon any of these imperatives, in response to Hitler's victory at Auschwitz, would be to hand him yet other, posthumous victories.[100]

The political implications of this position are clear: Maintaining Jewish identity, including loyalty to the land and state of Israel "as a moral necessity," is the only way to insure that Hitler and all his anti-Jewish imitators are permanently defeated.[101] That defeat was implicit in the actions of the few "righteous Gentiles" who protected and defended Jews in Europe and was explicit in the armed resistance of Jews themselves, such as the fighters in the Warsaw Ghetto who refused to succumb to the "Nazi logic of destruction." Their resistance is the "emergence from powerlessness" that was completed in the establishment of the state of Israel.

Far from the mystical ideal of reuniting the divine being, what Fackenheim means by tikkun olam is restoring Jewish trust in the rest of the world from a position of strength. "What then is the *Tikkun*? It is Israel itself. It is a state founded, maintained, defended by a people who—so it was once thought—had lost the arts of statecraft and self-defense forever."[102] By refusing to submit as sacrificial victims and asserting political power over their homeland, Jews can heed the "voice of Auschwitz" to preserve themselves. Fackenheim concludes with the story of a Warsaw Ghetto survivor who dedicated himself to adopting Jewish orphans, caring for them until they were old enough to marry and continue the people of Israel for generations to come.

Fackenheim and his generation of post-Holocaust thinkers transfer the mitzvoth of sacrifice from ritual worship of God to practical donations of time, wealth, and even life to the good of Israel, both people and state. What it means to be Jewish, whether one is religious or secular, is to be Zionist. While rabbinic tradition maintained that Jewish migration to the land of Israel and "holy war" in its defense were not allowed before the return of Messiah, the victory of the state of Israel in 1967 convinced Orthodox Jews that the messianic redemption had begun. Thus, mass emigration of Jews to Israel was part of the divinely authorized conquest of the land. Jewish scholar Reuven Firestone notes, "Combined, traditional religion and modern utopian nationalism created a powerful activist and thoroughly postmodern messianism."[103]

But a basic transformation in the meaning of sacrifice occurs when its object is no longer a mysterious and capricious divine being, but the fallible human vision of a historical utopia. Then the old tension between giving up the concrete for the sake of the abstract resurfaces—and so do screams of protest. It is now poets who return to the story of the Akedah to raise questions about the sacrifice of young lives for the sake of the nation of Israel.

Sacrifice and Critique of Israeli Nationalism

The Israeli literary critic, Yoseph Milman, argues that "from all shades of the political spectrum the Sacrifice [Akedah] is conceived as a symbol most accurately representing the essence of the Zionist ideal." His comment deserves to be quoted at length:

> Although it is no longer God who commands the sacrifice, and the readiness to sacrifice and to be sacrificed does not derive from religious devotion, the sentence on the national destiny is conceived by this generation as no less authoritative than the religious belief; and the *halutziut*—namely, the voluntary subordination of the individual and complete ascetic devotion to the national destiny—is regarded as an almost mystical addiction no less absolute than any devotional act of faith.[104]

Yael Feldman, professor of comparative literature, points to the irony that the secular Zionist movement appropriated the biblical story of the Akedah as the basis for its appeal to sacrifice in defense of the Jewish homeland. She points out that "since the 1940s, the Akedah has become a key figure in Zionist thought and Hebrew letters. Paradoxically, it gained its prominence because of its double semantic potential (like korban, it was understood to connote a state of 'victimization' and/or 'self/sacrifice'), and came to represent both the slaughter of the Holocaust and the national warrior's death in the old-new homeland." In this way, the Akedah "became part of Israel's 'civil religion,' articulating a modern ethos of national sacrifice."[105] Since the time of the Crusades, Isaac has served as a powerful exemplar of martyrdom and the trope has gained strength through its application to fallen Israeli soldiers in the wars of 1967 and 1973. The sense of duty to give oneself in defense of the homeland is pervasive in Israeli society, made inescapable by the requirement of military service. The religious ideal of sacrifice lends authority to the political demand to kill, and if need be to die, for the sake of the nation.

In contemporary Hebrew "anti-sacrificial poetry of protest," however, Milman notes, the call of Zionism is challenged in a reading of the Akedah as a story against the call to sacrifice in defense of Israel. For example, in his poem, "The Real Hero of the Sacrifice," Yehuda Amicahai cites the ram "who didn't know about the conspiracy between the others," a reference to Israeli youth whose lives were lost in the Six Day War. He ends by describing "the unscrupulous Abraham" who has "split long since," totally unaffected by the issue, and God, who has also departed—the two of them leaving "empty places." Citing Buber's warning against the danger of sacrificing human lives in an idolatry of empty abstractions, Milman concludes, "Only the magic of canonical myths keeps this deception alive and according to the protest poets, only the violent undermining of those myths in a deliberately provocative and alienating way can expose this deception and discard it."[106]

In his novella, *Early in the Summer of 1970*, Israeli author A. B. Yehoshua offers an ironic retelling of the Akedah story as a myth of national sacrifice in the context of the 1967 war where "young Israeli soldiers are posited as an offering for the older generation's ideological vision." In this novella the father, anxious to retain his authority as a teacher of the Bible, confronts his son on the battleground only to become the sacrifice himself —his Zionist ideology defeated by his son's idealism, expressed by the word "peace" inscribed on the younger man's knife.[107]

The brief poem by Shin Shifra, called simply "Isaac" (1962), exemplifies another subversive reading of the Akedah from the perspective of a dying soldier, who heard no divine voice of rescue but only God's derisive laugh. Feldman comments, "Here, the poet brazenly questions the necessity of national sacrifice. God's laughter, which evokes Sarah's famous laughter in Genesis upon learning she will have a son, becomes the malicious mockery of a god who accepts human sacrifice. In Shifra's version, no angel will come to stay Abraham's blade." One might add, as no angel extinguished the furnaces of Auschwitz—nor is there likely to be a restraining voice from heaven to prevent nuclear war in the Mideast, if such would be launched to defend the imaginative constructs of Land or State or Religion generated by any of the communities inspired by the sacrifice of Abraham.

Perhaps it is the voice of Jewish poets and novelists, reading the ancient story against itself, who issue the call for the end of sacrifice as a political strategy and as a religious ideal. In their verses and stories we detect an echo of Sarah's scream.

4

Sacrifice in Christian Tradition

And it is by God's will that we have been sanctified
through the offering of the body of Jesus Christ once for all.
—Hebrews 10:10

I appeal to you therefore, brothers and sisters,
by the mercies of God, to present your bodies as a living
    sacrifice,
holy and acceptable to God, which is your spiritual worship.
—Romans 12:1

At no time is the persistence of sacrifice more evident than when traditions declare the "end of sacrifice." Like the phoenix, the moment of
death marks rebirth. Sometimes the primal religious gesture returns
in attenuated forms of substitution and sometimes in intense acts of
imitation. No matter what the occasion for ending sacrifice, it is never
catastrophic enough or so decisively final that sacrifice becomes there-
after impossible. On the contrary, the very event that signals the end of
sacrifice often becomes the compelling model for continuing the practice. This process is illustrated in the history of Christianity. For most
Christians, the crucifixion of Jesus constituted the final sacrifice for the
forgiveness of sins and, at the same time, demonstrated the highest ideal
of loving self-denial that Christians are called to replicate. Christianity
declared the "end of sacrifice," while continuing to employ sacrificial
language to signify its primary virtues. What Stroumsa called "the
leaven of interiorization," transforming the practice of sacrifice in Judaism after the destruction of the Second Temple, Christianity declared
"spiritual worship."

Sacrifice in the Life and Writing of St. Paul

The attraction of sacrifice as religious ideal is particularly seductive for Christians who believe that Jesus's crucifixion was the ultimate sacrifice, making possible the redemption of the world. Through their own sacrifices they identify with Christ in his revelation of divine love for humanity. The apostle Paul set sacrifice at the center of Christian faith and practice. Writing from prison in Rome where he later died as a martyr, Paul compared his persecution to a drink offering sanctifying the sacrifices of other believers: "I am being poured out as a libation over the sacrifice and the offering of your faith" (Philippians 2:17). For Paul, Christian life entails unceasing sacrifice. He wrote, "I have been crucified with Christ; and it is no longer I who live, but it is Christ who lives in me" (Galatians 2:19–20). Paul's suffering is even represented as an extension of the redemptive offering of Christ in the claim that "in my flesh I am completing what is lacking in Christ's afflictions for the sake of his body, that is, the church" (Colossians 1:24).

This use of sacrificial imagery illustrates the point made by biblical scholar James Watts that *sacrifice* is not as much a description of ritual action as it is an evaluative term based on a narrative model: "Calling some act a 'sacrifice' is to claim that the act is comparable to some paradigmatic action in a hero's or villain's story."[1] In Paul's case the story is the crucifixion of Jesus as the highest example of self-giving. Further, Paul connects the imitation of Christ's suffering to the anticipation of sharing in the triumphant end of his story, that is, resurrection in the age to come. "I want to know Christ," he writes, "and the power of his resurrection and the sharing of his sufferings by becoming like him in his death, if somehow I may attain the resurrection from the dead" (Philippians 3:10–11).

It is significant that half the individual books in the New Testament are attributed to Paul, even though most scholars recognize only seven or eight as his compositions. Paul's genuine letters are the earliest books in the New Testament, mostly written or dictated during his missionary travels, on the fly and without meticulous attention to grammar and syntax. The letters address congregational problems and their theological passages are fragmentary. Still, it is remarkable that Paul records no parables of Jesus, none of his miracles, and ignores the Sermon on the

Mount, focusing instead on his sacrificial death and resurrection. Alternative interpretations of Jesus's central significance, such as wonder worker or teacher of moral wisdom or revealer of heavenly secrets, were literally anathema ("accursed") to Paul. As he warned the churches in Galatia, "But if even we or an angel from heaven should proclaim to you a gospel contrary to what we proclaimed to you, let that one be accursed!" (Galatians 1:8).

The interpretation of the death of Christ as sacrificial offering to be replicated by self-giving became the dominant Christian view. This understanding eventually provided the "deep symbol" by which Christian orthodoxy expressed its highest values and against which it measured competing interpretations.[2] The Church came to teach that Christ offered himself as the perfect and final sacrifice that satisfied the justice of God and allows those who believe in him to receive forgiveness of sins and eternal life. In Paul's words, "since all have sinned and fall short of the glory of God; they are now justified by his grace as a gift, through the redemption that is in Christ Jesus, whom God put forward as a sacrifice of atonement by his blood, effective through faith" (Romans 3:23–25). While Paul does not develop a typological interpretation of Christ's death as the fulfillment of atonement foreshadowed in Israelite animal sacrifices, he draws imagery from Jewish tradition, particularly from the story of Passover, declaring that "our paschal lamb, Christ, has been sacrificed" (1 Corinthians 5:7).

Paul carried the message that Jesus is the *Christ* (the Greek equivalent of the Hebrew term for "anointed one" or "Messiah") beyond Palestine into the Hellenistic world. The churches Paul established in Asia Minor were composed primarily of "Gentiles" (from Greek *ethnoi*, meaning peoples or nations), those who were not part of the Jewish people. Their understanding of Jesus, consequently, was not shaped by Jewish religious categories. Paul vigorously defended the right of these Gentile Christians to be free from ritual requirements of Torah and strenuously opposed all attempts by the Jewish-Christian community in Jerusalem to impose upon Gentile believers the marks of Jewish identity, such as circumcision and kosher food laws.[3] In support of his position, Paul referred to Abraham, whose faith in God's promise to give him countless descendants was accounted as righteousness *before* he was circumcised (Genesis 15:5–6). From this chronological point, Paul concluded that

Abraham was "the ancestor of all who believe without being circumcised" (Romans 4:11).

Abraham believed that he and Sarah would have children despite their advanced age, and Paul preached belief in "him who raised Jesus our Lord from the dead." Still, for Paul the principle was the same: God counts faith as the ground of justification (or being declared righteous before God). Paul does not comment on Abraham's obedience to the divine call to sacrifice his son, perhaps because the story of the Akedah could be construed to mean that Abraham was not justified by faith, after all. That position is expressed in a later epistle, written under the name of the apostle James: "Was not our ancestor Abraham justified by works when he offered his son Isaac on the altar?" (James 2:21). But the distinction between faith in Christ and obedience to Torah, sharpened by Martin Luther into a point of absolute difference between Christianity and Judaism, is surely exaggerated in the case of Paul. As biblical scholar Pamela Eisenbaum persuasively argues, Paul remained a Jew throughout his life and embraced a "covenantal theology" in which one's ethical life is "the way one worships God."[4] Paul fully expects Gentile Christians to live, as he does, by the moral standards of Torah, even as he recognizes they are not obligated to fulfill those commandments that define distinctive Jewish identity. In that spirit, he likened Gentile Christians to Isaac in an allegory to illustrate their "freedom in Christ" from the "yoke" of Mosaic laws given to Jews (Galatians 4). It seems that Paul's interest in Abraham is primarily polemical, to demonstrate that non-Jews can be "grafted" into the tree of Abrahamic lineage through faith in Christ (Romans 11:13–19).

Similarly, he uses the Greek title *Kyrios*, meaning "Lord," to refer to Jesus, as part of his rhetorical appeal to non-Jews. Kyrios was particularly useful because it was also the term used for the personal name of God (YHWH, transliterated as *Yahweh*) in the Greek version of the Hebrew Bible and designated in English translations by small capitals (LORD). To Greek-speaking Jewish Christians, kyrios would associate Jesus with the Creator-God of Jewish faith; but in the Hellenistic cities where Paul preached, kyrios would be known as the title of the god of a mystery religion. These secret religious societies were each organized around a deity, such as Dionysius or Mithras or Isis, whose worship included sacrificial rites.

Membership in "mystery religions" was voluntary and one was free to join as many secret societies as one had time and money to pursue. Each cult offered its devotees access to supernatural knowledge and power through secret rites of initiation. For example, one devotee was initiated into the cult of the Egyptian goddess Isis by elaborate ceremonies of purification, including offering sacrifices and fasting. The rite culminated in his being dressed in "a new linen robe" and led to "the most secret and sacred place of the temple." The ritual involved a reenactment of the myth of the cult deity, a play in which actors took the roles of various characters, usually in a drama of dying and rising to new life. The performance was preceded by offering sacrifice and concluded with the narrator Lucius confessing his inadequacy to offer "sufficient praise" to Isis, specifically noting that not even the offering of all the property he inherited from his father would be enough, confessing that "my patrimony is unable to satisfy thy sacrifices."[5]

Sacrificial ceremonies reached their most gruesome form in the *taurobolium*, the ritual of initiation for the high priest of the cult of the Great Mother Cybele, whose most devoted male followers castrated themselves and joined the procession of her worship as transvestites. In a description of the taurobolium by a disapproving Christian poet of the fourth century, named Prudentius, we find details no doubt dramatized to evoke repugnance in his readers. The high priest in full beard and silken toga descends into a pit over which a wooden floor is placed with wide spaces between the planks and holes bored to make a lattice. Then a huge bull, adorned with garlands and gold leaf, is led onto the platform and slain. The sacrificers "pierce its breast with a sacred spear; the gaping wound emits a wave of hot blood, and the smoking river flows into the woven structure beneath it and surges wide." The priest below raises his head to catch the flood of the bull's life blood until his beard and clothing are drenched. He then emerges from the pit, "horrible in appearance" but reborn into divine life, and "all hail and worship at a distance" in respect for his sacred authority.[6]

Initiates into the cult of Dionysus received eternal life through participation in the god's sacrificial death by means of a ritual meal. According to Greek myth, Dionysius was the son of Zeus born of a human woman. He was worshipped in orgiastic rituals which culminated in female devotees ripping apart the body of a sacrificial victim, representing the deity, and then feasting on its raw flesh. While historians question many of the sensational accounts of *bacchanalia* (celebrations of Dionysius as the god of wine and ecstasy), the myth of the dying and rising god who brings salvation through his sacrificed body was widely known in the ancient world.[7] Those who heard Paul speak of dying with Christ and being raised to eternal life through faith in his sacrificial death would have recognized the language. As the editors of a recent volume on sacrificial practices in Paul's world note, within "this complex mix of Roman, Greek, and Jewish sacrificial practices and concepts . . . Christians were just as invested in sacrifice as their neighbors."[8]

Thus, Gentiles who were ignorant of Jewish tradition would first understand Christ as the central deity of a cultic community, not as the Messiah sent to fulfill God's promises to the Jewish people. Paul's challenge was to preserve the unity of Jews and Gentiles in a community of believers in one God whose agent of universal salvation was Jesus, both *Christ* and *Lord*. What both audiences had in common was the "deep symbol" of sacrifice as the means of securing a right relationship with the sacred, whether through animal sacrifices offered in a temple or ritual participation in the death and resurrection of an incarnate deity. Even Paul acknowledges that understanding Christ's death as an atoning sacrifice was not original with him, but was already part of the tradition that he received and was handing on, namely, "that Christ died for our sins in accordance with the scriptures" (1 Corinthians 15:3).

Another tradition that Paul hands down from earliest Christian worship is a hymn in praise of Christ Jesus, "who, though he was in the form of God, did not regard equality with God as something to be exploited, but emptied (*ekenōsen*) himself, taking the form of a slave, being born in human likeness. And being found in human form he humbled himself and became obedient to the point of death—even death on a cross" (Philippians 2:6–8). Scholars refer to this passage as the "kenotic" hymn, from the Greek root (*kenōsis*) of "emptying." These words may have been among those Christians sang daily at their dawn worship services. What the hymn suggests is that these Christians regarded the incarnation of the preexistent Christ as a sacrifice, in which he gave up the "form of God" to assume "human form," including becoming subject to the power of death. The second stanza of the hymn describes the outcome of this divine self-giving: God exalted Jesus above the entire cosmos (heaven, earth, and underworld) so that all should worship him, confessing that "Jesus Christ is Lord." Here the incarnation is not the means of embodiment that made it possible for Jesus to die as a sacrifice; rather, the incarnation *is* sacrifice. In emptying himself of "equality with God" Christ relinquished his transcendent status to enter human history and suffer the fate of all humanity.

According to what Paul calls "my gospel," sacrifice is not only the act of Christ, but the ideal of every Christian as well. Salvation requires dying to one's former way of life and being raised to a new life free from the power of sin. It is through the initiatory ritual of baptism that the believer enters into the life of the risen Christ, as Paul writes, "all of us who have been baptized into Christ Jesus were baptized into his death. . . . if we have been united with him in a death like his, we will certainly be united with him in a resurrection like his" (Romans 6:3–5). For Paul, immersion in water represents death to one's natural life and rebirth into the divine life of Christ. Paul draws on primeval associations of water with womb and tomb: Every human is preceded into life by a gush of water and anyone caught beneath its surface meets death. For Paul, baptism is an act of self-sacrifice, dying to former desires and ambitions with the hope of emerging reborn, beyond the power of death in future resurrection.

For Paul, baptism initiates the new Christian into a life of unending sacrifice, crucified with Christ and bound to deny bodily passions in obedience to divine will. "But now that you have been freed from sin and enslaved to God, the advantage you get is sanctification. The end is eternal life" (Romans 6:22). The logic of sacrifice is clear: Give up the right to make personal decisions and accept servitude in exchange for immortality. To become sacred or sanctified requires relinquishing personal autonomy. In this spirit Paul introduces himself as a servant or slave (*doulos*) of Christ and, by extension, the slave of others as well. He writes to the church at Corinth, "For we do not proclaim ourselves; we proclaim Jesus Christ as Lord and ourselves as your slaves for Jesus' sake" (2 Corinthians 4:5).

Baptism is a clear symbolic sacrifice, but there is an even more dramatic representation of the life of Christ, and of the Christian, as sacrifice, and that is the ritual meal known as *Eucharist* or "thanksgiving." Among the earliest Christians this ceremony involved eating an entire meal together, which they called the "love feast." Later Christian practice limited the "feast" to a sip of wine and a wafer. The ritual was also later interpreted as a *sacrament*, or means of grace, that must be administered in certain prescribed ways by ordained men. The control of the Eucharist by a formal priesthood resembles the ancient Israelite regulations governing animal sacrifices.

The ritual of Eucharist reenacts the story of Jesus's last supper with his disciples and his subsequent death on the cross. It thus recreates the sacred time in which the Christian faith was founded by recalling the community's common *memory* and reaffirming its common *hope*. Paul combines these elements in his instructions for the Eucharist: "For as often as you eat this bread and drink the cup, you proclaim the Lord's death until he comes" (1 Corinthians 11:26). Paul presents the ritual meal as an occasion for Christians to live out their commitment to sacrifice for one another. Elsewhere, in a letter written under Paul's name, Christ's death is presented as an example of the love Christians should show to one another. The author urges his fellow believers to "live in love, as Christ loved us and gave himself up for us, a fragrant offering and sacrifice (*thysian*) to God" (Ephesians 5:2).

Paul insists that his preaching centered on Christ's death, writing to the Corinthians, "I decided to know nothing among you except Jesus Christ, and him crucified" (1 Corinthians 2:2). In another letter he vows, "May I never boast of anything except the cross of our Lord Jesus Christ, by which the world has been crucified to me, and I to the world" (Galatians 6:14). Yet Paul's focus on sacrifice is sharpest when he talks about identifying with Christ in suffering and weakness rather than triumph.[9] He writes from prison to the church in Philippi, "I want to know Christ and the power of his resurrection and the sharing of his sufferings by becoming like him in his death, if somehow I may obtain the resurrection from the dead" (Philippians 3:10–11). Paul regarded suffering as the mark of his servitude to Christ, confirmed by scars from lashings he received from persecutors. "From now on," he ends his fierce letter to the Galatians, "let no one make trouble for me; for I carry the marks of Jesus branded on my body" (Galatians 6:17).

Throughout his correspondence with the church in Corinth, Paul defiantly defends his authority as an apostle of Christ against detractors who charged that he lacked the divine power to work miracles. His challengers said that Paul was physically unimpressive and his oratory fell flat. According to Paul, they charged that "his bodily presence is weak and his speech contemptible." By contrast, they performed wonders to back up their superior rhetorical skill in persuading the Corinthians of their version of the gospel, namely, that every believer should already enjoy the glory of the resurrection. The evidence of true faith, then, should be power over natural forces and the ability to speak with the tongues of angels (*glossolalia*). In short, every believer and *a fortiori* any apostle should exhibit material and spiritual perfection. They were the prototypes of today's preachers of "prosperity theology." Paul sarcastically calls them "super-apostles" (*hyperlian apostolōn*) and counters that their message is inspired by Satan as a deception to lead believers into arrogance and delusion.

By contrast, Paul presents the opposite set of credentials for his apostolic authority. The proof he offers that he is a "better" minister of Christ than his opponents is a résumé of his sufferings as a missionary: floggings; stoning; shipwreck; threats by storms and bandits; betrayal; insomnia; hunger and thirst; lack of shelter; anxiety about his congregations; and a chronic physical ailment he calls a "thorn in the flesh" (possibly glaucoma).[10] Clearly, for Paul suffering in the service of Christ constitutes *sacrifice* in which he is the victim. It is important to note that the afflictions he bore in the course of his missionary work were not self-imposed, as ascetic disciplines. Paul exposes himself to these dangers with uncertainty about his own survival but with full confidence that the risk is necessary to complete his identity with Christ. In his appeal to the Corinthians Paul writes, "For Christ was crucified in weakness, but lives by the power of God. For we are weak in him, but in dealing with you we will live with him by the power of God" (2 Corinthians 13:4). In daily vulnerability to pain and death, in sacrificial self-giving, Paul found his vocation and identity.

In his historical context Paul would not have been alone in locating personal identity in suffering. Classics professor Judith Perkins demonstrates that in "the late Hellenistic period and the early Roman Empire, the suffering body became a focus of significant cultural concern and this gave rise to the creation of a new subjectivity—the self as sufferer." She argues that the discourse of suffering focused attention on the body as the locus of individual identity requiring attention and care.

In fact, she notes that the exemplary martyr Ignatius of Antioch taught that "suffering was not simply something that happened to a person. Rather, it was the means of achieving real selfhood." The construction of the suffering subject prepared the way for the development of Christian institutions, such as hospitals and aid agencies for the poor. Along with sacrifice as religious practice, the suffering self as cultural subject is another "deep symbol" that supported the Pauline ideal of identification with Christ's passion. As Perkins writes, "even pagan contemporaries who knew almost nothing about Christianity knew that Christians were sufferers. This knowledge marked the point where pagan and Christian cultural preoccupations met in their attention to suffering."[11]

Still, suffering was not an end in itself. For Paul a life "in Christ" (one of his favorite phrases) does not offer reward in the present, but holds out hope that God will in the future bring about redemption. Paul writes, "I consider that the sufferings of this present time are not worth comparing with the glory about to be revealed to us" (Romans 8:18). Beyond the limits of this life, believers who have shared in Christ's sacrificial self-giving may hope to share in the unimaginable perfection of a redeemed universe. For Paul, as much as for the visionaries of Kabbalah, God's ultimate goal is the salvation of the entire cosmos. In the meanwhile, far from enjoying the lavish riches of paradise the super-apostles boast to possess, "God has exhibited us apostles as last of all, as though sentenced to death. . . . we are hungry and thirsty, we are poorly clothed and beaten and homeless" (1 Corinthians 4:9, 11). In poverty and misery so severe Paul says it is like dying anew every day, he lives in hope of the resurrection to come. He is confident that his daily sacrifices invest him with the authority to say, "Be imitators of me, as I am of Christ" (1 Corinthians 11:1). For Paul, his gospel, his authority as an apostle, and his conduct are one, united by the principle of sacrifice. His faith was formed under the sign of the cross and for him any account of Jesus's life must drive to that spectacle of violence as its redemptive climax—as do the four Gospels included in the New Testament.[12]

Sacrifice in New Testament Gospels

Paul was so successful in promoting the view that Christ's death was redemptive sacrifice which every believer should replicate in daily life that his view eventually became the dominant interpretation of Christian faith and his letters acknowledged as divinely inspired. Already by the late first century, in a writing attributed to the apostle Peter, Paul's letters are praised as written with wisdom. Although at points "hard to understand," the author includes them with "the other scriptures" (2 Peter 3:16). Another epistle written during the same time also cites sayings of Jesus as "scripture" (1 Timothy 5:18). "Thus," concludes the biblical scholar Bart Ehrman, "by the beginning of the second century some Christians were ascribing authority to the words of Jesus and the writings of his apostles."[13] What is of interest here is the strong consistency between Paul's focus on the sacrificial death of Jesus and the narrative structure of the Gospels.

Each Gospel was believed to have been written by one of Jesus's apostles (Matthew and John) or by someone closely associated with an apostle (Mark as the secretary of Peter and Luke as the personal physician of Paul). While varying in perspective and addressed to different audiences, what these works also have in common—and what sets them apart from other early accounts of the life of Jesus that were claimed to be written by apostles—is emphasis on Christ's sacrificial death. They each bring the story of Jesus to its dramatic climax at his crucifixion.

The first three Gospels are called "synoptic" because they "see" the story of Jesus "together." Most scholars agree that Mark was the first written (around the time of the fall of Jerusalem) and that Matthew and Luke follow and expand Mark's order of events—moving relentlessly through Jesus's career as an itinerant healer and teacher in Galilee to his trial and execution in Jerusalem. To Mark the purpose of Jesus's life is as a prelude to his crucifixion: "For the Son of Man came not to be served but to serve, and to give his life a ransom for many" (Mark 10:45). A noted feature of Mark's Gospel is that Christ's identity is concealed until the moment of his death. Only at the foot of the cross is the "messianic secret" disclosed by a Roman centurion, awestruck by the way Jesus died: "Truly this man was God's Son!" (Mark 15:39). Mark sustains the mystery, however, by ending with three women at the empty tomb, terrified, amazed, and afraid (Mark 16:8). Readers are left in suspense to decide whether the sacrifice was effective (a lack of resolution that was quickly supplied by editors who added longer endings with resurrection appearances of Jesus).

Matthew and Luke fill out Mark's spare and episodic story line with selections of Jesus's teachings drawn from a common "sayings source" (known to scholars as Q from German *Quelle* or "source") and their own independent traditions. But the additional material is not allowed to distract from the trajectory of the story, driving toward its climax in Jerusalem. Luke notes in his narrative of Jesus's infancy that, as the firstborn son of Joseph and Mary, he is presented to God in the temple in Jerusalem and there redeemed by the sacrifice of two birds (Luke 2:22–24). From the beginning, then, Jesus is associated with Israelite ritual and the story of the Akedah, his own young life spared from God's claim on it by a sacrificial substitute. Yet the Gospel story ends with Jesus becoming the sacrifice, reluctantly submitting to divine will as had Isaac on Moriah. In Gethsemane on the night of his arrest Jesus prayed: "Father, if you are willing, remove this cup from me; yet, not my will but yours be done" (Luke 22:42). This time no angel intervened, no animal stand-in was provided, and Jesus went to his death by Roman hands.

In the Gospel of Matthew, Jesus shares a last supper with his disciples on Passover, associating Jesus's death with the Israelite sacrifice of a lamb in remembrance of the deliverance from slavery in Egypt. Further, Matthew provides Jesus's words that give the ritual meal explicit sacrificial meaning. After breaking bread and giving it to the disciples, Jesus said, "Take, eat; this is my body." Then he passed around a cup of wine, with the explanation that "this is my blood of the covenant, which is poured out for many for the forgiveness of sins" (Matthew 26:28). Matthew found these words of institution already in the Gospel of Mark, where they are followed by an eschatological reference: "Truly I tell you, I will never again drink of the fruit of the vine until that day when I drink it new in the kingdom of God" (Mark 14:25).

In the Gospel of John the Eucharist is presented as a communion sacrifice in which believers partake of the victim's body *and blood* (in violation of Jewish ritual prohibition). Further, the victim is none other than Jesus himself: "Those who eat my flesh and drink my blood have eternal life, and I will raise them up on the last day; for my flesh is true food and my blood is true drink. Those who eat my flesh and drink my blood abide in me, and I in them" (John 6:54–56). Further, biblical scholar Elaine Pagels notes that in John the "last supper" occurs, not on

Passover, but on the eve of Passover: "John's version of Jesus' death dramatizes his conviction that Jesus himself *became* the sacrificial lamb."[14]

While Paul taught that participation in Christ was through imitation of his sacrificial love in acts of self-denial and service to others, the Gospel writers highlight the institutional form that participation would take in ritual performance of the Eucharist. In that way they continue the focus of Christian devotion on sacrifice as the means of obtaining divine favor. This close correspondence between the letters of Paul and the Gospels indicates that the sacrificial interpretation of the significance of Christ may have served as the basis for the widespread use of these writings in the worship of the early church and thus indirectly contributed to their eventual inclusion in the New Testament.

The formation of the New Testament as a fixed and authoritative collection of writings (or canon from the Greek *kanōn*, meaning "measuring rod") depended on many historical factors and continued through the first four centuries of Christian history. But the letters of Paul and the Gospels were already widely acknowledged as sources of Christian belief and practice by the end of the second century.[15] As biblical scholar Harry Gamble notes, "Paul's letters must have been preserved chiefly out of a persistent devotion to Paul's teaching."[16] As we have attempted to show, a central lesson in that teaching was Paul's interpretation of Jesus's death as "a sacrifice of atonement by his blood" (Romans 3:25). Despite all their differences from Paul and from one another, the Gospel writers share a sacrificial view of Christ's crucifixion, making it the climactic moment in their accounts of his life.

Death of Christ as Sacrifice in Epistle to the Hebrews

Sacrifice is so prominent a feature of Christian tradition that it is easy to forget that it was once a highly contested interpretation of the significance of Christ and the salvation he made possible. The major issues in that ancient contest can be conveniently recovered through a comparison of the New Testament *Epistle to the Hebrews* and some Gnostic writings against sacrifice.

For the writer of Hebrews the death of Christ is foreshadowed by the rituals of sacrifice in Israelite practice and constitutes their ultimate fulfillment and displacement: Christ "entered once for all into the Holy

Place, not with the blood of goats and calves, but with his own blood, thus obtaining eternal redemption" (Hebrews 9:12).[17] Christ offers himself as the gift that establishes a "new covenant" between God and humanity; his death is final and requires no repetition The author states that Christ "has appeared once for all at the end of the age to remove sin by the sacrifice of himself" (Hebrews 9:26). For the writer, the point of contrast between the annual cycle of sacrifices stipulated in Exodus and the single sacrifice of Christ is of paramount importance. "And every priest stands day after day at his service, offering again and again the same sacrifices that can never take away sins. But when Christ had offered for all time a single sacrifice for sins, 'he sat down at the right hand of God'" (Hebrews 10:11–12).

The author of Hebrews refers to the same prophetic critique of animal sacrifice that Rabbi Yohanan had; but he draws a very different conclusion, namely, that the sacrificial system had *never* been efficacious: "For it is impossible for the blood of bulls and goats to take away sins" (Hebrews 10:4). Rather than substituting prayer and Torah study and good deeds as new forms of sacrifice in the post-temple age, this Christian writer announces an apocalyptic discontinuity with the older system. Only the sacrifice of Christ's body, made in "these last days" by the one who is "the exact imprint of God's very being" could bring about "purification of sins" (Hebrews 1:2–3). In Hebrews Christ is represented not only as the uniquely perfect sacrificial victim, but also as the high priest who offers himself as the sacrifice. But he is not a priest in the line of Aaron or Levi, whose priesthood was provisional. Christ belongs to the "order of Melchizedek," the mysterious king and priest of "God Most High" who offered bread and wine to Abram and to whom Abram paid tithe (Genesis 14:18–20). In Psalm 110 Yahweh promises the Messiah, "You are a priest forever according to the order of Melchizedek." The writer of Hebrews draws on this textual tradition and plays on the fact that neither Melchizedek's birth nor death are recorded to bolster the claim that his priesthood is eternal (Hebrews 7:3).

In another bold move of textual appropriation, the author places words from Psalm 40 attributed to David in the mouth of Jesus when "he came into the world" (presumably referring to the debut of his public ministry and not his birth). In the Hebrew Bible the psalmist pledges that he will bring the offering of his obedience to God rather than animal sacrifices, and he notes that God "opened" (literally, "dug out") his ear so that he might attend to divine instruction. The author of Hebrews quotes the psalm from the Septuagint, the Greek translation of the Hebrew Bible which, according to legend, was prepared by seventy scholars and is thus represented by the Roman numeral LXX. The copy our author used translated the Hebrew word for "ear" with the Greek term for "body." The author retained that scribal choice because it served his theological interest by emphasizing that God prepared Christ's *body* as the perfect sacrifice and did not simply open his *ear* to divine law.[18] Further, he omits the poetic parallelism between doing God's will and obeying God's law in the Septuagint version to suggest that Christ performs the divine will by offering himself as the final sacrifice. Compare the two readings:

> LXX: Sacrifices and offerings you do not desire,
> but you have given me an open ear;
> Hebrews: *but a body you have prepared for me*

> LXX: Then I said, "Here I am; in the scroll of the book it is written of me.
> I delight to do your will, O my God; your law is within my heart."
> Hebrews: *Then I said, "See God, I have come to do your will, O God (in the scroll of the book it is written of me)."*

In offering his body in fulfillment of prophecy, Christ demonstrates that it is God's will to abolish the sacrificial system of ancient Israel and replace it with "the offering of the body of Jesus Christ once for all" (Hebrews 10:10).

Despite the announcement of the end of sacrifice, however, Hebrews concludes—in typical epistolary style—with moral exhortations. The author counsels his readers to endure the suffering of persecution, accept divine discipline, and "offer to God an acceptable worship with reverence and awe; for indeed our God is a consuming fire" (Hebrews 12:28–29). Just as Jesus suffered outside the gates of Jerusalem, so Christians should join him and "bear the abuse he endured." In short, Christians should *continue sacrificing* by following the exhortation to "not neglect to do good and to share what you have, for such sacrifices are pleasing to God" (Hebrews 13:16). Here the "end of sacrifice" as the means of redemption marks the beginning of sacrifice as the ideal of self-giving, including the possibility of sharing in Jesus's sacrifice through a martyr's death.

Polemic against Sacrifice in Gnostic Christian Writings

Some early Christians, however, rejected the idea of sacrifice as the Christian ideal. They are known collectively as *Gnostics*, although scholars identify many different schools within that general category.[19] For these Christians the purpose of Christ's coming into this corrupt world was to awaken the immortal spirits within a select company, including Jesus's disciples and those who would later read the teachings he left with them. Gnostic writings express a version of the faith that does not find religious significance in the passion of Christ, rejects the hope of resurrection of the body, affirms the divinity of every believer, and finds in revealed knowledge the basis of immortality. Gnostic Christians largely ignored, or actively resisted, the Jewish tradition that formed the background of religious belief for Jesus and his disciples.

Where did these alternative views come from? In Upper Egypt in 1945 a farmer digging in the side of a hill for fertilizer struck the sealed top of a jar with his shovel. The spot was near the modern city of Nag Hammadi and the jar concealed a collection of ancient books. Besides Gospels, the cache contained magical incantations, philosophical treatises, and texts representing a form of Hellenized Judaism marked by dualistic opposition between matter and spirit. Written in Greek from about 120–200 CE, they were translated by Christian monks in Egypt into Coptic. They were preserved in leather-bound books (called codices), fifty-two texts in total.

Their survival is remarkable because, after the early Christians decided on the Gospels they accepted as authoritative, church leaders sought to destroy other versions of the life and teachings of Jesus. Irenaeus, bishop of Lyon in the second century, issued a five-volume condemnation of Gnostic teaching, *The Destruction and Overthrow of Falsely So-called Gnosis*, denouncing Gnostic writings as "an abyss of madness, and blasphemy against Christ." In that spirit, Athanasius, archbishop of Alexandria, ordered all books of heresy destroyed. Disregarding the order, monks of the monastery of Pachomius (290–348), founder of Christian communal monasticism, buried these copies around 370. Why would Christian monks preserve writings condemned by Church authorities?

One plausible answer is that they found in them ideas compatible with their own spiritual quest. For example, the Coptic *Gospel of the Egyptians* is dedicated to the "the Great Invisible Spirit" from whose "living silence" issued the series of *aeons*, an intricate network of divine beings, through whom one must pass after death with the knowledge of proper incantations. According to this Gnostic writing, the first man, *Adamas*, generated Seth, who became the father of an incorruptible race. In resistance to the evil *archons* (cosmic powers) Seth takes on the *persona* of Jesus and instructs the elect in renouncing the world and reciting the secret names of the divine powers. As a result, "these will by no means taste death."[20] Immortality through contemplation is the obsession of Egyptian spirituality, and the desert eremites developed spiritual disciplines to match that theology of divinization.

In the monastery he established, Pachomius became a spiritual master by systematically occupying each "chamber" of his mind with thoughts of spiritual matters, so that no room remained for distracting temptations to arise. Pachomius sought a vision of God that would be the spiritual equivalent of immortality: an immutable consciousness, exempt from change, disturbance, or decay. It was said that "because of the purity of his heart he was, as it were, seeing the invisible God as in a mirror."[21] Since the consciousness of immortality and an immortal consciousness are finally the same, the devotions of the desert monks shared the goal of esoteric wisdom with the Gnostics. The monks of the order of Pachomius worshipped Christ as the bearer of divine illumination rather than the victim of divine vengeance, as revelation not sacrifice. They sought knowledge of God through inner stillness—and not through the agony of self-tortures in imitation of Christ's sacrifice. For them, the Gnostic texts were guilty pleasures.

The Jesus who emerges from Gnostic writings is not the Christ who is uniquely one with God and saves humanity from sin and death by his sacrificial suffering. The Gnostic Jesus urges believers to find God within themselves, to acknowledge the authority of their own religious visions, and to recognize that all distinctions in the world are illusory—even the one between Jesus and his disciples. The ideal disciple is the one who "drinks in" the Savior's words, as in a kiss. For some Gnostic Gospels, the ideal is represented by Mary Magdalene as the disciple whom Jesus loved more than the others, his "companion" in the quest for eternal truth, and he "used to kiss her often on her [mouth]."[22] It is clear that for the author Jesus loves Magdalene because she comprehends his esoteric meaning.

Among the first of the Gnostic writings to become public was the *Gospel of Thomas* in which Jesus says, "I disclose my mysteries to those [who are worthy] of [my] mysteries." As heavenly revealer, Christ came to earth to instruct receptive humans in divine knowledge, the *gnosis* that imparts immortality: "Whoever discovers the interpretation of these sayings will not taste death."[23] *Thomas* claims to be the "secret sayings" of Jesus given to his twin brother. Elaine Pagels interprets this statement as referring to the Gnostic reader who becomes Jesus's "double" by appropriating the knowledge in his sayings. Those who possess this special knowledge themselves become "like God." In the Gnostic view the destiny of humans is to claim equality with God through a process of taking in the words of Jesus, just as Magdalene did. "Jesus said, 'He who will drink from My mouth will become like Me. I myself shall become he, and the things that are hidden will be revealed to him'" (Thomas, 108).

For Gnostics wisdom, not sacrifice, cancels the guilt of sin and overcomes the power of death. They were convinced that such divine insight lay within the human soul and could be discovered through profound reflection, apart from the mediation of the institutional church, its approved scriptures, hierarchical authority, and ritual practices, including the sacrificial meal of Eucharist. To make clear their opposition to the Church as a cultural institution, some Gnostics identified with Seth, as the renewed image of Adam after the death of Abel and the exile of Cain, while others emulated Cain and those biblical figures who resisted the will of the Creator of this world, such as the men of Sodom and the serpent in the Garden of Eden.[24] Gnostics believed that the emphasis on Jesus's sacrificial death cast Christian faith in erroneous terms of ancient Israelite religion, worshipping the Creator of this world and seeking to thank and placate him through sacrifice. They preferred to think of themselves as embraced by Christ, drinking in the insight flowing from his mouth, rather than crucified with him in God-forsaken darkness.

For one community of Sethian Gnostics, the disciple who discerned the true meaning of Christ was Judas Iscariot, who betrayed him into the hands of Roman authorities. In the recently restored and translated text of the *Gospel of Judas* Jesus commends Judas for his role in making the crucifixion possible, but not as a sacrifice for sins. Christians have always expressed some ambivalence over Judas since, without his betrayal of Jesus, there would have been no atonement for sin. Nevertheless, the New Testament condemns him for his act; and no branch of the Christian church has made him a saint, despite some proposals to do so. Further, throughout Christian history his association with Judaism (his name, Judas, was linked to Judea) inspired persecution of Jews as "Christ killers."[25]

By contrast, these Gnostics honored Judas as the one who arranged the conditions under which Christ could be relieved of the "garment" of the body, escape the material world created by Saklas (their name for the deity worshipped by Jews), and return to unity with the supreme Spirit. Thus, Jesus praises Judas as the greatest of his disciples. "Truly [I] say to you, Judas, [those who] offer sacrifices to Saklas [. . .] God [three lines missing] everything that is evil. But you will exceed all of them. For you will sacrifice the man that clothes me."[26] In a reversal of the representation of Judas in the New Testament as possessed by Satan (Luke 22:3) and cursed by God (Mark 14:21), the Gospel of Judas describes Judas as the only disciple who understood the hidden wisdom of Christ and arranged for his escape from the material world through death.

Further, the Gospel of Judas offers a sustained polemic against proto-orthodox teachers, represented by the disciples, by comparing them to Israelite priests offering sacrifices at the altar in the temple of Jerusalem. By continuing to worship the Creator of this world and misleading believers into thinking that Jesus's death was a sacrifice offered to that deity, their false teachings turn ordinary Christians, whose spirits are led into fatal error, into sacrificial victims. Jesus says to his disciples, "Those you have seen receiving the offerings at the altar—that is who you are. That is the god you serve, and you are those twelve men you have seen. The cattle you have seen brought for sacrifice are the many people you lead astray before that altar." Then Jesus issues this blunt command: "Stop sac[rificing]."[27]

For some Gnostics the stark prohibition extended to the Eucharistic meal understood as a re-enactment of the sacrificial death of Jesus. The *Gospel of Philip* declares of the Creator of this world, "God is a cannibal. Therefore human beings are [sacrificed] to him. Before human beings were sacrificed, animals used to be sacrificed, because those to whom they were sacrificed were not gods."[28] In this Gnostic interpretation of Christian faith the meaning of sacrifice is turned on its head: *from* a means of securing forgiveness of sins and resurrection in an immortal body *to* a deluded gesture that binds the spirit tightly to the realm of ignorance and death created by lesser deities. For Gnostics the true sacrifice is that of the physical body. Thus, Jesus reassures Judas that he is greater than all the disciples because "you will sacrifice the man that clothes me."

Throughout the Gospel of Judas Jesus often laughs, usually at the disciples' inability to understand his teachings. In other Gnostic texts, Christ laughs as his spirit ascends, leaving the body of Jesus writhing on the cross and crying out, "My God, my God, why have you forsaken me?" Jesus seems amused by the irony of seeking spiritual salvation through elements of the material world, including the body of a sacrificial victim.[29] In Irenaeus's work *Against Heresies*, he records a summary of the teachings of the second-century philosopher Basilides that includes the claim that Jesus did not suffer, but that Simon of Cyrene, who was forced to carry his cross, was mistaken for Jesus and crucified in his stead, "while Jesus, for his part, assumed the form of Simon and stood by, laughing at them." Irenaeus adds that Basilides taught that "anyone who confesses the man who was crucified is still a slave and is still under the authority of the beings that created bodies; while anyone who denies him . . . is freed from them."[30] These testimonies to an alternative version of Christianity were silenced at the dawn of the tradition, yet they have recently generated much interest in their non-sacrificial rendering of the faith.

But we must be careful not to oversimplify our reading of these fragmentary and elliptical texts. Philippa Townsend, biblical scholar at the University of Edinburgh, argues that the Gospel of Judas, for example, may condemn sacrifice only as practiced by the author's opponents, both Jews and proto-orthodox Christians. The author's own community may have retained ritual participation in Christ's sacrifice as a means of constituting their new kinship group or "race." Drawing on Nancy Jay's theory that blood sacrifice generates a patriarchal line of descent that defines the family, Townsend concludes that in the Gospel of Judas "it seems plausible that the sacrifice of Jesus plays a role in generating the holy race that will eventually be 'raised up.'"[31] In this nuanced reading, ritual sacrifice persists along with the claim of the finality of Christ's sacrifice in the flesh. If Townsend is right, not even Gnostics can escape sacrifice as the marker of their membership in the heavenly race.

The Gnostic way entails another kind of sacrifice as well since the cost of eternal unity with the Supreme Spirit is the forfeiture of individuality. One Gnostic text teaches that "the thought of those who are saved will not perish, the intellect of those who have acquaintance with such an object will not perish."[32] The problem is that the prospect of being constituted entirely by awareness of an eternal object raises the question of the disembodied soul: How can an individual exist with no limits provided by a body? Without any material element, the soul has no relation to space and, as immediate and comprehensive consciousness, it has no relation to time. The problem is exacerbated by Gnostic claims that spiritual awareness is of unified, eternal, immutable truth. That is, all spirits would have the same consciousness, since there can be no variations within absolute truth. Thus, death releases one's spirit to merge seamlessly with all other enlightened spirits in the same eternal thought. That apotheosis constitutes the ultimate sacrifice, the shattering of markers of identity set by embodiment. The Gnostic acquisition of divine knowledge is a form of spiritual martyrdom.

Sacrifice in Early Martyrs: Polycarp and Perpetua

Despite the appeal of Gnostic teaching, Paul's insistence that Jesus died as an atoning sacrifice prevailed in Christian history and promoted the ideal of sacrifice that inspired early martyrs. One of the first was Polycarp (69–155), bishop of Smyrna, a church in Asia Minor to which one of the letters in the New Testament Apocalypse was addressed with reference to martyrdom: "Do not fear what you are about to suffer. . . . Be faithful unto death, and I will give you the crown of life" (Revelation

2:10). Written at the end of the first century of the Common Era, the book of Revelation reflects threats to Christians in certain regions of the Roman Empire and anticipates the apocalyptic destruction of Rome at the end of history. At this time, however, persecution of Christians was not official policy and the punishment of Christians who refused to denounce their faith was at the discretion of local magistrates.

In Smyrna the populace urged the Roman proconsul to treat Christians harshly. They are recorded as shouting after one young man was executed: "Away with the atheists! Make search for Polycarp!"[33] The charge may sound odd, but Christians rejected the ancient deities that provided Rome with its authority by refusing to offer sacrifices to them, at the same time presenting no images of their own God.[34] From the Roman perspective, Christians inexplicably refused to honor the imperial cult which "united all quarters of the empire and was instrumental in the sustenance and stability of it." Not surprisingly, the crowd in the arena accused Polycarp of being "the destroyer of our gods, who teaches many not to sacrifice nor to worship." In addition, Christians refused to respect Roman courts, practiced what Romans regarded as "superstition," and met in secrecy that encouraged scandalous and salacious gossip about them.[35] Christians were suspected of practicing incest (sharing a "holy kiss" with "brothers and sisters") and cannibalism (eating the body and drinking the blood of the "holy child" Jesus).

The full slate of charges against Christians was answered by Athenagorus, most likely a philosopher of Athens, in A Plea Regarding Christians set before Roman rulers around 176. Athenagorus provides evidence that Christians are innocent of slanders against them and appeals for an end to their persecution and official recognition of the same right to practice their religion as was granted to other citizens of the empire, even though Christians lacked the cultural marker of a religion, namely, public sacrifice to gods. Athenagorus likens the Christian God to Plato's single eternal source of all beings. "If, then, Plato is not an atheist when he considers the one uncreated maker of the universe to be God, neither are we atheists when we recognize and affirm him to be God by whose Word all things were created and by whose Spirit they are held together."[36] In this sentence Athenagorus identifies the God of Christians with the transcendent and immutable One of Plato and, at the same time, with the immanent ordering principle of the universe the

Stoics called Mind (*nous*). Athenagorus then moves to the absurdity of offering sacrifices to such a God: "The creator and Father of the universe does not need blood or the smell of burnt offerings or the fragrance of flowers or incense." Athenagorus proclaims that "the greatest sacrifice in his eyes" is grateful prayer to the creator and providential guide of the world. Athenagorus sets Christian theology on the same side as philosophers who found the crudely anthropomorphic deities of the Greek and Roman pantheons laughable. It was a masterful defense, but history contains no record of the imperial response—only an ongoing narrative of martyrdom of Christians, such as Polycarp, for being "atheists."

According to tradition, Polycarp was a disciple of the apostle John who lived to an advanced age in Ephesus and invested Polycarp with apostolic authority. Polycarp took that commission seriously. Irenaeus knew Polycarp as a child and praised him in his work against heresies for resisting the Gnostic teacher Valentinus and records his calling another heretic "the first-born of Satan." Polycarp's place in Christian history was secured, however, by his death. He was the first martyr of record outside the New Testament, following Stephen, who died from stoning in Jerusalem while beholding the risen Jesus in a vision (Acts 6:8–7:60). The story of Polycarp's arrest and immolation by Roman authorities was recounted in an encyclical letter, passed down by a series of transcribers who are named at the end. What is of interest here is that the narrative of Polycarp's ordeal was intended to demonstrate "a martyrdom conformable to the gospel," that is, in imitation of Christ (*imitatio Christi*). This first martyr story sets the pattern for those to follow and echoes Paul's conviction that identification with Christ is confirmed by sharing his suffering. To that end every detail in *The Martyrdom of Saint Polycarp* has parallels in the account of Jesus's passion in the Gospel of John—with one exception. Polycarp was burned alive as a literal sacrifice from whose body wafted "a sweet aroma as the breath of incense."

Literary form and theological interest always shape historical reporting in writing about saints (hagiography), and this narrative is no exception.[37] Polycarp did not seek martyrdom, but retired from the city at the urging of friends. The night before his arrest in a country house he dreamed that his pillow burst into flames. He awoke and said to his companions, "I must be burned alive." His foreknowledge parallels Jesus's prophecies of his own death in Jerusalem. Polycarp's hiding place was revealed by a slave under torture. Nevertheless, the narrator regards his act as parallel to Jesus' betrayal by one of his disciples, writing that "the very ones who betrayed him were of his own household." Even the arresting official "chanced to have the same name as Herod" and acted so that Polycarp would be "made a partaker with Christ." Polycarp's pursuers, "with their customary arms, set out as though 'hasting after a robber.'" Here the narrator quotes Matthew 26:55 from a passage that describes Jesus's arrest. Polycarp could have escaped but instead quietly submitted with words like those of Jesus in the Garden of Gethsemane: "God's will be done." Polycarp was led into the city on a donkey, as Jesus entered Jerusalem, and at first remained silent as the authorities urged him to profess Caesar as Lord. Then, in a final flash of irony, he directed the charge against him at the crowd. The narrator records that "groaning and looking up to heaven, he said, 'Away with the atheists!'"

The crowd's response was to "shout with one accord" that Polycarp be burned alive, even as the New Testament Gospels record the unanimous cries of the crowd in Jerusalem that Jesus be crucified. Then the narrator shifts from the model of Jesus's passion to older imagery. Polycarp vowed to remain in the pyre without moving, so his executioners did not nail him to the wood but bound his hands behind his back, "like a noble ram out of a great flock ready for sacrifice, a burnt offering ready and acceptable to God." The allusion to the Akedah links the martyr with Isaac as a prototype of Christ. In his final prayer Polycarp thanks God for allowing him to partake "in the cup of thy Christ" (a reference to Jesus's acceptance of the "cup" of suffering in Luke 22:42), and asks to be received into God's presence "as a rich and acceptable sacrifice" in the name of "the eternal and heavenly High Priest, Jesus Christ."

What follows, according to the narrator, was a confirming miracle. The flames formed an arch around Polycarp's body so that he did not appear as burning flesh, "but as bread baking or as gold and silver refined in a furnace." Enraged, his persecutors stabbed him with a dagger and so much blood poured from the wound that it put out the fire. These details parallel the account of Jesus's death in which a soldier pierces his side with a spear and "at once blood and water came out" (John 19:34). After the centurion ordered Polycarp's body burned, his companions gathered up his bones, beginning the Christian tradition of venerating relics on the ground that the holiness of the saint permeates the body as well as the soul. That sanctity is the result of the conformity of the saints to the model of Jesus, as the narrator confesses, "we love the martyrs as disciples and imitators of the Lord." For the narrator, the chain of replication continues through the account of Polycarp, "whose martyrdom all desire to imitate as one according to the gospel of Christ." Paul once urged his converts, "Be imitators of me, as I am of Christ" (1 Corinthians 11:1). In similar fashion martyrs became models for living sacrificial lives (thus all early martyrs were declared saints for their virtue) and for suffering exemplary deaths.[38]

The power of their examples depends upon clear analogy between their stories and the Gospel accounts of Jesus's passion. *The Martyrdom of Polycarp* sets the precedent for narratives of martyrdom by making the parallels transparent. The narrator also recognizes that the authority of Polycarp as a model Christian depends on the reliability of the transmission of his story. Thus, the account ends with a recitation of those who preserved and handed it on, beginning with Gaius, who copied it from the papers of Irenaeus, the famous heresy hunter, "who was a disciple of Polycarp." The final transcriber is one Pionius, who was led to the manuscript by a vision of Polycarp himself. Pionius then passed on the account "in order that the Lord Jesus Christ might bring me also with his elect unto his heavenly Kingdom." With due caution not to read too much into a conventional profession of piety, we might find in this closing line the suggestion that preserving the narrative of Polycarp's martyrdom was an act of redemptive merit. By extension, telling the story of any martyrdom as *imitatio Christi* is a way of participating in the sacrifice. Even under conditions of relative security, then, Christians cherish and transmit stories of martyrs as literary sacraments. Not only writing the "lives of martyrs," but also reading them—as much as consuming the bread and wine in the Eucharist—allows imaginative entry into a world of ghastly suffering and noble endurance where salvation is secured through sacrifice.

One of the most widely read and analyzed accounts of martyrdom is that of Vibia Perpetua, a twenty-two-year-old woman of noble birth, and her slave Felicitas, who were martyred in Carthage under imperial order in 203.[39] Despite urgent pleas by her father that she have pity on her infant son, Perpetua proceeded unwaveringly to her death. She, Felicitas, and three male slaves were baptized before being imprisoned and condemned to death by wild beasts: a boar, bear, and leopard for the men; a wild cow to gore the women. Perpetua was permitted to nurse her son in prison, while Felicitas delivered a child there and gave it to another Christian woman to raise. As Polycarp, Perpetua had visions of her impending doom, with images of her victory over Satan and her ascension to paradise. She also saw her brother, who had died in childhood as a pagan, raised to health and released from punishment as a result of her fervent prayers. She was, even before her martyrdom, effectively interceding for others as a saint to secure their salvation. According to tradition, Perpetua wrote down her experiences in prison and eyewitnesses completed the story of her martyrdom. As in other accounts, there are parallels to Jesus's passion: visionary foreknowledge of her death; sharing of a last meal which the martyrs treated as an *agape* or "love feast," an early form of Eucharist; singing psalms on the way to the arena; scourging ("they indeed rejoiced that they should have incurred any one of their Lord's passions"); and, after mauling by the cow, receiving a sword thrust in her side. Even then, her endurance was such that the narrator marvels, "Possibly such a woman could not have been slain unless she herself had willed it."

Perpetua's determination to preserve her faith by resisting the demand to "offer sacrifice for the well-being of the emperor" has made her a hero of Christian tradition, but also a model of female agency in a world where women were subjected to patriarchal order. Judith Perkins reads the account of Perpetua's martyrdom as a narrative of female empowerment in a cultural context where individual identity, both pagan and Christian, was defined by suffering. Christian narrative constructed "Christians as a community of sufferers. . . . it scripted subjects who embraced death and rejected conventional social life." Perkins points to Perpetua's rejection of her father three times—a narrative strategy of finality—as her victory over male authority: "Perpetua's new identity, as a Christian, allows her to begin her narration by presenting herself as overcoming her father, the *pater familias*, the pivot of legitimate authority in the Roman system."

Following his initial demand that his daughter renounce her faith and return home, Perpetua's father finally throws himself at her feet and begs her not to persist for the sake of her baby, calling her "not daughter, but lady" through his tears. Perkins finds this scene particularly significant as representing "a radically reversed hierarchy—a father at a daughter's feet, calling her mistress."[40] Classical scholar Mary Lefkowitz notes that the Latin phrase is *non filiam sed dominam* to emphasize that Perpetua achieves power (dominance) over her father in a "sexually defined conflict with authority." Lefkowitz concludes her essay: "In seeking martyrdom she was as much concerned with solving problems in this life as with attaining perfection in the next."[41]

Feminist interpretations of accounts of women's self-sacrifices have illuminated indications of female agency otherwise hidden in the texts. Their sacrifices are conventionally represented as exemplary self-giving on behalf of community or family, acts that sanction and sustain the very social forms that constrain women within passive and subordinate roles. But that representation is from the viewpoint of the community, not necessarily from the self-understanding of the one sacrificing herself. Religious studies scholar Matthew Recla argues that from the standpoint of the martyr, her violent death "should be understood first as an act of self-formation, not self-sacrifice" for the sake of her community or institution.[42] That moment, however, is also marked by the liminal passage from life to its unknown aftermath. The paradox in the martyr's intention is that self-willed death (*autothanatos*) is both absolutely final and radically open. Even as an act of free agency, martyrdom entails the risk of sacrifice.

Perpetua was a strong and independent woman, who directed her fate with such power that it seemed to the one concluding her story that "such a woman could not have been slain unless she herself had willed it." Nevertheless, it is still possible to raise the question whether her act should be considered in isolation from other actors in her drama. The account is presented largely as the work of Perpetua, representing herself as a model Christian martyr, willing to defy not only conventional social order but natural attachment to her own child. She tells her story as one who is gifted with visions, sustained by unwavering faith, and nearly impervious to pain. It is a tale of a spiritual hero (like Abraham) who abandons natural affection and familial ties in order to pursue an intangible, although richly imagined, reward.[43] Here, as we have seen elsewhere, the exchange of the concrete for the abstract is the heart of religious sacrifice.

If we were to read this text against itself, however, we might hear the one voice in the narrative that protests sacrificial transaction, one who speaks on behalf of the child and takes him out of harm's way, that of Perpetua's father. Suppose his action is not a petulant assertion of patriarchal authority to claim the child, but a desperate attempt to rescue one life from the chamber of death constructed by Christian piety. He moves from imperious demands to tearful pleading, hoping to move his daughter from her determination to die. She, in turn, does not even record his name. "The father" registers in her text, as in many academic interpretations, as a mere abstraction representative of oppressive social order. But suppose that his tears are as genuine as Sarah's screams, that his cries also express horror at sacrifice and disbelief in its redemptive value. Suppose this pagan grandfather, by refusing to assign the honorific name of *sacrifice* to his daughter's recalcitrant self-assertion, is giving voice to human protest within the narrative of martyrdom designed to silence him?

Sacrifice in Orthodox Theology: Athanasius and Anselm

By early in the fourth century, Paul's emphasis on Jesus's death as redemptive sacrifice and his resurrection as the basis of eternal life was enshrined in the creed produced by the ecumenical Council of Nicea (325). Bishops from the ancient centers of Christianity gathered in Asia Minor at Nicea, site of Iznik in modern-day Turkey, at the order of the Roman emperor Constantine. Constantine had accepted the Christian God as his patron deity after a vision of a cross of light with the inscription, "Conquer by this." His subsequent victory over the forces of the ruler Maxentius led to his entering the city of Rome and proclaiming himself emperor of the West. After consolidating his power over the eastern empire as well, Constantine turned to the problem of uniting the churches throughout his realm. To that end, he presided over the Council of Nicea and established its formulations of orthodox faith as normative for his Christian empire.[44]

The statement of beliefs composed at the Council of Nicea retained Paul's version of the gospel of Christ's sacrifice over alternatives by writing it into official documents of the institutional church with imperial sanction. The primary champion of the new orthodoxy was Athanasius (296–373), the young presbyter who assisted the bishop of Alexandria at Nicea and later assumed his position. Athanasius insisted that Christ's sacrificial death is "the very center of our faith." The eternal Word entered the body of Jesus so that "He might offer the sacrifice on behalf of all, surrendering His own temple to death in place of all, to settle man's account with death and free him from the primal transgression." In Athanasius's Platonic interpretation, because the incarnation informs one human body with the divine Word, all individuals can regain immortality through participation in that divinized humanity. He writes, "For the solidarity of mankind is such that, by virtue of the Word's indwelling in a single human body, the corruption which goes with death has lost its power over all."[45]

The historical specificity of the death of Christ, however, limits the potentially universal efficacy of the incarnation. Humans are not automatically divinized by the immortal Word entering the body of Jesus. The claim of death over individuals must still be cancelled by Christ's sacrifice—and each must place faith in that sacrifice. Athanasius writes, "Now that the common Savior of all has died on our behalf, we who believe in Christ no longer die." The "common Savior of all," it turns out, is available only to "we who believe in Christ," that is, those initiated into the church by baptism and sustained by Eucharist. Only those who partake in the sacrifice of Christ and pledge loyalty to his community can receive salvation.

Still, the question persists, why was the death of Christ the *necessary* condition for securing God's forgiveness? The Benedictine monk Anselm of Canterbury (1033–1109) explained the necessity of Christ's sacrifice in terms of the feudal relation between serf and master. Because human sin affronts the honor of God by failing to respect his laws, the offense is impossible to repay; it is of infinite gravity. The penalty facing the transgressor could only be the same as that for a peasant poaching deer in the lord's forest: death. It was not that the master was harmed in his person; his feasts would proceed without the venison. It was that his sovereign preserve was invaded; his authority was challenged and his honor violated. Nothing the serf possessed could possibly compensate for the lack of respect shown to the master, any more than any human effort could compensate for violating divine law and thus bringing dishonor to God.

Further, even if we possessed something of infinite value to sacrifice, we could not do so with proper intention since our nature is already corrupted. As Anselm put it, "a sinner cannot justify a sinner."[46] Since the satisfaction of divine justice, then, is that "which none but God can make and none but man ought to make, it is necessary for the God-man to make it."[47] Only the sacrifice of Christ, the God-man, is of infinite value and is given freely for human salvation. But the logic then follows that recipients of that forgiveness owe the only comparable gift within their power: their entire lives as vassals in the service of their lord. The economy of gift exchange requires that those for whom Christ died to satisfy divine honor must now reciprocate by unconditional submission to divine authority. As Paul wrote to the Christian assembly in Rome, "you, having been set free from sin, have become slaves of righteousness" (Romans 6:18). The terms had changed by Anselm's time, but the relationship was the same. Whether slave or serf, the believer whose spirit is redeemed by sacrifice must give back to God the body—its passions and pleasures, its freedom and imagination, its autonomy and privacy. Far from marking the end of sacrifice, then, the death of Christ established the condition under which ongoing sacrifice would become the only condign response to divine forgiveness.

But is there an alternative reading of Anselm's theory that interprets the meaning of "God-man" in a different way? Suppose that the incarnation of God in Jesus signifies not the intention to make a bloody sacrifice of a man but to reveal that God is present among us *as human*. Suppose we are redeemed not by sacred violence, but by following our natural affinity for other human beings, by engaging with them in creative enterprises, by forming communities of mutual respect, by reflecting the divine image within us, by promoting unity rather than division, peace rather than war, and forgiveness instead of retribution. Suppose that Christians focus, not on the death of Christ, but on his life, specifically on his compassion and healing and forgiveness. Consider Jesus's description of the final judgment in which the Messiah welcomes into the kingdom those who fed the hungry, welcomed the stranger, clothed the homeless, and visited the prisoner—even though they did not know they were serving him by doing so (Matthew 25:31–46). What is remarkable is that Jesus imagines the Messiah applying no theological test or requiring any particular religious affiliation to enter the kingdom but rewarding simple acts of caring for others as mercy shown directly to him. Matthew records Jesus as saying, "just as you did it to one of the least of these who are members of my family, you did it to me." On that basis, Christians can affirm the redemptive value of moral virtue, sacrifice for others, as practiced throughout the human family.

Displacement of Sacrifice: Abelard

One medieval philosophical theologian who thought about the death of Christ in this alternative way was Peter Abelard (1079–1142), known for his love of Héloïse, a student whom he seduced in her uncle's home under pretext of furthering her education. She became pregnant and bore him a son. Her uncle was furious by the betrayal and punished Héloïse so severely that Abelard arranged for her to join a convent. The uncle then took his revenge by ordering his servants to castrate Abelard, a disgrace that led to his entering the abbey of St. Denis as a monk. Disaffected by the worldliness of the monastics there, he withdrew into a hut and attracted a large number of students. He constructed an oratory and consulted with Héloïse on the administration of the religious community gathered there. Héloïse later became an abbess, widely honored for her piety and wisdom.

According to Abelard's autobiography, fittingly called *Historia Calamitatum: The Story of My Misfortunes*, his envious fellow monks resented his teaching theology on the basis of what he called "rational and philosophical explanations," including the principle that "nothing could be believed unless it could first be understood."[48] On that principle he wrote a book on the Trinity for his students which his rivals condemned before an ecclesiastical council. The book was burned and Abelard was confined for a year to the monastery. By his account, wherever he went he encountered opposition from monks whose conspiracies against him enlisted the aid of church officials. His later rejection of beliefs that humans inherit original sin and that Jesus died as a ransom to the devil aroused the fierce condemnation of Bernard, abbot of Clairvaux (1090–1163). Bernard is known for his devotional hymns and his support of the Second Crusade. The combination of mystical conviction and vengeful disposition made Bernard a formidable opponent, against whom Abelard's philosophical arguments were impotent. Bernard attacked the older man mercilessly before the council of Sens in 1140, accusing him of interpreting the creed by reason rather than accepting its statements by faith alone. Abelard set out to seek vindication in Rome, but collapsed on the way and later died in the priory of St. Marcel.

Abelard's story can be read as classic tragedy, with his role that of a flawed hero whose pride led to his eventual downfall. But even allowing for Abelard's enhanced sense of his own intellectual and moral superiority, a trait that certainly contributed to his troubles, what specific interpretation of Christian belief aroused such opposition to him? The answer lies in his challenge to the "satisfaction" theory of atonement developed by Anselm. According to the historian of theology, Gustaf Aulén (1879–1978), in the medieval church "the Mass was interpreted primarily as a sacrifice for sins."[49] By contrast, Abelard denied that the sacrifice of the human body of Jesus on the cross could be of infinite value, as Anselm insisted.

Further, as a philosophical nominalist, Abelard held that the reality of a thing depends on what arbitrary name (*nomen*) we give it, rather than on the necessary universal it represents. Thus, God could designate anything as sufficient to satisfy his honor, making the death of Christ unnecessary for human salvation. Here Abelard touched upon the most sensitive spot in the body of sacrificial theology: Why would an all-loving and omnipotent God require the tortured execution of Jesus in order to forgive human beings for their sins, when he could name any event as the ground of salvation? Further, how could any human action so impugn the honor or sovereignty of the infinite being as to require "satisfaction"? Anselm's scheme of redemption by bloody sacrifice implicated God in the petty resentments and cruel vengeance of human rulers. It is little wonder that Abelard's contemporaries winced at such questions and struck out against him.

If not by sacrifice, though, how *did* Abelard think that Jesus brought God and humans together? In the words of Aulén, "Christ is the great Teacher and Example, who arouses responsive love in men; this love is the basis on which reconciliation and forgiveness rest."[50] For Abelard, Christ's death provides the supreme example of patient obedience and suffering love. Christ reconciles humans to God, not by offering himself as a sacrifice to uphold divine honor, but as a model of virtue to inspire us to imitate divine goodness. He could find support for his interpretation in the New Testament: "But if you endure when you do right and suffer for it, you have God's approval. For to this you have been called, because Christ also suffered for you, leaving you an example, so that you should follow in his steps" (1 Peter 2:20–21).

As a philosopher, Abelard argued that Christ redeemed humans, not by fulfilling an objective condition set by God, but by effecting a change in their subjective response to Christ's dramatic self-giving. The persuasive power of Christ's example arouses the desire to imitate him by conforming one's will to God's righteousness, thereby becoming justified. In his later work *Collationes*, a three-way dialogue between a philosopher, a Jew, and a Christian, Abelard enunciates the moral principle behind his thinking in the philosopher's critique of expiatory sacrifice. He reasons that "when true love of God and neighbor has made someone just, there is no longer any guilt for sin in him which would require spiritual purification."[51] While the philosopher has ancient Israelite practice in mind, Abelard also applied the principle to criticize medieval interpretations of Christ's death.

In his own day, Abelard failed to persuade church authorities to adopt his non-sacrificial view of Christ's role in redemption. His voice of protest against sacrifice could not be heard above the pervasive religious discourse of medieval Catholicism. But when the deep symbol of sacrifice began to surface and be examined critically in the modern period, his "moral influence" theory of atonement began to resonate with Christian theologians and social activists, whose views we will consider near the end of this chapter. For now we turn to the persistence of the sacrificial version of Christianity in two mystics who identified with Christ through sharing his physical suffering and spiritual distress.

Mystical Self-Sacrifice: Thomas à Kempis and Teresa of Avila

The term *mysticism* is related to the Greek root *muein*: to close (the eyes) or to shut (the mouth). The mystical experience is an unmediated apprehension of God, often described as darkness or silence. God is not seen or heard, but directly intuited. Mystics say the experience can never be fully rendered in images or expressed in language. While there has been an intense debate in academic circles over the question whether all mystics share the same experience, there is no way to resolve the question. Since mystics of different traditions often speak different languages and employ diverse symbols of transcendence, however, it is likely that a given mystic's "religious experience" is shaped by history and culture the way all our experiences are. What is similar is that nearly every religious tradition has a mystical strain, with emphasis on individual experience, critical of ritual and dogma, and resistant to institutional authority.

Roman Catholic mystics often develop their practice in monasteries, where their ecstatic visions and intense devotion are out of public view and subject to official regulation. There is a subversive element in mysticism that is viewed with some suspicion by church authorities, especially when it leads to heretical theology or innovation in practice. We will consider two Christian mystics whose paths to union with God are marked by self-sacrifice. Thomas à Kempis sought a personal communion with Christ by sharing his suffering. Teresa of Avila sought a personal relationship with Christ leading to ecstatic union with God.

Thomas à Kempis (1379–1471) was an Augustinian monk in the Netherlands, who lived a quiet life as sub-prior of his monastery engaged in copying manuscripts and composing books on piety. Thomas regards suffering by self-denial in imitation of Jesus as the way to unite in spirit with him by losing the ego in the service of Christ. His manual of Christian practice became one of the most widely read devotional tracts in Christian history. In *The Imitation of Christ* he counsels cultivating friendship with Christ: "Love Him and hold Him for thy friend."[52] Thomas's desire to enter into personal communion with the divine is clear from his use of a category that was rarely employed in Christian thinking about Christ. Perhaps it was thought presumptuous, but Thomas applies the trope of friendship to indicate affection, loyalty, courage, and shared danger: in short, major elements of male bonding. (In contemporary terms, Thomas's "intimate love for Jesus" constitutes a spiritual "bromance.")

For Thomas, the test of friendship with Jesus is meeting the challenge of his sacrifice with one's own: "Set thyself, therefore, like a good and faithful servant of Christ, to the manful bearing of the Cross of the Lord, who out of love was crucified for thee . . . Drink thou lovingly thy Lord's cup if thou desirest to be His friend and to have thy lot with Him" (Book II, XII, 10). Thomas has contempt for fair-weather friends of Jesus who love his kingdom and wonder at his miracles, but shrink from "the royal way of the holy cross." They are mere "mercenaries" in his judgment, perhaps not realizing that his fidelity to the crucified one also has an eye to his own resurrection: "For if thou be dead with Him, thou shalt also live with Him."

Thomas acknowledges two other aspects of note about his sacrificial bonding with Christ. First, confidence is not constant. Sometimes Thomas feels "deserted by God's favor," but he regards moments of desertion as temptations to be overcome through rigorous "denial of self" (Book II, IX, 6). Similar doubts haunt other mystics and the sense of occasional absence seems to intensify their desire for divine presence. Second, self-sacrifice is contrary to nature. As Thomas notes, with considerable understatement, "It is not in the nature of man to bear the cross, to love the cross, to keep under the body and to bring it into subjection" (Book II, XII, 9). Consistent with his conviction, Thomas was reported on certain days to have scourged himself "as part of his private discipline."[53] He stuck mainly to his cell, even advising readers to avoid taking walks as natural beauty distracts the mind from devotion.

The mystic quest demands that we love what our natural instinct for self-preservation teaches us to avoid. In this sense, Thomas does not call for quiet contemplation but active giving up of earthly desires and ambitions to share in the project of his heavenly friend. In that bond of shared labor, he prepares "for bearing the cross more than joy" (Book II, X, 1). Sacrifice is the only means of attaining the mystic goal, but it requires supernatural assistance. Thomas offers this prayer, "Make possible to me, O Lord, by grace what seemeth impossible to me by nature" (Book III, XIX, 5). While other mystics celebrate the beauty of creation, Thomas's program of spiritual formation is an example of what Žižek calls "violent derailment of nature" by spirit.

The model was set by earlier Christian ascetics, such as the fierce fourth-century scholar and monastic, Jerome, who developed what Veronika Grimm calls "ascetic propaganda" to promote an ideal of Christian perfection that included extreme fasting, ruthless suppression of sexuality, and denial of natural affection for family. The aim was "total freedom from social constraints" that encouraged ascetics to "upbraid the foibles of urban society."[54] We might add that their rejection of material luxuries and denial of personal satisfactions freed them from the specific constraint of economies of productive value. Ascetics "destroy" their bodies *as bodies* by denying their basic needs, rejecting their attraction to other bodies, and refusing to engage in material productivity, yet without killing themselves. Their practice illustrates Bataille's claim that sacrifice need not annihilate what is offered, but only liberate it from systems in which its value is determined by social benefit and its meaning derived from completion of constructive projects. Christian ascetics offer their hunger and thirst and sexual desire as the "accursed share" of an economy of devotion. Without regard to the historical future, they "give up" their bodies in a never-ending process of "living sacrifice," with an eye on "treasure in heaven."

Another mystic who sought "intimate love of Jesus" was Teresa of Avila (1515–1582), Spanish nun, founder of the order of Discalced Carmelites (those without shoes like Francis of Assisi), who was canonized in 1622 and declared a Doctor of the Church (one of two women honored in this way) in 1970. St. Teresa taught the way to God through prayer: vocal, mental, and contemplative. She encouraged the nuns under her charge to use their imaginations to create mental pictures of Christ that reflected their moods, thus lending dramatic realism to their devotion. It was a practice she followed as well.

According to her personal testimony, Teresa entered the divine sphere through ecstatic self-sacrifice. Speaking of the angel who appeared to her in a vision, she wrote, "I saw in his hand a long spear of gold, and at the iron's point there seemed to be a little fire. He appeared to me to be thrusting it at times into my heart, and to pierce my very entrails; when he drew it out, he seemed to draw them out also, and to leave me all on fire with a great love of God. The pain was so great that it made me moan; and yet so surpassing was the sweetness of this excessive pain, that I could not wish to be rid of it."[55] Earlier, Teresa used explicit sacrificial imagery to describe her devotion: "It is not we who apply the fuel; the fire is already kindled, and we are thrown into it in a moment to be consumed." Lanced through the heart, eviscerated, cast into flames, and writhing in exquisite agony, Teresa became what her namesake, Mother Teresa of Calcutta, called herself, a "victim of Christ."[56]

In his sculpture illustrating this passage from St. Teresa's autobiography the Italian artist Giovanni Lorenzo Bernini (1598–1680) captured the rapturous moment of sacred violence and human surrender. While conventional sensibilities may be offended by hints of orgasmic swoon in the saint's face, sexual imagery is often used to describe mystic union, including commentary on the *Song of Songs* in the Bible. Further, Teresa was not innocent of the power of erotic imagination to promote spiritual devotion. She counseled younger nuns under her direction to form in their minds attractive images of Jesus as their heavenly "spouse" to intensify their love for him and to encourage their speaking directly to him in prayer. "You will find it very helpful if you can get an image or a picture of this Lord—*one that you like*—not to wear round your neck and never look at but to use regularly whenever you talk to Him, and He will tell you what to say."[57] Teresa cautioned that the highest level of prayer or contemplation carried the risk of loss of self-control through excess of emotion; yet her own account seems to record precisely such abandonment, embracing the "sweetness" of the "excessive pain" of ecstasy with moans. As she later reflected, "It is not bodily pain, but spiritual, though the body has a share in it—indeed a great share." So, bodily pain after all.

The historian Maureen Flynn argues that "late medieval mystics exploited sensory pain as a mechanism for identifying with the suffering savior." Their ascetic torture of the body was also their means of focusing the mind on immaterial reality; the more the agony of flagellation faded from their consciousness, even as they punished themselves more brutally, the more convinced they were that they were entering the timeless perfection of pure spirits. For Teresa in particular, "pain constituted proof that her human nature was being purified. . . . In this theology of ecstasy every tinge of corporeality implied the beginning of the end of temporal existence."[58] Flynn's essay sheds light on the often overlooked connection between asceticism and mysticism, particularly in mystics who seek a unitive melding of their individual beings with infinite transcendence in a total immolation of the self. Flynn comments on Teresa's contemporary, St. John of the Cross, that he required monks under his guidance not only to eliminate all physical sensations, but all mental images as well: "To pass the threshold of eternity required that the hapless monk cross into total oblivion" on a "path of psychological nihilism."

These mystics put into practice the principle of negative or *apophatic* theology that one can say nothing positive about God, only what God is not. The classic text of this tradition is *Mystical Theology*, probably written by a monk in Syria early in the sixth century. The work was composed under the pseudonym, Dionysius, a member of the Court of the Areopagus, the governing council of the city of Athens, who converted to

Christianity in response to a sermon by Paul (Acts 17:34). According to our author, known as Pseudo-Dionysius, the precondition of achieving mystical union is "an undivided and absolute abandonment of yourself and everything." In that moment the highest degree of insight possible for a finite being may emerge "in the brilliant darkness of a hidden silence." The goal is self-erasure: "Here, being neither oneself nor someone else, one is supremely united to the completely unknown by an inactivity of all knowledge, and knows beyond the mind by knowing nothing."[59]

Metaphors of "dazzling obscurity" and radiant darkness in this work allude to the New Testament declaration: "It is [God] alone who has immortality and dwells in unapproachable light, whom no one has ever seen or can see" (1 Timothy 6:16). Expressed in symbolic language, the reason no one can see God, visually or cognitively, is that it would be like trying to stare directly at the sun. The result would be blindness, a plunge into darkness caused, not by an absence of light, but by an overwhelming *excess of light*. In this classic statement of apophatic theology, the divine darkness stands for the utter alterity of God before which all language is sacrificed, reduced to ashes.

The method of approaching God by negation is a process of abstraction, of removing from the mind, in a systematic and comprehensive way, all that is *not* God. Dionysius compares the *via negativa* to the way a sculptor shapes a statue by chipping away everything that does not express the form he discerns in the marble. In an analogous way the mystic seeks "that unknowing which itself is hidden from all those possessed of knowing amid all beings." This claim is the epistemological counterpart to the metaphysical claim that God is finally beyond all representations, including personal images. God is not a being, not even the Supreme Being, but what Thomas Aquinas called the "power" of being or what the Lutheran mystic Jacob Boehme (1575–1624) identified as the *Urgrund* or "originating ground" of all beings or what the Dominican theologian and mystic Meister Eckhart (1260–1328) called *Gottheit*, the Godhead beyond the personal Trinity.

The mystic's goal is to reunite with divine reality beyond all description in a state of total eclipse of individual awareness. The final result of ascetic contemplation is not discourse about the nature of God, but passage from speech into absolute silence. "There is no speaking of it, nor name nor knowledge of it." And there is this chilling fact: "Existing beings do not know it as it actually is and it does not know them as they are."[60] The mystic swoons in ecstasy, unknowing and unknown.

Teresa attests that the agony of union with God is suffering that arises from the intensity and transience of union with the transcendent. It is the pain that accompanies reflection on human intercourse: the agonizing awareness that the moment of satisfaction cannot be sustained. The loss of the beloved is inevitable; *thanatos* (death) always accompanies *eros* (love). As Bataille commented, "The truth is that between death and the reeling, heady motion of the little death [*le petite mort* is a French euphemism for sexual climax] the distance is hardly noticeable."[61] The proximity of the two in mystical ecstasy brings us back to sacrifice.

A recurring theme of this book is that mystical experience involves radical self-sacrifice. Whether associated with ascetic discipline or not, the mystic relation to transcendence is only completed with the consumption and disappearance of the human participant. In Teresa's case, at the moment of mystical consummation the angel struck her heart with a flaming spear and penetrated her body, withdrawing her internal organs, then setting her "all on fire with a great love of God." It is hard to imagine a more graphic description of the preparation and offering of a sacrificial victim. What is striking in this account of mysticism, then, is not so much images of transient sexual ecstasy but explicit references to the violence of sacrifice: The mystical union with God is the moment of the psychic death of the saint. Until that consummation, moments of doubt and the sense of spiritual desertion come to all mystics and demonstrate the conditionality and suspense of religious sacrifice.

Eucharist as Sacrament or Memorial: Aquinas, Calvin, and the Second Vatican Council

For most Christians, however, the mystery of Christ's sacrifice does not evoke inner torment and desolation. Partaking in the Eucharist is more likely to evoke repentance, gratitude, or worship; and the ritual performance is in part designed to allay anxiety and promote confidence in the efficacy of Christ's death to achieve redemption for the communicant. The Eucharist is practiced throughout the world, but the three main branches of Christianity differ in their views of how or whether it is the offering of Christ as a sacrifice.

Roman Catholic and Eastern Orthodox churches agree that at some moment in the ritual the bread and wine undergo an essential change into the body and blood of Jesus. Thus, by breaking the bread and pouring out the wine, the priest reenacts Christ's death on the cross, and by receiving the consecrated host, believers ingest by faith the immortal body of Jesus and so receive divine life. For both traditions, the elements of the Eucharist act as the "medicine of immortality." Many Protestants, however, do not believe that the bread and wine transform into the "real presence" of Jesus's body. Rather, the communion ritual is a memorial in which the elements signify, but do not become, the body and blood of Christ. Through the communal act of remembering Christ's sacrificial love, most Protestants participate in his reconciling presence through the Spirit of their fellowship as the assembled "body of Christ." Their views were shaped during the Reformation in Europe in dissent from Catholic interpretation.

Roman Catholic theology of the Eucharist as ritual sacrifice of Christ developed over time. By the second century Justin Martyr explained the Eucharist as the fulfillment of Israelite sacrifices and an expression of thanksgiving for Christ's death and resurrection. Irenaeus added that it also signified the self-offering of believers. The association of the Christian life with sacrifice became explicit in the writing of Augustine (354–430), bishop of Hippo in modern-day Algeria, who was proclaimed a saint by popular acclaim and declared a Doctor of the Church in 1298. In his magisterial work, *The City of God*, he called a sacrifice "the visible sacrament or sacred sign of an invisible sacrifice," namely, the inner surrender of one's own interests for the good of others as counseled in the Epistle to the Hebrews. Such generosity fulfills the words of the prophet Hosea: "I desire mercy rather than sacrifice." Thus, Augustine defined a true sacrifice as "every work which is done that we may be united to God in holy fellowship, and which has a reference to that supreme good and end in which alone we can be truly blessed."[62] For Augustine, "the whole redeemed city, that is to say, the congregation or community of the saints, is offered to God as our sacrifice through the great High Priest, who offered Himself to God in His passion for us. . . . And this is also the sacrifice which the Church continually celebrates in the sacrament of the altar, known to the faithful, in which she teaches that she herself is offered in the offering she makes to God."[63] Yet Augustine is clear that the Eucharist also signifies the sacrifice made by Christ: "He is both the Priest who offers and the Sacrifice offered. And He designed that there should be a daily sign of this in the sacrifice of the Church, which, being His body, learns to offer herself through Him."[64]

The same dual emphasis on sacrifice as the redemptive offering of Christ and the reciprocal gift of believers to his kingdom appears in Thomas Aquinas (1225–1274), architect of medieval Christian thought, who was canonized in 1323 and declared a Doctor of the Church in 1567. In his massive work, ambitiously titled *Summa Theologica*, Thomas discusses sacrifice as one of the cardinal virtues, indeed, a "natural law" inasmuch as "at all times and among all nations there has always been the offering of sacrifices" as acts of homage to rulers. Christians, however, offer sacrifices as outward representations of "inward spiritual sacrifice" owed to God alone as "the sovereign Ruler of the whole universe." For Thomas the sign that an offering is a sacrifice is that "something is done to it," that is, it is burned or consumed rather than used for the support of "ministers of Divine worship." What distinguishes a sacrifice from other gifts is that it is removed from productive use, "destroyed in worship of God, as though it were being made into something holy."[65] Only offerings freed from human utility and purpose can signify God, who transcends all earthly calculation and understanding.

While sacrifice is an act of inner submission to God, it requires an external sign: an object "destroyed in worship of God." But how can the Eucharist re-enact the sacrifice of Christ if his body is absent, returned to heaven in glorified form never to die again? Thomas answers that the Eucharist is called "Sacrifice" because it "represents the Passion of Christ, but it is termed a 'Host' inasmuch as it contains Christ, Who is 'a host of sweetness.'"[66] The quotation is from Ephesians 5:22 where the writer uses the Greek term *thysia* for "sacrifice," but Thomas translates "host" using the Latin *hostia*, which means "victim." For Thomas the logic is simple: There is no sacrifice without a victim. But where is Christ in the elements of the Eucharist?

Thomas turns to his trusted source of philosophical insight, Aristotle, for the answer: a theory of substantial transformation. According to Aristotle, all beings consist of *substance* (nature) and *accidents* (characteristics). While the nature of a thing is general and abstract, its characteristics are specific and concrete. Thomas interprets the ritual consecration of the bread and wine in the Eucharist as the moment when the substance of the elements is transformed into the body and blood of Christ, while the elements' outward characteristics remain the same. The change is not observable nor has it any other examples in nature for, according to Thomas, "it is entirely supernatural, and effected by God's power alone." Thomas concludes that the change in being is "not a formal, but a substantial conversion; nor is it a kind of natural movement: but, with a name of its own, it can be called 'transubstantiation.'"[67] As a result, the bread contains "the entire body of Christ, that is, the bones, the nerves, and the like." By the miracle of consecration the Eucharist becomes a sacrifice with a real victim on the altar/cross, whose invisible body can be daily offered up in commemoration of his visible crucifixion that cannot be repeated.

It was a subtle distinction that one prominent leader of the Protestant Reformation rejected, insisting that Christ's body was located in heaven and could not also be present in the Eucharist. The foremost scholar among the sixteenth-century Reformers, trained in classical humanism, John Calvin (1509–1564), dismissed "the monstrous notion of ubiquity."[68] He confessed he could not explain the mystery of Christ's presence in the sacrament, but that he would "rather experience than understand it." Typical of Reformation emphasis on biblical authority, Calvin held that the sacramental elements were not made efficacious through "a silent action, as has happened under the pope's tyranny," but by "lively preaching" from the Bible and the communicants' acceptance of the promise of redemption. Rather than receiving the immortal body of Christ, believers "bear away from this Sacrament no more than they gather with the vessel of faith" (xvii.33).

At the height of polemical fervor, Calvin charges that Satan "blinded nearly the whole world with a most pestilential error—the belief that the Mass is a sacrifice and offering to obtain forgiveness of sins" (xviii.1). He is incensed that Catholics regard the elements as "an expiatory victim, by which they reconcile God to themselves." What purpose, he asks, is there for "the Mass, which has been so set up that a hundred thousand sacrifices may be performed each day, except to bury and submerge Christ's Passion, by which he offered himself as sole sacrifice to the Father?" (xviii.3). After the unique and final sacrifice of Christ on the cross, God has given believers "a Table at which to feast, not an altar upon which to offer a victim; he has not consecrated priests to offer sacrifice, but ministers to distribute the sacred banquet" (xviii.12).

For Calvin, the Eucharist is not a sacrifice, but "a kind of exhortation" to believers to live in harmony as one body with disparate members, just as the bread is composed of many grains. The purpose of the ritual is to create "communion" by remembering "when Christ, giving himself to us, not only invites us by his own example to pledge and give ourselves to one another, but inasmuch as he makes himself common to all, also makes all of us one in himself" (xvii.38). Calvin believes that communal participation is essential for the Eucharist and charges that private performance of the Mass, usually in chapels within the estates of the wealthy, "dissolves and tears apart this community." "For the petty sacrificer, about to devour his victim by himself, separates himself from all believing folk" (xviii.7). To Calvin the Mass violates the moral duty of believers to worship in community.

On the last point, Calvin was not so far from his opponents. Thomas, who Calvin regarded as among the "saner Schoolmen," called for the assembled church to present itself together before God as an offering of gratitude. Thomas also defined Christ's death as a sacrifice because he gave himself up for the honor of God, "in order to appease him" and out of his love for humanity.[69] Beyond their sharp differences over interpreting the Eucharist, it is significant that both Thomas and Calvin set sacrificial love as the model for Christian conduct. Thomas discusses sacrifice in the section of his work devoted to moral theology, and Calvin distinguishes Christ's sacrifice of expiation from sacrifices of thanksgiving that include "all the duties of love." For Calvin, "doing good and sharing are called sacrifices that are pleasing to God (Hebrews 13:16) . . . and thus all the good works of believers are spiritual sacrifices" (xviii.16).

In Calvin's reading, every exercise of virtue *is* a sacrifice, a subordination of personal interest and suppression of natural desires, in imitation of Christ. If sacrifice is the ground of Christian conduct, then even the most casual act of kindness is a mystic crucifixion. As a religion of Abraham, Christian tradition, in all its forms, cannot escape the shadow of Moriah. For Protestant interpreters, Isaac served as a prototype both of Christ offered in sacrifice and also of the believer sacrificed with Christ.

The beginning of the Protestant Reformation is often dated at 1517, when a young Augustinian monk named Martin Luther (1483–1546) posted ninety-five theses for debate on the door of the Wittenberg Castle church. Formally titled "Disputation on the Power and Efficacy of Indulgences," most of the propositions challenged the medieval practice of granting remittance of mortal sins (those deserving eternal punishment in hell) and reducing the suffering for venial sins (those that can be forgiven over time) for souls in purgatory. Originally granted to Crusaders and pilgrims, by Luther's time indulgences were part of a corrupt trade. Pope Leo X cut a deal with regional bishops that half the money collected from the sale of indulgences would be sent to Rome for the construction of St. Peter's basilica. Still, to ordinary believers, who are neither saints nor demons, but somewhere in between, purgatory made common sense: A merciful God provides a second chance to make up for garden-variety transgressions. The good news is that those who awaken after death in purgatory can be assured that they will eventually reach heaven.

Further, if believers' donations can relieve the agony of loved ones, then their sacrifices contribute to the economy of salvation—even though mediated through brokers of the church. That was precisely the system Luther set out to dismantle: "Christians are to be taught that if the pope knew the exactions of the pardon-preachers, he would rather that St. Peter's church should go to ashes, than that it should be built up with the skin, flesh and bones of his sheep."[70] For Luther, the sacrifices of the living, as sheep offered on the altar, cannot achieve salvation for the dead, "even though the pope himself were to stake his soul upon the assurance."

For Luther, the only sacrifice sufficient for justification is the offering of Christ on the cross and the only sacrifices sufficient for sanctification are the sufferings Christians endure for the sake of Christ. As Luther writes in his commentary on Hebrews, the person of faith is "lifted up in Christ and crucified."[71] Luther insisted that his was a "theology of the cross," and disciples of Christ should expect to share in his passion. Perhaps this emphasis owed something to Luther's belief in the total depravity of all humans. The unbeliever has to "die" since there is nothing of virtue within that could be repaired or rehabilitated. Luther's catch phrase was that humans are "not able not to sin" (*non posse non peccare*). To Luther "it is absolutely clear that the entire will of the natural man is wicked and evil." Therefore, he concludes, "to love God is to hate oneself.["72] The evangelical emphasis on Christian faith as requiring spiritual death and rebirth stems from this negative view of human nature. On this point, Reformers rejected the principle of Thomas Aquinas that "grace perfects nature" in favor of the claim that "grace recreates nature." Thus Luther asserted that "the love of God cannot exist side by side with a love of the created world." It would be hard to find a clearer example of self-sacrifice as a religious ideal utterly opposed to self-interest as a natural good.

Luther's rejection of the Mass as a sacrifice of Jesus was the mirror image of his view of the total depravity of human nature and led to his rejection of the efficacy of church ritual to accomplish the supernatural act of redemption. For these teachings and others, Pope Clement VII excommunicated Luther and the formation of separate "reformed" churches began throughout Europe. The Roman Catholic Church responded to Protestant criticisms by calling a council to address what were by then acknowledged as problems in doctrine and practice. The council was held at Trent and Bologna in northern Italy between 1545 and 1563.[73] The Council of Trent issued judgments on most Protestant criticisms and explicitly denied Luther's teaching of justification from sin by faith alone, insisting that human will cooperates with divine grace in redemption (as Thomas had taught). Accordingly, the assembled bishops interpreted original sin as a privation of grace inherited from Adam, but not voluntary and removed by infant baptism. The Council reaffirmed the dogma of transubstantiation and the ritual of the Mass as sacrifice, issuing a condemnation (*anathema*) of anyone who says "that in the Mass a true and proper sacrifice is not offered to God."[74] While the bishops recognized that prayers, alms, and penance are called "sacrifices," they insist that there is only one "true and real sacrifice of the Mass" and that is performed only by male priests as representatives of Christ on earth.

That judgment stood for 750 years until Pope John XXIII convened the Second Vatican Council (1962–1965) and called for *aggiornamento* or "bringing up to date." The pope used the dramatic image of opening windows to let fresh air blow through the Catholic Church to represent engaging the cultural and intellectual challenges of the modern world. Among the changes were revised relations with other religious communities. Vatican II removed the charge of deicide ("God killers") from the Jewish people, exonerated Protestants from the charge of heresy (and thus assignment to hell as schismatics), established a Secretariat for Christian Unity, affirmed an essential relation to Judaism and Israel, and offered to initiate dialogue with Orthodox churches. As important as these adaptations were, for most Catholics the changes in the theology and ritual performance of the Mass may have been most striking.

The use of vernacular languages in the celebration of the Mass reduced the mystery many felt from Latin recitation, greater participation by laity in congregational singing and praying shifted focus from the sacrificial ritual to the gathered community, and the priest turning to face participants rather than offering the elements of bread and wine to God alone suggested that the gift of Christ's sacrifice was *for* the communicants as much as *to* God to secure their forgiveness. The formulations of the Second Vatican Council seem designed to hold together the view of the Mass as a double offering: that of the body and blood of Jesus as atoning sacrifice and that of the believing community as a gift of devotion and service to God.

Since then three popes have swung the pendulum of sacrificial imagery back and forth. Pope John Paul II (1978–2005) embraced most of the reforms of Vatican II, while resisting "liberation theology" because its attention to the poor and disenfranchised was focused through the lens of Marxist analysis. Pope Benedict XVI (2005–2013) reaffirmed that "the reality of the Eucharistic sacrifice has always been at the heart of Catholic faith," then added to an Anglican audience, "called into question in the sixteenth century, it was solemnly reaffirmed at the Council of Trent against the backdrop of our justification in Christ."[75] On the other hand, Pope Francis (2013–), the first pontiff from Latin America, calls for the Church to sacrifice its own resources for the sake of the powerless. His program of reform recalls the phrase from Vatican II that inspired liberation theologies in Latin America and elsewhere: "preferential option for the poor." The meaning of sacrifice for him seems to find its primary application in the self-giving of the church as the "body of Christ" in history, and he has led the way by giving up much personal luxury that he might enjoy as the head of the largest religious institution on earth.[76]

He emulates the saint whose name he assumed, Francis of Assisi, who lived in poverty and deprivation and bore on his body *stigmata*, marks of his literal sharing of the sacrifice of Christ. Pope Francis seems to have chosen the saint's name to identify with his way of life, even if he finds "Jesus' wounds in carrying out works of mercy."[77] A few days after his election, he said, "For me, [Francis] is the man of poverty, the man of peace, the man who loves and protects creation . . . the poor man. . . . How I would like a Church which is poor and for the poor." He emphasizes that "authentic power is service . . . service which has its radiant culmination in the Cross." The redemptive power of Christ's self-sacrifice, then, lies in its disclosure of divine love. "If I embrace this love, then I am saved; if I refuse it, then I am condemned, not by him, but my own self, because God never condemns; he only loves and saves."[78]

While Pope Francis remains committed to the Eucharist as the ritual offering of Christ's body to God for the expiation of sins, comments like this one suggest that he also understands the sacrifice to have a compelling influence on the participants: They are saved by embracing the divine love Christ reveals in his suffering. Francis also understands *imitatio Christi* as responding to his example: "Let us ask ourselves: How do I follow Jesus?. . . . He reminds us every time that following him means going out of ourselves and not making our life a possession of our own, but rather a gift to him and to others." While still Cardinal Bergoglio, he wrote that Christian love is "generous and concrete. A decidedly generous love is a sign of faith and an invitation to faith."

Serving others, as Christ did, is its own form of persuasion, a way of "proclaiming the Kingdom and making it present." Visiting a homeless shelter, Pope Francis applied the point by insisting that "to love God and neighbor is not something abstract, but profoundly concrete: it means seeing in every person the face of the Lord to be served, to serve him concretely. And you are, dear brothers and sisters, the face of Jesus."[79] For Francis, the second meaning of sacrifice—as service to others, the gift of believers to the world—is explicitly concrete. Christians do not sacrifice for the sake of an abstract ideal, but to meet the immediate needs of concrete persons before them. Christ died to provide the example of love that compels his followers to act with compassionate generosity. It is an interpretation Abelard would have found congenial.

Sacrifice as "Moral Influence": Horace Bushnell to Martin Luther King, Jr.

The persistent question in Christian tradition of whether the sacrifice of Christ was intended to affect believers by inspiring their love for others and devotion to his kingdom or to appease God's justice and avert divine wrath presents a challenge to Protestant theologians as well. The interpretation of Jesus's sacrifice as the flawless example of patient suffering of injustice with a spirit of forgiveness toward his persecutors and a refusal to return their violence with violence has appealed to one strand of American theologians and social activists. In accordance with the precedent set by Peter Abelard, these Christian leaders argue that the sacrifice of Christ was not offered to convince God to forgive humanity but to persuade humans to reconcile themselves to divine love for all beings.

A leading proponent of this view in nineteenth-century America was the Congregational minister Horace Bushnell (1802–1876), who found himself as Abelard had, facing opposition. Bushnell was caught between Calvinist orthodoxy which insisted that Christ died "under the frown of God" to avenge divine wrath against sin and Unitarian rationalism that rejected such ideas out right. In 1848, Bushnell addressed the Unitarian stronghold of Harvard Divinity School on the subject of atonement; it was an audition for appointment to the Hollis Chair in theology. The stakes were high, and Bushnell knew what his audience wanted to hear; but he proceeded to lay out his mediating position on Christ's sacrifice, affirming both subjective and objective meanings to it, thereby offending both sides in the controversy and destroying his chances to teach at Harvard.[80] What he developed was a view of Christ's sacrifice as exerting moral influence, a view that was mediated through the personalist theology of Boston University to one of its most prominent graduates, Martin Luther King, Jr.

Bushnell's objection to traditional teachings that Christ's death was a sacrifice to satisfy divine justice or restore divine honor or maintain divine moral government was that attributing guilt to the innocent so that the guilty can go free is a fundamental injustice. Rather, Bushnell argued that the purpose of Christ's mission on earth is to create "a moral effect" on humanity, specifically, "to renovate character."[81] This subjective transformation is achieved by the power of Christ's endurance—"he bears the concentrated venom of his crucifiers with a lamb's patience"—to overcome sinful resistance to the divine will. "Before this cross, we feel ourselves weak in evil" and acknowledge the compelling virtue of the innocent. In this way, Christ reconciles to God those who respond to his sacrifice by taking on his way of self-giving. The test of faith is the response to Jesus's sacrifice by giving oneself in service to divine love.

Such response is not mere "self-culture," but a recognition that Jesus's life and passion affect the inner life of God. Bushnell professes the deity of Christ, despite making his Unitarian audience squirm, in order to affirm that the tragedy of the passion is one in which "God is the Chief Character, and the divine feeling, moved in tragic earnest—Goodness Infinite manifested through Sorrow" (205). "It is not that the suffering appeases God," Bushnell repeats, "but that it expresses God—displays, in open history, the unconquerable love of God's Heart" (216). To orthodox ears attuned to echoes of heresy, that declaration sounded like the teaching known as *patripassianism* (suffering of the Father). Early church councils rejected the idea that God could be affected by human affliction because the divine being is *impassible* (incapable of suffering) and *immutable* (without change). For Bushnell, however, "there must be some kind of passibleness in God, else there could be no genuine character in him. . . . A cast-iron Deity could not command our love and reverence." While God is spirit and not subject to physical pain, he is "morally passible" to the feelings of his creatures. His compassion is "co-passion. It suffers with its objects, takes their burdens, struggles with their sorrows." The crucified Christ "shows God in self-sacrifice, because he brings out and makes historical in the world God's passive virtue. . . . he opens our human feeling, bad and blind as it is, pouring himself into its deepest recesses and bathing it with his cleansing, new-creating influence."[82]

Bushnell argued orthodox theology denied the central Christian claim that Jesus revealed divine love in his suffering. In his later treatment of atonement, he declares that "the whole deity" is in the sacrifice of Christ. Bushnell attributes the significance of Christ's suffering not to "the writing body of Jesus, but to the very feeling of our God." Tracing suffering back to the inner experience of the Trinitarian God was a bold move, but one that illumined the kind of power divine love exercises: not coercive force, but persuasive influence. It is the latter, "the Moral Power of God," by which Jesus's life and passion sway human will to bring about "internal new creation."[83] He illustrated the principle by the image of Christ as a shepherd leading his flock rather than driving them. "He goes before them, bearing all the bitterest loads of sacrifice and facing all the fiercest terrors himself, only calling them gently to come and follow."[84] In this way, the example of Jesus "works out the recovery of transgressors by the transforming power of sacrifice."[85] The dynamic of human forgiveness depends upon the offended party forgoing resentment and continued wounded feeling. In his final book, Bushnell applies that dynamic to God as well, maintaining that "nothing will ever accomplish the proposed real and true forgiveness, but to make cost in the endeavor, such cost as new-tempers and liquefies the reluctant nature."[86] That cost is paid by the suffering of the one who forgives, whether human or divine.

During Bushnell's career that proposition was dramatically illustrated in the agony of the Civil War (1861–1865) during which more than 600,000 combatants and civilians died. As in nearly all discourse about war, the language of sacrifice was prominent. For some, the carnage was the price the nation was required to pay to realize fully its commitment to personal liberty: sacrifice for emancipation. That was the theme sounded by Abraham Lincoln in his Second Inaugural Address: "Yet, if God wills that it continue, until all wealth piled by the bondman's two hundred and fifty years of unrequited toil shall be sunk, and until every drop of blood drawn with the lash, shall be paid by another drawn by the sword, as was said three thousand years ago, so still it must be said, 'The judgments of the Lord are true and righteous altogether.'" That reading, while generous, tended to simplify the moral question by implying that Union forces were agents of divine justice whose deaths were redemptive, while Confederate troops had died in an unjust cause. Bushnell's orations also conveyed such sentiments, and historian Drew Gilpin Faust interprets his "accounting" as a form of theological economics in which survivors owe a debt of obligation to those who died to secure victory for the Union.[87]

In "Our Obligations to the Dead," published in 1881, Bushnell demonstrated one use of sacrificial language to talk about the value and moral significance of death in combat: Those who die impel us to continue the cause for which they gave their lives. The discourse of war has a self-sustaining logic that promotes further conflict to insure that our fallen warriors do not die "in vain." The response Bushnell believes the sacrifice of Civil War soldiers should inspire is to continue the project of reunifying the nation on the basis of moral principles and religious faith. Bushnell does not ask how those loyal to the Confederacy should respond to the example of the sacrifices of their soldiers, and thus reveals a moral blindness to the symmetry of pain in his theological analysis of sacrifice. While Bushnell fell short in other political and social views, including patronizing racism and misogyny, his best theological writing illumines the power of patient suffering to "melt hearts," in his sentimental language, and thus potentially to transform social order. His ideas, resisted in his own time, filtered through liberal Protestant thought, and eventually found theological expression in the Social Gospel movement and transforming power in the career of Martin Luther King, Jr., for whom sacrifice was the primary instrument of seeking justice and demonstrating love.

Dr. Martin Luther King, Jr. (1929–1968) was a Baptist minister, civil rights leader, and winner of the Nobel Peace Prize. After graduating from Morehouse College, he entered Crozer Seminary, where his interest was aroused by critical biblical study and liberal theological works, including Bushnell's *Vicarious Sacrifice* and Walter Rauschenbusch's best-selling tract of the Social Gospel movement, *Christianity and the Social Crisis*. On the question of atonement, King followed Bushnell, arguing that "Christ's death was not a ransom, or a penal substitute, or a penal example: rather it was a revelation of the sacrificial love of God intended to awaken an answering love in the hearts of men."[88] At Boston University, he continued his study of liberal Christianity, publicly breaking with the traditional Baptist views of his father. But as revisionist historians of King's development have stressed, his views were decisively shaped by his formative years in the black Baptist church. A large part of that influence was the content and style of the King James Bible. In its pages we find important background for King's view of sacrifice as a means of exerting moral influence capable of redeeming social order.

For example, in the prophet Isaiah the people of Israel are designated as the suffering servant of Yahweh, through whose affliction salvation will come to the world. In this interpretation suffering is exemplary and redemptive. Individual suffering thus finds its "meaning" in the larger context of the suffering of the chosen people, those who are called to bear witness to their covenant with God by their collective patience and hope. Israel is comforted in suffering by the promise of the power of their witness to redeem the whole world: "Even the captives of the mighty shall be taken, and the prey of the tyrant be rescued. . . . Then all flesh shall know that I am the Lord your Savior and your Redeemer, the mighty One of Jacob" (Isaiah 49:25–26). That desired outcome, however, depends upon one critical premise, namely, that evildoers are receptive to the moral suasion of suffering.

That premise underlies all noble attempts to confront evil with non-violent resistance. It is the foundation of the moral influence of sacrifice. King claimed the moral authority of innocent suffering and predicted the success of its exercise in one sermon:

> To our most bitter opponents we say: "We shall match your capacity to inflict suffering by our capacity to endure suffering. We shall meet your physical force with soul force . . . Throw us in jail, and we shall still love you. . . . But be ye assured that we will wear you down by our capacity to suffer. One day we shall win freedom, but not only for ourselves. We shall so appeal to your heart and conscience that we shall win *you* in the process, and our victory will be a double victory."[89]

It would be hard to cite a more robust statement of faith in the moral influence of sacrifice—and there is no question that faithful suffering does, on occasion, transform the oppressor. When the Persian ruler Cyrus released the Israelites and allowed them to return to their land and rebuild their temple, Isaiah declared that God moved Cyrus: "He is my shepherd, and he shall carry out all my purpose" (Isaiah 44:28). When protests persuaded President Lyndon Johnson to sign the Civil Rights Act into law, many Christians interpreted the event as another powerful ruler moved to do what is right by the unjust suffering of God's servants. While suffering without retaliation can sometimes break the cycle of violence, many people regard the cost as too high.

Under conditions of racism, oppressed groups often respond by refusing to recognize the humanity of oppressors and by organizing violent acts of retaliation that confront power with power. But King read the Gospels in light of Mahatma Gandhi's campaigns of nonviolent resistance to British rule in India. So he argued that violence leads only to greater alienation, more severe oppression, and finally, to self-destruction. "Have we not come to such an impasse in the modern world that we must love our enemies—or else? The chain reaction of evil—hate begetting wars, wars producing more wars—must be broken or we shall be plunged into the dark abyss of annihilation." Rather than retaliating for wrong done, "we must in strength and humility meet hate with love." To those who objected to that strategy as impractical, he continued:

> My friends, we have followed the so-called practical way for too long a time now, and it has lead inexorably to deeper confusion and chaos. Time is cluttered with the wreckage of communities which surrendered to hatred and violence. For the salvation of our nation and the salvation of mankind, we must follow another way. . . . While abhorring segregation, we shall love the segregationist. This is the only way to create the beloved community.[90]

While King emphasized the nonviolence of Jesus, turning the other cheek, absorbing the wrong of the oppressor, he also insisted that reconciliation was *not* capitulation. The "beloved community" can be created only by the synthesis of love *and* justice. King demanded that the oppressed abandon neither their rights nor their identity as human beings, but also that they refuse to break relations with the oppressors, continuing by their sacrifices to issue a call to repentance. Love is "the only force capable of transforming an enemy into a friend," and justice is the only authentic basis for lasting friendship.

But how can justice be achieved in a world in which there are not only unjust persons, but also unjust laws, providing governmental sanction for immoral policies? King believed the answer is that humanity is flawed, but redeemable. In even the most callused bigot, there is a soft spot of conscience. In even the most calculating bureaucracy, there are human beings in authority who can be persuaded by moral appeal. The problem as with all acts of sacrifice is that there is no guarantee of success and no assurance that the ideal will appeal to all the oppressed. As theologian James Cone comments, "Only God could empower black Christians to love hateful whites, and even God could not guarantee that they would return love for hate, nonviolence for violence."[91] Still, even after his home in Montgomery was bombed, King expressed profound faith in the final victory of sacrificial love to overcome human cruelty embedded in racist hatred. He embraced the vision of his famous "dream" of a day when "justice will roll down as a mighty river" in an integrated American society. He died as a martyr to its cause just short of his fortieth birthday. Perhaps the most impressive evidence of the moral influence of sacrifice is the continuing power of his example to inspire forgiveness and reconciliation.

Yet sacrifice was, and still is, a risky enterprise, filled with moral ambiguity. Those who lynched black victims in the southern United States offered them up, often in celebratory settings, as sacrifices to maintain the purity of the "white race" and the power of white supremacy. Black poets and artists saw the grim irony in the fact that, as Cone notes, "the clearest image of the crucified Christ was the figure of an innocent black victim, dangling from a lynching tree." Their works named the tragic deaths as "sacrifice" and constituted screams of protest against the spectacle. The poet James Andrews makes the connection explicit, comparing a lynching victim to a calf brought to a "lonely tree," as if to an altar.

> Upon a newer Cross he dies,
> And smoke ascends toward the skies:
> Burnt offering.[92]

What Abraham nearly achieved on Mount Moriah, the killers of the teenager Emmet Till (1955) and the bombers of four girls in Birmingham (1963) accomplished: the death of a child for the sake of an abstraction. In one Syriac homily from the fifth century, Sarah says to Abraham, "You are drunk with the love of God—who is your God and my God—and if He so bids you concerning the child, you would kill him without hesitation."[93] Those who witness or hear of such intoxicated devotion can only join Sarah in a scream of horror.

Finally, however, a scream is not enough. The catharsis of protest eases the conscience and maintains the moral innocence of the powerless. Yet without active resistance to injustice and political authority supporting reform, nothing changes. That is the limitation of self-sacrifice as nonviolent endurance of evil that hopes to transform the character of the persecutor through moral influence. The uncertainty of reciprocity that attends all sacrifice is deepened in the gamble of Christian sacrifice. Not only is the divine recipient beyond human control, but also those one seeks to persuade by patient suffering may obdurately refuse to mend their ways or cede their coercive power over others. Thus, Christian sacrifice requires hope in eventual divine vindication in the coming kingdom of God on earth or in the perfection of eternal life in heaven. That is, sacrifice in Christian tradition depends on eschatological redemption and so shares in the suspense and conditionality of sacrifice in general.

Immanuel Kant warned, in his moral outrage at Abraham's choice "to slaughter his own son like a sheep," that with all visionary faith "the *possibility* ever remains that an error may be discovered in it."[94] In that possibility lies the tragedy of sacrificing concrete human goods for abstract visions of heaven on earth. It is easy now to condemn those who lynched black men in cruciform poses to pursue illusions of racial purity, but what other fantasies must be rejected before they inspire other sacrifices? Christian tradition is peculiarly susceptible to the lure of redemptive violence because of the centrality of sacrifice in its theology and ethics. The challenge is to keep focused on the love of actual neighbors, fellow human beings who are near, and never presume to sacrifice them for whatever distant utopia beckons.

5

Sacrifice in Islamic Tradition

Pray to your Lord and sacrifice to him.
—Qur'an 108.1

We have made camels a part of God's rites.
Their flesh and blood does not reach God; it is your piety
 that reaches Him.
—Qur'an 22.36–37

As in Jewish and Christian traditions, so also in Islamic tradition, *sacrifice* carries a double meaning: the literal offering of a victim and the inward gift of devotion and gratitude. The "leaven of interiorization" that Guy Stroumsa detected at work in Jewish and Christian views of sacrifice also moves within Islam. With words that echo Hebrew prophets, Muhammad proclaims that the bodies of sacrificed animals do not affect God; only human devotion to divine will evokes Allāh's compassion and mercy. We should note that the Arabic term transliterated as *al-ilāh* means simply "the God." It is related to the Hebrew *El* and its plural *Elohim*. In the Qur'an, God is designated by plural personal pronouns, the "royal we," to indicate his status as sovereign of the world.

What is distinctive about Islamic practice is that Muslims continue to offer animal sacrifices, once a year during the pilgrimage (*hajj*) to Mecca, one of the five duties of a Muslim, conventionally called the Pillars of Islam. The first is the confession of faith (*shahāda*): "There is no god but God, and Muhammad is the messenger of God." The remaining three are daily prayers (*salāt*), charitable giving (*zakāt*), and fasting during the month of Ramadān. Regarding sacrifice of animals during hajj, the Qur'an directs, "Pronounce over them the name of God as you draw them up in line and slaughter them; and when they have fallen to the ground eat of their flesh and feed the uncomplaining beggar and the demanding supplicant" (22.36).[1]

Sacrifices of 600,000 cows, goats, sheep, and camels are performed in abattoirs on the plain of Mina north of Mecca on the tenth day of the month of pilgrimage, the last on the lunar calendar. The meat is processed and shipped to needy Muslims in thirty countries.[2] Muslims around the world also offer animals in their homes or at local gatherings on the appointed day of sacrifice, *ʿīd-al-adhā*. Most pilgrims prefer qualified specialists in ritual slaughter to cut the throats of the animals, but some undertake the task themselves.[3]

Sacrificers lay hands on the victims to signify their submission to divine law and their gratitude that God accepts the animal as a substitute for their own lives. That thanksgiving for divine mercy is a response to the story of Ibrāhīm (the name of Abraham in Arabic) offering his son and the ram being killed in his stead. For Muslims, as well as for Jews and Christians, Ibrāhīm is the exemplar of faith and the call to sacrifice his son is the test he passed, showing the way to please God.[4] As Muhammad testifies, "My Lord has guided me to a straight path, to an upright religion, to the faith of saintly Abraham, who was no idolater" (Qur'an 6.161).

Sacrifice as Test of Faith: Ibrāhīm and His Son

The story of Ibrāhīm and the near-sacrifice of his son is also recounted in the Qur'an. After God granted Ibrāhīm's prayer for "a righteous son," and the son had "reached the age when he could work with him, his father said to him: 'My son, I dreamt that I was sacrificing you. Tell me what you think.' He replied: 'Father, do as you are bidden. God willing, you shall find me steadfast.'"

> And when they had both submitted to God's will, and Abraham had laid down his son prostrate upon his face, We called out to him, saying: "Abraham, you have fulfilled your vision." Thus do we reward the righteous. That was indeed a bitter test. We ransomed his son with a noble sacrifice and bestowed on him the praise of later generations. "Peace be on Abraham!" Thus do We reward the righteous. He was one of Our believing servants. (Qur'an 37.100–113)

These verses appear in the *sūrah* or chapter with this title: "Those Who Set the Ranks or Draw Themselves in Ranks" (as in battle formation).

The reference is to believers who resist evil by bearing witness to the one God, particularly those prophets who came before Muhammad.

The opening *āyāt* or verses of this sūrah set the narrative template for the stories of Noah, Abraham, Moses and Aaron, and Elijah: The prophet appears and rebukes unbelievers, they refuse to repent, God delivers the prophet and his faithful followers from calamity, judgment is pronounced on evildoers, and the prophet is praised as one who performed righteous deeds and was a "believing servant" of God. Then the text shifts abruptly to confront challenges to Muhammad's message by those who claimed that Allāh has sons (or a son, as in Christian faith) or daughters (as in popular Arab belief). Muhammad and those standing with him, "who draw themselves out in ranks," take up the defense of the unity of God. These messengers of divine warning are in formation with all the prophets and they advance in confidence that "most surely Our host alone shall be the victorious ones." In this sūrah the passages about Ibrāhīm place him in the prophetic phalanx holding the line against idolatry and demonstrating heroic faith.

When we place the account of Ibrāhīm and his son in this wider literary setting, we see that both are represented as belonging to the ranks of true messengers and, like their fellow prophets, are tested. As a young man, Ibrāhīm attacked idols in his father's house, sarcastically calling on them to eat the offerings of food made to them. Like a Hebrew prophet, he accused the crowd that gathered of worshipping perishable works of their own hands rather than the divine creator of all things.[5] The enraged idolaters attempted to burn him alive, but God rescued him from the fire. In Kenneth Cragg's colorful rendering, Allāh says, "They meant to get him in their clutches but We made them bite the dust."[6] This record of Ibrāhīm's defense of God's supremacy is followed by his asking Allāh for a son who will be "righteous" (a moral precondition that foreshadows the son's obedience) and God gives him "news of a gentle son."

The drama of the sacrifice begins when the son reached the age of responsibility and thus the capacity to give consent. Ibrāhīm then discloses his terrible secret: "My son, I dreamt that I was sacrificing you. Tell me what you think." It is noteworthy that in the Qur'an God does not directly command Ibrāhīm to sacrifice his son. Rather than hearing the divine voice, Ibrāhīm "sees" the act in a dream. Then he asks what his son thinks, apparently seeking confirmation of the vision. The son declares himself "patient," willing to be acted upon as in his father's dream. In their mutual agreement, both father and son prove themselves to be "submitted." The father placed the son on the ground so that the victim was prostrate with his forehead touching the earth, as in the position of prayer. Only then does God interrupt the proceedings, which have taken on ritual form, to declare Ibrāhīm deserving of the reward of the restoration of his son. The divine voice confirms that the vision was "a bitter test" and that God himself "ransomed" the son with "a noble sacrifice," apparently referring to the animal substitute.

The ram caught by its horns in a thicket plays an important role in Jewish interpretation of Genesis 22, but the animal is not mentioned in Qur'an 37. Only in a later tradition do the horns of the ram feature in reports that they were hanging from the *Ka'bah*, the stone cube in the center of the Sacred Mosque in Mecca around which pilgrims circumambulate as part of the rituals of pilgrimage. Some commentators take this account as proof that the son in Qur'an 37 must have been Ismā'īl (the name of Ishmael in Arabic). According to Islamic tradition, the first Ka'bah was built by Adam and later restored by Ibrāhīm and Ismā'īl, whereas Ishāq (the name of Isaac in Arabic) is never reported to have been in Mecca. Further, Islamic tradition understands the phrase, "your only son" to refer to Ismā'īl since he was born fourteen years before Ishāq.

Jewish commentators, however, argue that Isaac was the only son *left* to Abraham, since the patriarch had earlier banished Hagar and Ishmael, giving them up for dead. Further, the account of the sacrifice is immediately followed in the Qur'an by reference to Ishāq, using the same phrase to describe God's announcement of his birth that was used to announce the birth of the son of the sacrifice: "We gave him the good news of Ishāq." Ishāq is also named "a prophet among the good ones" (Qur'an 37.112), a status that the actions of "the son" in the earlier story would seem to merit. Muslims, however, counter that the reference to Ishāq comes only after the story of the near sacrifice; therefore, that son must have been Ismā'īl.

Debate over the identity of the son continued for centuries.[7] Today most Muslims assume that the son was Ismā'īl. One consequence of this identification is that Ismā'īl is drawn into the ranks of the prophets by undergoing the test of faith. The Qur'an does not mention an altar or an upraised knife, but Ibrāhīm is prepared to kill his son when God calls off the sacrifice. As in Genesis, without the divine voice, the son would have died. But there are important differences in the two accounts. First, Ismā'īl is not a mere victim, but an agent who consents to his own death in submission to divine will. Second, Ibrāhīm's intention is not concealed in secrecy or "indirect discourse." He is entirely transparent about his dream and even asks Ismā'īl what he thinks about it. For his part, Ismā'īl is not perplexed about the absence of a lamb because he knows he is to be the victim. Third, neither in the Qur'an nor in later exegesis (tafsīr) does a dissenting voice interject a cry of horror at the prospect of the sacrifice. The only note of grief is sounded in a version of the story recorded by the tenth-century commentator al-Kisā'ī in which Sarah asks to be comforted after the sacrifice by receiving the bloody shirt of her son, identified in this account as Ishāq.[8]

Other misgivings about the deed are curiously represented by non-human objects that resist the sacrifice of the son. In a version transmitted by Al-Tabarī (d. 923), Ibrāhīm drew the knife across Ishāq's neck but hit only a protective copper sheath God placed there. In the retelling by al-Kisā'ī, the knife turned away from the throat of the son, saying, "Do not blame me, O prophet of God, for thus am I commanded to do!" Then the ram spoke up, offering itself for sacrifice in place of the son, and identifying itself as the same ram offered by Hābil (the name of Abel in Arabic), son of Adam. In the meanwhile it had been grazing in Paradise awaiting this moment of redemptive surrogacy. (Recall the rabbinic tradition that the ram had been waiting to be sacrificed since the dawn of creation.) When Ibrāhīm turned to untie Ishāq, he found his bonds already loosed by God and Ishāq ready to offer up the ram. White fire flared from heaven, consuming the ram—all but the head, which father and son took home with them. Upon hearing their story, Sarah fell on her face in grateful prayer to God.

Other versions of Sarah's response in the commentarial tradition also represent her as fully compliant with divine command. In one, Shaytān (Satan in Arabic) informs her of Ibrāhīm's plan and she first responds with disbelief; but when she learns that God ordered the sacrifice, she replies, "It is best that he obeys." She thus aligns herself with the parallel responses of Ibrāhīm and Ishāq and indicates her sharing their surrender to divine will. In another rendering, the son is Ismā'īl, and Iblīs (proper name for Satan in Arabic) informs his mother Hagar of the impending sacrifice. She protests that Ibrāhīm loves his son too much to harm him; but when Iblīs tells her that God commanded it, she answers, "If his Lord commanded him to do it, then one should surrender to the command of God."

In the Qur'an and Islamic interpretive tradition, Ibrāhīm's near-sacrifice of his son is treated as an example of the generic testing to which God submits every prophet and the prophet's family, not the singular nightmare of ethical contradiction that kept Kierkegaard awake nights. The Qur'an has no more interest in the subjectivity of its protagonists than does the Bible, except to make clear that neither Ibrāhīm nor Ismā'īl suffers from a divided mind. Ibrāhīm submits directly to divine will and for that he receives the reward due "the righteous." Whether his act deserves moral approval does not arise for most Muslims. Since God has the final word on what constitutes "the good," there is always harmony between obedience to God and ethical duty. From the position of Islamic tradition, Ibrāhīm can be moral *only* by enacting the vision of sacrificing his son.

Given that moral assurance, does Ibrāhīm offer the sacrifice in any suspense at all? One clue is that Ibrāhīm acted on the basis of a vision rather than a direct command. As vivid as the dream may have been, and as reassuring as Ismā'īl's compliance must have been, Ibrāhīm has no certainty that the sacrifice is required, let alone that it will enhance his relation to Allāh. The devil also knows how to stir imagination in the night. So the spare account in the Qur'an leaves the reader with the impression that Ibrāhīm undertook risky business that day. The explanation of the dream as a "test" only underscores that fact. Tests, unless they are rigged, cannot determine who will pass and who will fail. When Ibrāhīm cast his son into the dust, he could not know what would happen next. As it turned out, God spoke at that moment, "Abraham, you have fulfilled your vision." As in Jewish and Christian traditions, the story has a happy ending and both Ibrāhīm and his son emerge as heroes of faith.

As a result of his unconditional obedience, God designated Ibrāhīm "a leader of mankind" and issued the challenge, "Who but a foolish man would renounce the faith of Abraham?. . . . When his Lord said to him, 'Submit,' he answered, 'I have submitted to the Lord of the Universe'"

(Qur'an 2.124, 131). This terse dialogue signifies faith as total surrender of human inclination to divine will. The patriarch does not hesitate nor does the son protest; their absolute submission is the measure of the purity of their faith. Here it is important to note that the Arabic words for Islam, peace (*salaam*), and submission (*muslim*) are built on the same root, represented by *s-l-m*. Thus, Islam is conventionally represented as a religion that seeks peace through surrender to divine law. That representation is often extended to interpret "submission" as blind obedience to authoritarian rulers and to depict Muslims as passive followers with no critical minds or independent wills. That stereotype has been thoroughly criticized, beginning with Edward Said's groundbreaking work, *Orientalism*.[9]

What we can add to that critique in light of this story is that both father and son exhibit decisive agency in their agreement to carry out the sacrifice. The critical issue is not whether the decision fully engaged their wills—it clearly did—but whether their willingness to offer the · son's life on the basis of a dream evoked any ambivalence. Since Islamic versions of the story represent the same exchange of concrete value for abstract vision as in Jewish and Christian traditions, are there also ways to read Islamic texts "against themselves" for indications of reservations about the sacrifice? For example, scholar of comparative religion Yvonne Sherwood discusses interpretive traditions in both Judaism and Islam which portray the son as concerned that he might reflexively resist the knife or that his father might falter out of pity for him.[10]

Sherwood also reminds us that in Jewish *midrashim* it is Sarah, "specifically, the body of the mother," that becomes "a major site of ethical opposition to the 'sacrifice.'" She notes that in Jewish and Islamic interpretations, "Abraham and obedience to God as 'hypergood' are held in tension with the protests of the 'sacrificed' in the graphic, audible form of Isaac's kick and Sarah's scream." In Islamic texts, it is Sarah who "utters a scandalized 'Why?' when told what Ibrāhīm is up to, or angrily accosts him on his return, 'You would sacrifice my son and not inform me?,' so castigating the patriarch who thinks that he lives in the rarefied a-social air of the mountaintop where men live alone with their sons and their God." Sherwood comments that in Sarah's scream "the proclamation of redemption and its subversion collide in the very same breath." In one Shiite rendering of the story, Sarah inspected her son and "saw the mark of the knife scratched into his throat. She complained bitterly, and a sickness appeared which killed her."[11] As in Jewish tradition, Sarah dies in protest against her husband's choice to kill their son to fulfill his dream of what God required.

In her groundbreaking study of sacrifice in the kingdom of Morocco, anthropologist M. Elaine Combs-Schilling (1949–2016) argued that the "Islamic myth of Ibrāhīm poses the dilemma of life and death as a battle between God and nature . . . the myth elicits the opposition by demanding that the natural father slay the natural son at divine command." She continues, "The myth then offers the means by which the ultimate conflict between eternal God and transient earth can be resolved, by males of faith sacrificing. Males are established as the worthy link precisely because they can distance themselves from earthly concerns. The cry of nature would be to spare the son; the call of God is to slay him." Combs-Schilling interprets the story as setting the basis for male authority to negotiate with the sacred and to exclude women from religious leadership because they lack the spiritual strength to rise above nature to achieve "transcendent birth." Moroccan women she interviewed typically said that Hagar, who remains unnamed and unnoticed in the story, would have tried to save her son and, while understandable, her action would have "lost for all humanity the hope for divine connection." By contrast, the story establishes the superior cultural position of men "who must handle collective decision making and transcendent questions precisely because they can distance themselves from nature."[12]

Combs-Schilling explicitly rejects the theory of sacrifice as gift in favor of interpreting sacrifice as "an active attempt at intercourse with the sacred" (the knife piercing the ram's throat acting as a substitute for the phallus penetrating the vagina) by a displacement of female childbearing with spiritual rebirth through male mediation. As a consequence, "the Ibrāhīm myth and the ritual of sacrifice build a male-paved pathway to transcendence." After this trenchant analysis, she issues the challenge of considering an alternative means of mediation, namely "that females could make the divine connection on behalf of the whole and that their ability to give natural birth specifically prepares them for doing so." This counter-reading of the story suggests that the divine may be reached through natural creativity and affection, as Grace Jantzen later argued. In these feminist readings, sacrificial death is displaced as the means of reaching transcendence by the creative power of flourishing life.

In a further exercise of reading the texts against themselves, Sherwood highlights the voice of Satan in raising questions about the sacrifice, particularly the wisdom of setting a precedent that could lead other fathers to decide that offering their sons is what God requires. Satan's "recurring presence in retellings of the sacrifice seems to indicate . . . that the 'sacrifice' is his greatest opportunity, for it is at this point that God's case (and scripture) seems to be at its most vulnerable." Satan is always at his best when he brings divine principles into contradiction with themselves. Here he exploits the moral dilemma to its fullest extent, as if, Sherwood slyly suggests, "he somehow got his hands on an advance copy of *Fear and Trembling*." But one does not need to be a modern philosopher to detect the tension between natural morality and religious faith in this story, as its series of interpretive retellings in the tradition demonstrates.

Despite the representation of all the actors as pious submitters to the divine call, what should we make of the indications of resistance to the sacrifice? The knife refuses to cut, the ram offers itself as a more fitting victim, the son is apprehensive, the mother is devastated, and even Satan has reservations. Carol Bakhos notes that Muslim sources, as well as Jewish and Christian, "carry with them voices, cries, whimpers, and shouts, muffled by the sweep of time, that resist the ungodly Godly command."[13] By setting up Ibrāhīm as "a leader of mankind," Islamic tradition cannot escape the same moral ambiguity about sacred violence that Jewish and Christian traditions do in designating Abraham as an exemplar of faith.

Because Ibrāhīm lived before Moses or Jesus, Islamic tradition presents his belief in one God and his surrender to God as the original form of worship and service to which all humanity should return. Jews and Christians, called "people of the book" because both traditions possess written revelations, are particularly urged to accept the universal monotheism of Ibrāhīm's faith and the community around Muhammad as the custodians of true belief. "Abraham was neither Jew nor Christian. He was an upright man, one who surrendered himself to God. He was no idolater. Surely the men who are nearest to Abraham are those who follow him, the Prophet, and the true believers" (Qur'an 3.68). Muhammad had hoped that Jews and Christians would accept his message as the culmination of the history of divine revelation that began with Torah and continued through Jesus's prophetic teachings in the Gospels, but he encountered fierce resistance from both—as well as from worshippers of desert spirits (*jinn*) and deities in Mecca.

Sacrifice as Defense of Community: Muhammad in Medina

The radical nature of the monotheism proclaimed by Muhammad is indicated by the Arabic phrase, *lā ilāha illā Allāh*, meaning "No god but God!" Over twenty-three years Muhammad received revelations and followed what he considered divine instruction to "cry," or recite, the message to the people. That recitation contained guidance for both individual life and social order. Muhammad's preaching in Mecca was done in the center of the city, near the great stone enclosure called the Ka'bah, which housed images of the deities and spirits worshipped in Mecca and those honored by people of other lands who visited while there on caravan business. It was also a traditional pilgrimage site and place of sacrifice. Muhammad later made it the center of Islam after he had removed and destroyed all the idols.

Muhammad was not an overnight success, but after a decade of preaching he had won enough converts to alarm the nobility in Mecca, and they began to plot against his life. Muhammad escaped from Mecca in the *hijrah* or "migration" of 622 CE to Yathrib, a city later called Medina (from *madīnat al-nabī* or "city of the Prophet"), where he formed the first Muslim community (*ummah*). Because this date marks the beginning of Muhammad's organizing the first Islamic government, it is the point at which the Muslim calendar begins. Muslims mark the dawn of the new, and final, era of history at the first complete enactment of divine law in political, social, and religious order. In Medina divine unity (*tawhīd*) became manifest in cultural form; the revelations Muhammad recited (*al-Qurān* means "recitation") provided the prescription for human conduct.

In Medina, Muhammad united Arab and Jewish tribes under a constitution which provided that the Muslims "and those who follow and are attached to them and fight alongside them . . . form a single community to the exclusion of all [other] men." Further, "to the Jew who follows us belongs help and equality. He shall not be wronged nor shall his enemies be aided. The peace of the believers is indivisible."[14] It was a lofty ideal of mutual support and harmony that proved impossible to sustain. During this time Muhammad also received the revelation to change the direction of prayer (*qiblah*) from Jerusalem to the sacred mosque in Mecca (Qur'an 2.144), further distinguishing Islamic religious practice from that of Jews and Christians. Of the three Jewish tribes brought under the Constitution of Medina, two were eventually exiled and forced to leave their goods behind.

The third, known as the Bani Quraiza, colluded with Meccans in the key Battle of the Trench in which the Muslims narrowly escaped defeat. According to a traditional story (*hadīth*) transmitted by the prophet's wife 'Ā'isha, Muhammad retired to his tent to bathe when the warrior angel Gabriel appeared, his head still covered with dust from the battlefield. Gabriel challenged the weary prophet: "You have put down your arms! By Allāh, I have not put down my arms yet." Muhammad replied, "Where (to go now)?" Gabriel said, "This way," pointing toward the tribe of Bani Quraiza. "So Allāh's Apostle went out towards them."[15] Thus assured of divine guidance, Muhammad's forces laid siege to the Jewish encampment. After the Quraiza surrendered, all six hundred males were executed and the women and children sold into slavery. While the historian of religion Karen Armstrong recoils from the "horrible incident," she interprets it in the context of the struggle for survival by the early Islamic community. By showing no mercy to traitors, Muhammad sent a strong warning to any other groups in Medina who resisted his leadership. She emphasizes, however, that the hostility was not extended to Jews in general, only to the rebellious tribes.[16]

The scholar of Islam, Malise Ruthven, observes that Muhammad regarded the elimination of "ideological opponents" as necessary because the new allegiance to Islam took precedence over loyalties based on kinship.[17] The Jewish tribe understood that as non-Muslims in Medina they were consigned to the status of *dhimmi*: under "protection," but subject to poll tax. They decided that, in the long run, their best interests would be better served under Meccan rule. How much military support they provided Muhammad's enemies is not clear, but their opposition to the terms of his government was forthright. Their collaboration with the Meccans undermined Muhammad's strategic goals, and their rejection of the conditions of his administrative order prevented the full implementation of Islamic law in Medina. That is, their political opposition ultimately threatened the fulfillment of the prophet's religious vision. The deaths of the Quraiza men, throats slit and heads severed from their bodies, were offered as sacrifices to redeem the Islamic ummah, not from its sins but from external threat to divine rule. In technical terminology, their sacrifice was not expiatory (to atone for sin), but apotropaic (to avert evil power).

John Esposito, the respected author on Islam, comments on the execution of the Quraiza that "it is important to note that the motivation for such actions was political rather than racial or theological."[18] While one appreciates the apologetic effort, it does not improve the moral judgment on massacre and enslavement to attribute them to politics rather than religion, especially since Islam offers guidance for the whole of life. As scholar of Islam Frederick Denny notes, "From Medinan times, Islam was considered both *dīn wa dawla*, 'religion and political order.'"[19] So the question is unavoidable: Were those tribes sacrificed for the sake of the vision of a utopian society? Whether we call the vision "political" or "religious" seems irrelevant. In either case, the sacrifices of Muslim fighters, enemy warriors, and traitors within were *all* required to protect the nascent Islamic community. According to one hadīth, Muhammad upon returning from battle said, "Know that Paradise is under the shades of swords."[20] Regardless of one's judgment about the Islamic vision of society under divine law, it is clear that the pattern of sacrificing concrete lives for an abstract ideal appears again.

Once Muhammad's place as a powerful chieftain was established, he sought peace with the Meccans to ensure safe passage to perform the pilgrimage. Only when the Meccans violated the treaty did Muhammad march on the city and receive the conversion of the city to Islam at the Ka'bah. He then removed from the stone house the images of spirits worshipped by the nomads and destroyed them. Muhammad returned to Medina, from which base he led Muslims in other battles and maintained administrative responsibility for the growing Muslim community. On his last pilgrimage to Mecca he exhorted his followers to remain unified in their loyalty to Islam.

Sacrifice as Religious Duty: Muhammad in Farewell Pilgrimage

In a recent study the scholar of religious studies, Gerd Marie Ådna, argues that during his last pilgrimage to Mecca, the only complete hajj he performed, Muhammad set the model of pilgrimage rituals, including sacrifice. Ådna defines sacrifice in Islam as a ritual act performed in obedience to divine command for the chief purpose of bringing the sacrificer closer to Allāh. As she points out, one prominent term for sacrifice in the Qur'an is *qurbān*, from the root *q-r-b*, meaning "to draw near." Ådna cites the claim of anthropologist Roy A. Rappaport (1926–1997) that ritual is the means human beings use to order and regulate their lives as distinctively human, and she applies it to interpret sacrificial rituals as confirming a Muslim "as a Muslim."[21] To be Muslim, Ådna avers, one must perform sacrifice, in solidarity with fellow Muslims, with the same sense of obligation that one offers daily prayers, in accordance with the Qur'anic imperative: "Pray to your Lord and sacrifice to him." She argues that Muslim identity is formed through ritual participation in accord with Rappaport's view that "by performing a liturgical order participants accept, and indicate to themselves and to others that they accept, whatever is encoded in the canon of that order."[22]

Ådna applies this principle by arguing that the proper intention (*niyya*) for performing hajj may be enforced through ritual enactments. She writes, "The Islamic sacrifice is understood as a bodily activity performed in a ritual way, expressing obedience toward the transcendent being called Allāh, who is not to be discussed or doubted by his followers."[23] That is, participation in sacrifice establishes a certainty of faith not possible on the basis of rational reflection alone because sacrifice is performed in the bodily arena where intention comes to consciousness.[24] Muhammad achieved such a unity of word and deed in his life, as indicated by the sobriquet assigned to him in early sources: "son of the two sacrifices." This curious title refers to the near-offerings of beloved sons by Ibrahīm and by the Prophet's grandfather, 'Abd al-Mutt'Ālīb, who nearly sacrificed Muhammad's father.

The earliest biographer of Muhammad, Ibn Ishāq (d. 767), recounts that 'Abd al-Mutt'Ālīb was digging the well of Zamzam (near what is now the Sacred Mosque in Mecca) when he vowed that, if he were granted ten sons, he would sacrifice one to God in gratitude. When his prayer was granted, he consulted a divination expert to select the victim by casting lots, using arrows as tokens. The expert consistently drew out the arrow indicating ʿAbd Allāh, the youngest and favorite son. Leading the boy by one hand and grasping a large knife in the other, his father prepared to fulfill his vow. Members of the family, however, protested that he should redeem the boy by sacrificing one hundred camels in his place.[25] In both this story and its Quranic prototype the son is spared by animal substitute. Ådna notes that the two sacrifices that formed the spiritual womb from which Muhammad was born "communicate the same message: obedience to Allāh is religiously praiseworthy, and willingness to perform such a hideous act is desired but stopped at the right point in time."[26] Clearly both the command and the cancellation were determined by God.

But why should the Almighty engage in such contradictory behavior? Why require sacrifice in the first place? Here Ådna is drawn to the proposal by William Robertson Smith that sacrifice is a means of communion between humans and divine beings, specifically a form of sharing that includes "especially the role of *receiving* blessings."[27] That interpretation of sacrificial offering, however, implies that the divine recipient might be *obligated* to reciprocate. The suggestion so offended Smith's belief in divine self-sufficiency that he rejected the view of sacrifice in ancient Israel as a gift that implied divine blessing in return. Ådna notes that in Islam God is also viewed as immutable and self-sufficient; therefore, sacrifice can neither benefit nor obligate him. Still, sacrifices are offered for a purpose and usually with some expectation of return on investment. Ådna acknowledges that the believer's hope to influence God by obedience is "an important and valid aspect" of sacrifice. She cites a charming hadīth in which Muhammad says God comes down from heaven each night, running toward sincere believers in eagerness to grant their requests. God's willingness to respond to believers' devotion with reciprocal blessings is a clear exercise of his mercy. Still, "in the Qurʾānic references to sacrifices there is a major ambiguity."[28] On the one hand, there is the explicit command to sacrifice; on the other, the statement that the "flesh and blood" of victims do not reach Allāh, only "your religious devotion will reach him." So why offer sacrifices at all?

Ådna finds in early Islam a clear answer to that question, namely, that sacrifice expresses gratitude and is designed to bring the one who offers the gift closer to God, who in turn acknowledges the gesture even if he does not need it. Further, in Islam the gift benefits those who *do* need it, the poor and hungry. In that way, the sacrifice of protein-rich animals, directed at divine command, nourishes those in need and restores them to full strength in the Islamic community. Thus, a sacrifice *to* Allāh becomes a gift *for* the house of Islam—and perhaps even enlarges it. In one hadīth, Muhammad makes sharing in the hajj sacrifice one of the actions that marks Muslim identity: "Allāh's Apostle said, 'Whoever prays like us and faces our *Qiblah* and eats our slaughtered animals is a Muslim and is under Allāh's and His Apostle's protection.'"[29]

The interpretation of sacrifice as a means of uniting Muslims in a common identity by sharing a meal, however, does not entirely satisfy Ådna. She insists the sacrifice "is not *only* inter-human communication that takes place in the Meccan context but also a communication between God and the believer(s) who praise and long for their Creator."[30] Ådna offers this resolution of the theological problem posed by sacrifice:

> My analysis does not show that the bloody sacrifice changes Allāh's actions, but it changes his *followers'* behavior and conduct and the relationship *between* the two entities, despite their differences in kind and ontological nature. . . . His people are obedient in order to fulfil their prescribed obligations, and they are not free to do whatever they want. *If they want to live in accordance with the divine law, they must follow Muhammad's rituals, including the sacrifice of one or more animals in the context of Mecca. The sacrifice is *not* an empty ritual but fulfilled when the believers empty themselves in obedience to Allāh.[31]

We cannot, of course, judge what does or does not "change Allāh's actions," but we can agree that those who follow the sacrificial rituals of Muhammad are shaped by their performance into more faithful Muslims.

As a divinely appointed prophet Muhammad is not only the one through whom God's will is revealed, but also the human model of submission to that guidance. Thus, his example was normative for the practice of sacrifice during hajj, settling such controversial topics as whether prayer or offerings of money could substitute for sacrifice (no), what animals are acceptable victims (domesticated sheep, goats, oxen, and camels) and how they should be killed: by turning the properly marked animal toward the *qiblah*, pronouncing the *bismillāh* ("In the name of God, the Compassionate, the Merciful"), and severing its jugular vein with a single stroke of the knife, then sharing the meat with others. One hadīth represents Muhammad as quite strict about the order of the prayer: "The Prophet said, 'Whoever slaughtered the sacrifice before the prayer, he just slaughtered it for himself, and whoever slaughtered it after the prayer, he slaughtered it at the right time and followed the tradition of the Muslims.'"[32] The insistence that the animal be consecrated *before* the sacrifice seems to enforce the religious significance of the action. Dedicating the victim to God, prior to slaughtering it for the poor, fuses tawhīd and ummah. Allāh remains the eternal and unchanging One; and through sacrifice (qurbān) Muslims "draw near" to him and to one another, united in their allegiance to Islamic faith.

Sacrifice through Alms (Zakāt) and Fasting (Sawm)

Two other pillars of Islam are intimately associated with sacrifice: *almsgiving* equaling 2.5% of income and *fasting* during daylight hours in the month of Ramadān. Daily prayers are not typically described in sacrificial terms as the smoke or pleasing odor of burnt offerings arising to God—as they are in Jewish and Christian traditions—since animals are not burned in the hajj sacrifice, but rather are slaughtered and their meat distributed to the needy. That difference is significant because it points to the functional value of animal sacrifice, made in obedience to divine command for the purpose of nourishing the community and providing the opportunity for believers to demonstrate compassion and generosity.

While prayer engages both mind and body in the worship of God, it is not regarded as a substitute for sacrifice nor for almsgiving and fasting. First, regarding almsgiving, "*zakāt* is a legal, obligatory act and considered part of one's service to God, as a technical part of worship. . . . *Zakāt* is not to be confused with charity. . . . Muslims are commanded to give charity often and freely, with emphasis on discretion and concern for the feelings of the recipients."[33] In the beginning of the ummah, wealthy people especially were expected to be as generous as possible. The daughter of Muhammad's close companion Abū Bakr consulted with the Prophet about the duty of almsgiving and he answered, "Do not shut your money bag; otherwise Allāh too will withhold his blessings from you. Spend (in Allāh's Cause) as much as you can afford."[34]

Charity as altruistic giving is necessary for maintaining community where there is disparity between rich and poor. To give on the part of the wealthy is a condition of their salvation; to receive with gratitude is a duty of those in need. Alms can even alleviate economic inequality. The wealthy of Medina are directed: "If your debtor be in straits, grant him a delay until he can discharge his debt; but if you waive the sum as alms it will be better for you, if you but knew it" (Qur'an 2.280). As for the poor, the tradition regards refusal to ask for help as unwillingness to accept one's lot determined by Allāh, and as obduracy that prevents others from exercising the virtue of charity. Only in utopian conditions immediately preceding the Day of Judgment will there be no one in need of almsgiving. In the meanwhile, the community depends upon the mutual support it signifies. Muhammad is reported to have said, "'A faithful believer to a faithful believer is like the bricks of a wall, enforcing each other.' While (saying that) the Prophet clasped his hands, by interlacing his fingers."[35]

The legal donation (*zakāt*) is required of all Muslims and must be a costly deduction from one's resources. As the Qur'an warns, "You shall never be truly righteous until you give in alms what you dearly cherish" (3.92). The original meaning of the term was "purification," and it may not be amiss to compare it with sacrifices of the "first fruits" of harvest in many cultures. The return of part of the bounty to God sanctifies the rest for ordinary use. The difference is that zakāt indirectly evokes divine approval by supporting the ummah that enacts God's will in the world. Zakāt is given *to* God *through* the poor. "Believers, give in alms of the wealth you have lawfully earned and of that which We have brought out of the earth for you; not worthless things which you yourselves would but reluctantly accept." Then, to emphasize that the donation assists others and does not enhance divine being, this addition: "Know that God is self-sufficient and worthy of praise" (Qur'an 2.267). The recipients are identified: "Alms shall be only for the poor and the destitute; for those that are engaged in the management of alms and those whose hearts are sympathetic to the Faith; for the freeing of slaves and debtors; for the advancement of God's cause; and for the traveler in need. That is a duty enjoined by God" (Qur'an 9.60). Like all sacrifices, goods given as zakāt cannot be retrieved. Muhammad said to one man who asked if he could reclaim a horse given to a poor man that "he who takes back his alms is like the one who swallows his own vomit."[36] Once given, the gift becomes "waste" to the giver.

While modern Islamic states, such as Pakistan, require Muslim citizens to pay a "poor tax" of 2.5% of assets, the amount of charitable donation above the obligatory zakāt is not limited. Although the tradition is clear that one must provide for one's own family first and the immediate community next, the degree of sacrificial giving beyond that reflects the measure of one's willingness to mirror divine compassion and generosity back to the divine source of all human possessions. The power of voluntary donation to the community is so great as to identify one as surrendered to God. One convert to Islam posed the question to Muhammad: "Before embracing Islam I used to do good deeds like giving in charity, slave-manumitting, and the keeping of good relations with kith and kin. Shall I be rewarded for those deeds?" The Prophet replied, "You became Muslim with all those good deeds."[37] The famous commentator on the Qur'an, Fakhr al-Din al Razi (1149–1209), linked reference to zakāt with the command to "pray to your Lord and sacrifice!" (Qur'an 108.2), where the precise verb for ritual slaughter (*nahar*) is used. In his interpretation, distributing the meat to those in need is necessary to fulfill the requirement to sacrifice.[38]

Fasting (*sawm*) is another ritual obligation of Islam by which, in Ådna's phrase, a Muslim is confirmed "as a Muslim." During Ramadān, the ninth month on the lunar calendar, every healthy Muslim is required to abstain from food, drink, and sexual activity from dawn to dusk. In modern times, restrictions also include refraining from smoking. Scholar of religion Glenn Yocum observed the month of fasting in late twentieth-century rural Turkey, where the Directorate of Religious Affairs in Ankara had issued the rigorous judgment that swallowing accumulated saliva was *makruh*, not forbidden (*haram*) but "disagreeable," and would detract from the religious reward of the fast.

Yocum's ethnography demonstrates not only the discipline of individuals, but also the collective nature of the deprivation. He observes that "fasting is fundamentally submission demanded of the body, the individual faster's body as well as the social body of the community." In short, fasting during Ramadān is an "extraordinary ritualization of central Islamic ideals of active, disciplined submission and egalitarian solidarity."³⁹ This particular case study demonstrates a theoretical understanding of collective sacrifice as creating social solidarity because all share in the rigors of self-denial, thereby strengthening their common bond.

Some of Yocum's respondents, however, emphasized the religious significance of fasting as a gift to God in gratitude for his receiving believers into paradise. The Qur'an makes the occasion for thankfulness the beginning of the revelations to Muhammad during the month of Ramadān. In one passage we read that God "desires you to fast the whole month so that you may magnify God and render thanks to Him for giving you his guidance" (2.185). Further, self-denial by fasting is held to have redemptive efficacy in a famous hadīth: "Fasting is a shield against hell."⁴⁰ One side of that shield is the expiatory power of fasting as compensation for wrongdoing. For example, a Muslim who kills another believer by accident must pay blood money to the relatives, except when the killer is indigent. In that case, "He that lacks the means must fast two consecutive months. Such is the penance imposed by God: God is all-knowing and wise" (Qur'an 4.95). Fasting, then, can evoke divine forgiveness, a standard function of sacrifice. In another hadīth Muhammad says that "whoever fasts in the month of Ramadān out of sincere faith, and hoping for a reward from Allāh, then all his previous sins will be forgiven."⁴¹

Thus, the other side of the shield of fasting faces paradise, as Muhammad promised, "There is a gate in Paradise called *Ar-Raiyan*, and those who observe fasts will enter through it on the Day of Resurrection and none except them will enter through it. . . . After their entry the gate will be closed and nobody will enter through it."⁴² As with other pillars of Islam, fasting can serve as a metonymic sign for the whole of submission to divine will, the sacrifice of self to the one God.

Sacrifice in Defense of Muslim Community: Jihād

Muhammad praised the sacrifice of those who died in the struggle or *jihād* to preserve the new faith. According to one often told story, upon returning from a battle Muhammad declared it the "lesser" jihād in contrast to the "greater" jihād of overcoming personal desires in submission to divine revelation.[43] Thus, sacrifice is early inscribed in Islam as a test of faith, and many examples are recorded in traditions about Muhammad and his companions. Only those who had conquered their own desires and ambitions were qualified to participate in active fighting on behalf of the Islamic ummah—and for them, engaging in jihād was of religious significance. Muhammad declared warfare justified to defend those displaced from their homes for professing faith in Islam: "Permission to take up arms is hereby given to those who are attacked, because they have been wronged. God has power to grant them victory: those who have been unjustly driven from their homes, only because they said, 'Our Lord is God'" (Qur'an 22.39). According to one hadīth, Muhammad said, "A single endeavor (of fighting) in Allāh's Cause in the forenoon or in the afternoon is better than the world and whatever is in it."[44] The reason is because, even if one is killed fighting for the cause of Islam, the heavenly world opens to receive the faithful warrior with eternal delights. Muhammad reassured those who mourned the fallen in battle: "Never think that those who were slain in the cause of God are dead. They are alive, and well provided for by their Lord . . . God will not deny the faithful their reward" (Qur'an 3.169).

A martyr who dies in pursuit of jihād is called *shahīd* or witness, one who testifies to the oneness of God (*shahādah*) and defends the truth of divine revelation, the authority and honor of the prophet Muhammad, and the peace and security of the Islamic community at the cost of one's life.[45] According to Islamic tradition, martyrs proceed directly to Paradise, where they enjoy gardens with running streams and "spouses of perfect chastity" (Qur'an 3.15), "bashful, dark-eyed virgins" (Qur'an 37.48), whom God created as "loving companions for those on the right hand" (Qur'an 56.35). The bloody clothing in which martyrs meet their death is not changed before burial so that they may bear the tokens of their suffering and courage into the divine presence. Then "they shall be decked with pearls and bracelets of gold, and arrayed in garments of silk" (Qur'an 22.23). They will drink from "rivers of wine delectable to those that drink it" (Qur'an 47.15), "purest wine (that will neither pain their heads nor take away their reason); with fruits of their own choice and flesh of fowls that they relish" (Qur'an 56.17). The extravagant descriptions of Paradise clarify the benefits to be expected for self-sacrifice in jihād.

The return of future reward for present suffering is a standard form of sacrificial exchange, the sort of trade-off we find in Christian tradition in Paul's speculation, "I consider that the sufferings of the present time are not worth comparing with the glory about to be revealed to us" (Romans 8:18). The problem that one cannot know with utter certainty what awaits after death is magnified by Islamic belief that only God determines the future. All matters, including the destiny of martyrs, depend on divine prerogative. For that reason, Muslims routinely end any statement about the future with the phrase, *in'shallāh* or "God willing." Despite the suspense that attends all sacrifice, the tradition represents Muhammad as so convinced of the efficacy of martyrdom that he expressed the hope to experience death in jihād repeatedly: "By Him in Whose Hands my life is! I would love to be martyred in Allāh's Cause and then get resurrected and then get martyred, and then get resurrected again and then get martyred and then get resurrected again and then get martyred."[46]

This robust enthusiasm for jihād is in tension with the recognition in the Qur'an that "fighting is obligatory for you, much as you dislike it" (2.216). Following Muhammad as the supreme example—the virtue called *imitatio Muhammadi* in parallel to the *imitatio Christi* in Christian tradition—requires setting aside personal preference and moral reservation in favor of divine command. Submission to Allāh's cause requires sacrifice of private judgment and acceptance of the affliction of the righteous: "Did you suppose that you would go to Paradise untouched by the suffering which was endured by those before you?" (Qur'an 2.214). Nowhere was this question more poignant than in the experience of those who split the early Islamic community after the death of Muhammad by their support of his son-in-law, Ali, as his successor. They are known as *Shī'at 'Alī*, from the Arabic phrase for "party of Ali"; and their history is marked by suffering and martyrdom.

Sacrifice of Martyrdom in Shī'a Islam

In 2003 the United States launched a war that defeated the regime of Saddam Hussein in Iraq. On June 28, 2004, the US-led coalition returned sovereignty to the Governing Council of Iraq, led by a president who was Sunni Muslim and a prime minister who was Shiite. The arrangement was an attempt to create a common government by political compromise. The strategy has not proven effective, in part because the original division of the two groups was precisely over the exercise of political authority. Such differences cannot be overcome by overlaying a European model of parliamentary cooperation because the political struggle is profoundly religious in its discourse. That is, Muslim politicians draw upon Islamic images and texts to legitimate their actions—just as politicians elsewhere appeal to "deep symbols" in their cultures.[47] When the Shīʿa split off and developed their own beliefs and practices, no one ruler could claim any longer to govern the entire "house of Islam." Thus, the ummah that Muhammad had labored to make the reflection of divine tawhīd was irrecoverably shattered, both in religion and politics.

For Shiites the "deep symbol" that expresses and sustains their identity as Muslims is *sacrifice*; and their paradigm of sacrifice is the martyrdom of Ali's son, Husayn, betrayed and killed by Sunni forces at Karbalā in Iraq in 680. The conflict began when the early Muslim community chose Muhammad's successor or *caliph*. Upon the death of a charismatic founder and leader, religious movements often face the choice between two types of successors: a member of the founder's family whose blood relation is a direct and tangible transmission of authority, or a loyal associate of the founder who shares the founder's vision and demonstrates skill in implementing it. In the case of the early Christian community, the choice came down to James, the brother of Jesus, who became leader of the church in Jerusalem, and Peter, Jesus's chief disciple. Muhammad had no surviving son, so the ummah had to choose between Ali, a member of Muhammad's family, and his faithful "companion," Abū Bakr.

According to one story, the choice became clear while the community was mourning the death of the Prophet. Entering the room filled with wailing, Abū Bakr declared, "If any of you has been worshipping Muhammad, let him know that Muhammad is dead. But if you have been worshipping God, then know that God is eternal and never dies." The story represents Abū Bakr as a wise upholder of the shahādah and faithful to Muhammad's testimony that "I am but mortal like yourselves" (Qur'an 46.6). It also implies that his choice as Muhammad's successor was a matter of consensus. Frederick Denny, however, points out that a small group, including Abū Bakr, selected him as leader and "presented this decision in a peremptory manner to the Medinan community, and it was accepted, but not without some degree of resentment."[48] While a vocal minority continued to support the claim of Ali, the majority accepted Abū Bakr as caliph.

Abū Bakr was elderly at the time of his appointment and in the two years of his rule countered early defections from the growing empire. His successor, 'Umar, was a highly effective military leader, the first caliph to be given the title, "commander of the faithful." The third caliph was 'Uthman, whose distinguishing achievement was to establish the official text of the Qur'an. 'Uthman gathered all extant written accounts of Muhammad's recitations, selected the versions he preferred, and then—in a master stroke of editorial power—burned all the rest. As a result, the text of the Qur'an was fixed; while debates over its meaning would continue, the content to be interpreted was rarely in question. 'Uthman, however, failed to inspire loyalty from fellow Muslims and was assassinated in his unguarded house by dissidents from Egypt.

Ali became the fourth caliph after the assassination of 'Uthman. His succession was disputed, however, because 'Uthman's relatives (including his nephew, Mu'āwiya, governor of Syria) believed that Ali had made no effort to defend 'Uthman and his family. In the tradition of blood vengeance, therefore, they sought Ali's life in compensation. Ali disappointed his supporters by agreeing to submit the matter of 'Uthman's murder to arbitration in which a judgment was given in favor of Mu'āwiya. Disappointed with what they regarded as Ali's weak leadership, some of his partisans withdrew support and became known as the *Khārijites* or "seceders." They were purists who tolerated no compromise and insisted that Ali had proven unworthy as a Muslim. Their armed resistance became a model for later reformers who fought Muslim rulers they considered corrupt. Ali was eventually assassinated by one of his own disillusioned supporters. The leadership of the Muslim community passed to his rival, Mu'āwiya, who established the Umayyad Caliphate in Damascus, beginning the long line of Islamic empires that ended with the defeat of the Ottomans in World War I. Because of this history, Shiites deny the authority of the first three caliphs and accept no hadīth transmitted through them.

Shiites continue to recognize only the authority of the descendants of Muhammad through Ali. They claim that Sunnis sought to eradicate the line of Ali, beginning with his eldest son, Hasan, who abdicated his right to the caliphate and retired to Medina. While many in the Party of Ali were disappointed, others explained his renunciation as an act of selfless compassion to avoid bloodshed among Muslims (the Syrian forces were overwhelmingly superior). Sunnis insist that Hasan died in his sleep, but Shiites charge that Mu'āwiya arranged to have one of his wives poison him and therefore regard Hasan also as a martyr. After Mu'āwiya's death, Shiites saw an opportunity to regain the caliphate from his son Yazīd. Ali's youngest son, Husayn, proceeded into Iraq with a small contingent of troops and his immediate family.

Some Shiites conclude that Husayn went knowingly into battle against hopeless odds because he intended to sacrifice himself in the hope of uniting Shiites in resistance to the government in Damascus. Encamped on the plain of Karbalā, west of the Euphrates River, Husayn's party was surrounded and cut off from their water supply. Negotiations failed when Husayn refused to pay tribute to Yazīd; in the ensuing battle all the Shiite fighters were killed. Husayn was holding his infant son, Abdullah, when an arrow struck the boy. Husayn raised the body above his head in a gesture of offering to heaven and cried, "Oh God, please accept this sacrifice (al-Qurban)." Political scientist Melissa Finn notes, "Abdullah was a *shaheed* (martyr and witness to excess and depravity) and *qurban* (sacrificial offering)."[49] Husayn's head was taken as a trophy and enshrined in the Grand Mosque of Damascus, where Shiites come to venerate his sacrifice.

Only a few family members survived the attack, including Husayn's sister, who was brought to Damascus and displayed in the mosque courtyard. But she defied Yazīd for his self-serving account of Husayn's killing. For her witness to the authority of the House of Ali she is revered by Shiites as Sayyida ("Lady") Zeinab. A shrine in her honor, financed by Iran, still stands in the Shiite neighborhood of Damascus despite bombing attacks by Islamic State fighters that have killed scores of people in the current Syrian civil war. The shrine has been a site of Shiite pride and the target of Sunni jihādist groups, so that Shiite pilgrims who dare to visit there today take upon themselves the risk of martyrdom. The possibility of suffering in defense of their faith is one that many Shiites already celebrate in annual re-enactments of the tragedy of Karbalā.

Shiites regard Husayn's slaying as a redemptive sacrifice and seek to participate in its efficacy on the anniversary of his death on 'Āshūrā, the

tenth of the first lunar month *Muharram*, with passion plays and processions of flagellants. The festival began in the tenth century with large
processions in Baghdad and became a major religious holiday during
the Safavid dynasty of Iran in the sixteenth century. The central ritual
event is the portrayal of the deaths of Husayn and his family in a passion
play or *ta'ziya*, a term signifying the "consolation" of mourning. The
actors are male, and women participate by funereal wailing or ingula-
tion. The ta'ziya extends over ten days and dramatically represents key
events on the plain of Karbalā, including the deaths of Husayn's sons
(one represented by an infant's coffin) and the capture of his sister and
other women. Spectators join in the ritual cursing of those responsible
for Husayn's death, agents of Yazīd who represent unjust rulers who op-
press defenders of true Islam, namely, the Shī'a.

Since 'Āshūrā rituals are performed in public in countries with Sunni-
dominated governments, such as Pakistan, they disrupt customary
diplomacy by revealing deep differences between Shiites and Sunnis.
According to the ethnographer Vernon Schubel, however, 'Āshūrā rituals "are not an invitation to hostility"; rather, they provide an opportunity for Shiites to demonstrate their personal allegiance to the "people
of the house" of Ali (*ahl al-bayt*), including his wife Fatima and Imams
descended from his line, "which [allegiance] is the core of Shi'ism."[50]

The climax of the passion play occurs when the actor portraying
Husayn dons his burial shroud, fully accepting his fate as a martyr. In
some locales, ritual identification with Husayn involves physical acts
of mourning, including self-laceration. Men and boys dressed in white
shrouds scourge their own backs with knives suspended from chains
connected to a wooden handle; some cut themselves with razors and
parade in the streets until their gowns are streaked with blood from
their wounded heads and torsos. Many cry in lamentation as they walk,
sometimes for as much as an hour. Their suffering testifies to their desire to identify with Husayn in his sacrifice for the sake of the house of
Ali and thus share in its expiatory effect.[51] Schubel emphasizes, however,
that he observed no visible signs of pain from the flagellants and no lasting injuries from their "wounds of devotion."

What Schubel concludes is that 'Āshūrā flagellation is different from
Christian scourging, which shares in the actual pain of Christ's suffering.
Shiite flagellation "is not a solitary act of pious mortification but rather

is the public performance of a deed of piety." As such, it serves two purposes: The participants "affirm to themselves the extent of their faith by risking personal bodily injury," and their protection from pain and infection provides tangible "proof of the miraculous intervention of the *ahl al-bayt* into this world, and this, they claim, constitutes proof of the entire Shi'i position." Like the martyrs of Karbalā, who entered Paradise directly, so the wounds of the flagellants "are in some sense as illusory as the deaths of the martyrs."[52] For those who object to the bloody display, Pakistan allows for the alternative of donating blood to hospitals. While this charitable action spares the participants public wounding, it retains the significance of the ritual inasmuch as "the shedding of blood symbolizes sacrifice (qurbān)."

Another aspect of 'Āshūrā rituals, as performed in Pakistan, which relates to sacrifice is fire-walking in imitation of the women of Ali's family at Karbalā who rushed into burning tents to rescue children. Schubel notes a precedent during colonial occupation of Pakistan when British officials colluded with Sunni rulers to block the way of the 'Āshūrā processions, "but miraculously the people were able to walk right through without being harmed." The story appropriates imagery of Karbalā to portray the persecution and suffering of Shiites under foreign and apostate rule. But there is an earlier allusion in the ritual of Shiite men and boys walking across live coals without visible pain or injury, namely, the rescue of Ibrāhīm from idolaters who sought to burn him alive. By emerging unscathed from the bed of coals, these believers identify with Ibrāhīm, who was saved from becoming a burnt offering by divine intervention, and with his son also rescued from death. Schubel concludes, "The miraculous element of these performances . . . acts to convince non-Muslims and non-Shi'a of the efficacy of Shi'i religious beliefs and thus is a form of proselytization as well as an act of devotion."[53]

As the scholar of Islam, Heinz Halm, observes, the martyrdom of Husayn at the time was little more than the incidental removal of a pretender to the caliphate by the superior ruler. But in Shiite tradition, the event was a turning point that transformed the Shī'a from a minor political movement into a distinctive religious community with an alternative version of Islam.[54] What is particularly important for this study is the central role sacrifice played in that development. In the words of Mahmoud Ayoub, Lebanese Shiite and professor of Islamic studies, Husayn's death "served as a source of sorrow and a lesson of true sacrifice in the way of God and the Truth. It has also served as an example for the pious to imitate in their struggle against wrong-doing and tyranny."[55] Sacrifice in Shiite understanding is *productive* suffering, not mere victimhood; it advances ideals of righteousness and justice within Islamic community and in the world beyond. Self-sacrifice is offered as witness to divine revelation and investment in the eschatological triumph of the Mahdī, the divinely guided leader in succession from Ali who will rule over the utopian society to come. It is a hope of redemption parallel to Jewish hope of the messianic age and Christian expectation that Christ will return to establish the kingdom of God on earth.

Belief in the redemptive power of suffering also shapes Shiite understanding of the story of Ibrāhīm's near-sacrifice of his son. According to one tradition, Ibrāhīm lamented the divine command to offer his son and asked to sacrifice a sheep instead. God asked Ibrāhīm whether he felt greater pain over killing his son or from his prophetic foreknowledge that the grandson of Muhammad would die unjustly at the hands of his enemies. When Ibrāhīm began to weep in sorrow over the "wrongful sacrifice" at Karbalā, God said, "O Abraham, I have redeemed the grief you would have had about your own son if you had sacrificed him with your own hand, for your grief about al-Husayn and his death; and I have [therefore] given you the highest level of reward for misfortunes." The narrator of the story continues, "This is the meaning of [God's] statement (Qur'an 37.107): and we redeemed him with a magnificent sacrifice." The scholar of comparative religion, Reuven Firestone, notes that this innovative interpretation applies the story of Ibrāhīm to "the foundational narrative of Shi'ite Islam" by identifying Husayn with the ram offered in the son's place and affirming that "Abraham's grief over the future death of Husayn is accorded divine merit."[56] The lesson is that vicarious sorrow is the means of gaining divine favor and accruing merit transferable to others. By sharing in the grief of Ibrāhīm through the rituals of 'Āshūrā, Shiites not only demonstrate their allegiance to Husayn, but also derive a portion of the merit produced by the suffering of the house of Ali.

Because Shiites are fiercely loyal to the family of Ali, they insist that their *Imams*, divinely inspired leaders and teachers of esoteric wisdom, follow in authoritative succession from Muhammad and that their authority to govern is grounded in the Qur'an. The scholar of Islam Fuad Khuri notes that this "textual Imamate" is traced to the command in 26.214: "Admonish your nearest kinsfolk." Shiites "insist that upon this revelation, the Prophet gathered his folk in his house, and after they had eaten, he said to them while pointing to Ali, 'This is my guardian and successor, listen to him and obey his order.'"[57] In support of Ali's claim to be Muhammad's caliph, Shiites cite the hadīth: "Whoever takes me as Lord, Ali is his. May God lend support to whoever bids him loyalty, fight whoever takes him enemy, dishonor whoever fails him, and turn the truth with him in whichever direction he turns."[58] The last phrase suggests that Ali, as recipient and custodian of Muhammad's esoteric wisdom, both mediates the truth and determines it.

Accordingly, Shiites do not accept the Sunni declaration (in the tenth century) that no further additions to the legal tradition are legitimate and that all future decisions about Muslim conduct would be decided on the basis of precedent.[59] Shiites, on the contrary, believe that their Imams are not only capable of reaching authoritative interpretations of the Qur'an and issuing binding judgments (fatāwa), but also that they are inspired by God to discern deeper meanings in the Qur'an and to receive new revelations of truth. The latter claim evokes judgments of "heresy" against Shiites that lead to their persecution in Sunni areas. The imaginative expansion of Islamic theology by Shiites, based on their faith in Ali's divine wisdom and Husayn's sacrifice in its defense, has made them vulnerable to becoming sacrifices themselves.[60]

For Sunnis there are no prophets with religious authority after Muhammad. Their imams are those qualified to lead prayers in the mosque with no other privileged authority. For Shiites, however, the rightful successor of Muhammad is both heir of the Prophet's political authority and also trustee of Muhammad's esoteric religious knowledge. As such, Shiite Imams (usually capitalized to mark the difference from Sunni prayer leaders) possess four distinguishing qualities: supreme wisdom to interpret divine revelation infallibly; sinlessness in conduct and piety; succession by family line through Ali; and authority to mediate between Allāh and the people. That mediation is often accomplished by sacrificial discipline and martyrdom.

Because of their profound differences from Sunnis, Shiites supported the Abbasid challengers to the Umayyad caliphate—even though they fared little better under the new rulers. Under conditions of continued persecution from established Sunni authorities, however, the last of the Imams in succession from Ali is said to have withdrawn from public view (a deliberate concealment called "occultation"), waiting to return in the last day as the messianic *mahdī*. He is known as the "Hidden Imam" and each of the different branches of the Shīʿa identify him with their founding figure, but they share the common conviction that human government will never escape injustice and oppression until the Mahdī appears to establish divine rule on earth. In the meanwhile, Shiites live in a state of "perpetual rebelliousness," dramatically signified by the rituals of ʿĀshūrā which carry the potential for expressive protest against injustice as well as passive mourning. Khuri demonstrates the point from a speech by Shaikh Mahdi Shamsuddin of Lebanon in 1983: "In every rebellion, there arises a martyr. . . . from this awareness, Husain chose the path of martyrdom, the choice that helped preserve Islam and the conquests of Islam." Then the shaikh went on to describe the entire life of the believer as unending self-sacrifice for "a cause linked to God and His teachings."[61]

A wide variety of views and practices are included under the umbrella term *Shiism*. Like American religious denominations and political parties, such as Methodists and Democrats, "Shiites" are not a monolithic bloc arrayed against "Sunnis" who are often also wrongly represented as united in a single normative point of view. Rather, both are marked by internal divisions and dissension. What most Shiites do share is a sense of estrangement from the larger world of religious apostasy and cultural decadence, fierce loyalty to the "House of Ali" through their Imams, and faith in the power of sacrificial suffering to resist injustice and purify the soul. The dominant Shiite group today regards the twelfth Imam as the last of the rightful successors of Muhammad. Known as Twelver Shīʿa, they are dominant in Iran and officially adopted Shiite rule after the revolution that overthrew Shah Reza Pahlavi in 1978. Twelvers recognize as the Hidden Imam a descendant of the House of Ali, Muhammad ibn al-Hasan al-ʾAskari, who disappeared at the age of five in the year 874. They believe that he went into occultation and selects representatives to guide in his absence until his return.[62]

Twelver Shiites believe that their Imams represent the Hidden Imam, and the most honored among them are called "sign of God" (*ayatollah*).

They are believed to possess esoteric insight into the mystical meaning of the Qur'an and, like Muhammad, some are also political leaders, such as the Ayatollah Ruholla Khomeini (1902–1989), leader of the Iranian Revolution and Supreme Leader of the Islamic Republic of Iran. He sent Iranian military forces against the secular regime of Saddam Hussein in Iraq during a protracted war, urging his fighters to accept martyrdom in the course of jihād in imitation of Imam Husayn. When Khomeini called for Iranian youth by the tens of thousands to join the jihād against Iraq, they responded by marching to their deaths against superior weaponry. To inspire their devotion, Khomeini used the sacrificial language of Karbalā. Many boys went into battle against tanks with little but Quranic passages on scraps of paper to protect themselves. They were the actual sacrifices, lambs led to the slaughter, offered for the sake of defending the ideal of Shiite government. In short, "the willingness to self-sacrifice and martyrdom, as has been preached for centuries, were instrumentalized for the revolution and the war against the Iraqi aggressors."[63]

Martyrs in defense of true Islam have been part of the tradition since the battles of the Muslims under Muhammad. What is relatively new is the willingness to take one's own life in suicide attacks on the objects of jihād, specifically, those who oppose Islam and those who abet injustices. In the present context, some Shiites understand those enemies to be Israel and the United States. Applying the conditions of jihād to their loss of homes and land, some have initiated their own deaths, despite the explicit prohibition in the Qur'an to not "with your own hands cast yourselves into destruction" (2.195). Members of the Shiite "Party of God" (*Hezbollah*) in Lebanon have made their intention and motivation clear by strapping on explosives to march in 'Āshūrā processions, thus displacing symbols of sacrificial suffering with signifiers of militant action. The 'Āshūrā rituals are sacrificial reenactments that create real sacrifice by placing martyrdom within the cosmic drama of the struggle between good and evil.[64]

Closely allied to Shiite belief in the hidden meaning of divine truth known to their Imams is the conviction that certain mystics, known as "friends of God," are gifted with insight beyond that available to ordinary believers. Their intense devotion and independence from conventional teaching and practice, however, mark them as anomalous—and for that reason Islamic tradition expresses mixed feelings toward them. For their piety they are revered as "saints," but their radical claims to unity with Allāh, as well as their antinomian conduct and erotic attachments, attract accusations of *shirk*, associating themselves with God and claiming freedom from external regulation. They often describe their religious way as sacrificial, even to the extent of being consumed in the divine presence. They are known as Sufis.

Sacrifice as Annihilation of Self (Fanā') in Sufi Islam

The term *sufi* comes from the Arabic for *wool* and refers to the coarse garments worn by the early Sufis, perhaps in imitation of Christian hermits in Syria.[65] The name may also be related to a group of pious companions of Muhammad, called *ahl al-suffa* or "people of the bench." They spent most of their time in the mosque, performing prayers and acts of devotion, and they lived in poverty and ascetic deprivation. One of them, Abū Dharr al-Ghiffarī, was exiled from Medina during 'Uthman's caliphate for teaching that no one could be a sincere Muslim who possessed houses, land, or gold.[66] The formal Sufi movement began in the eighth century as a protest against the institution of the caliphate, whose rulers Sufis saw as more interested in gaining and keeping power in this world than in seeking closer union with God.

Their spiritual aspirations and political critique ally them in many ways with the Shī'a, and their leaders, called *shaykhs* or *pirs*, like Shiite Imams, are regarded as transmitters of eternal insight and imagined as cosmic centers around whom the lives of their followers revolve. For members of the order of the Persian Sufi poet, Jalal al-Dīn Rūmī, the dance of slowly twirling dervishes around their pir in reverent silence is a demonstration of this mystical claim. Rūmī is said to have begun dancing one day while passing through a bazaar, moved by the rhythmic hammering of the goldsmiths to slowly dance in a circle. His movements provide the example for members of his Mevlevi order in Turkey to this day.[67]

British student of mysticism, Martin Lings (1909–2005), quotes the eleventh-century mystic and theologian, Abū Hāmid al-Ghazālī: "A bird I am: this body was my cage. But I have flown, leaving it as a token."[68] Al-Ghazālī's words could refer to death, but Sufis believe that such sayings have another level of meaning, a significance not evident on their surface, an interior meaning hidden from most readers. For the one who knocks adeptly and persistently, a door will open and, behind it, a foretaste of that spiritual ecstasy that awaits true believers in Paradise. In other words, one can achieve the transcendence of the material body without passing through death. This aspiration is the goal of other mystics we have noted in Jewish and Christian traditions: to experience directly and without mediation timeless divine unity. That experience is nothing less than the sacrifice of individual identity and consciousness without expectation of reward or virtue. Beyond the sacrifices that express gratitude or loyalty or that contribute to the defense or purity of the community or that provide charity to those in need, the mystical sacrifice is free from interest in its outcome or future. Such self-abandonment is the least encumbered instance of Bataille's claim that "sacrifice is the antithesis of production."

While the relation between mind and body is a murkily complex philosophical question, and despite recent interest in the inescapable effect of embodiment on all thought and emotion,[69] the fact remains that mystics consistently distinguish between body and spirit. Mystics may insist that there is "no-thing" beyond the confines of the material world; but if there is no other reality at all "over there," transcendent and eternal, then what is the point of devotional service and ascetic exertion? Why sacrifice the body, with its interests and desires, if spirit is nothing but an epiphenomenal awareness of the body? Whatever integration of body and spirit religious mystics achieve (or endure), they do not equate it with identity. If the body is the vessel in which the soul is restrained, the purpose of gaining religious knowledge (*gnosis*) is to release the soul so that it may "fly upward" or "journey inward" to find unity with God who is pure spirit.

At the point of total illumination, all distinctions are obliterated and the individual disappears. That self-annihilation or *fanā'* is for a Sufi the highest form of religious experience, the true meaning of *islām* as ultimate surrender to Allāh. At the point of fanā', a Sufi passes beyond cognitive understanding of the unity (tawhīd) of God and directly realizes the truth that "God is One. He has no associates." At the *exoteric* or public level of meaning (*zāhir*) that phrase is a warning against idolatry. At the *esoteric* or private level of meaning (*bātin*) it is a verbal symbol of the mystic intuition that the self cannot claim an "association" with God for it has no reality "but God."

The Sufi practice of fanā' is an enactment of the confession of faith that "There is no god but God" (lā ilāha illā'llāh). As scholar of Islam Annemarie Schimmel (1922–2003) notes, Sufis refer to the lā or "no" as a sword that cuts off everything that is not God or as a broom that sweeps the inner self empty of all distractions.[70] In one story that illustrates the point, a shaykh was tested by a group of assembled scholars, who challenged him to explain the shahādah. In response, he began to recite. "When he said lā ilāha, he disappeared and when he said illā'llāh, he reappeared. Again he said lā ilāha and disappeared, then said illā'llāh and reappeared. The third time he disappeared on lā ilāha and reappeared on illā'llāh. The fourth time he said lā ilāha the entire crowd including the examiners disappeared and when he said illā'llāh they all reappeared."[71] For this demonstration, the shaykh was recognized as a "great treasure." By using the "sword of lā," he exposed the transitory nature of the human self. The master's trick is a parable, an allegory, whose meaning is that there is no reality but what God sustains. In the words of the Dutch Sufi master Frithjof Schuon, the central truth of mystical Islam is disclosed only through "an indefinite play of veiling and unveiling."[72]

In Islamic tradition, as in Jewish and Christian communities, mystics are often unable to find orthodox language in which to express their deepest insights. That deficiency can prove fatal, as it did for the Sufi master of Baghdad, Husayn ibn Mansūr (858–922), known as al-Hallāj, or "cotton carder," from his family's profession. The honorific title also carried the spiritual meaning that the master combed through and sifted the inner thoughts and motives of others. Hallāj gained repute for his rigorous ascetic disciplines, including severe fasting. He traveled to India and there spread his message of mystical love. Upon his return to Baghdad, he met opposition from both Shiite and Sunni groups who supported the status quo and feared that a spiritual revival among the people would be "dangerous for a society whose religious and political leaders lived in a state of stagnation."[73] At one point, Hallāj declared, "I am Absolute Truth (anā'l-Haqq)" as a dramatic way of bearing witness to his utter loss of self in the divine reality. By referring one of the ninety-nine revealed names of God to himself, however, he was suspected of equating himself with Allāh and eventually charged with shirk or idolatry. Because such presumption is condemned as blasphemous in the Qur'an, "it was not surprising that Muslims were horrified by al-Hallāj's ecstatic cry."[74]

To compound the charge of theological deviance, Hallāj also taught the inner meaning of ritual actions, such as the circumambulation during hajj. Hallāj said, "Proceed seven times around the Ka'ba of your heart." In even more radical teaching, he advised people to forgo pilgrimage and spend the money feeding and clothing orphans.[75] His enemies charged him with wanting to abolish outer ceremonies altogether and thus fostering an antinomian attitude among the people, "inspiring them to question the formal religiosity of the caliphs and the [legal experts] who upheld their authority." While Hallāj taught in public little more than what other Sufis claimed in private, his charismatic appeal threatened religious and political order.

Sunni authorities imprisoned and condemned Hallāj to a protracted torturous execution. Throughout the long ordeal Hallāj maintained his composure, offering prayers and forgiving his enemies for offering him as "a sacrifice."[76] He had often called upon simple believers to release him from the body in a hymn that began with these words: "Kill me, o my trustworthy friends, for in my being killed is my life." We have encountered similar expressions of self-sacrifice as the path to rebirth or spiritual transformation in Jewish and Christian mystical traditions. For Hallāj, "the compensation for having offered God unconditional love was the beatific vision, without an intervening 'I'"; that was fanā', the erasure of self in surrender to God.[77]

While his inner exaltation moved him to dance in his fetters to the gallows, his physical suffering was horrific. His executioners amputated his hands and feet, cut out his tongue, suspended him from a gibbet and left him exposed for two days before he was decapitated; they cremated the body and threw the ashes from a minaret into the Tigris River. His last words were reported as "All that the ecstatic wants is to be alone with the One." Hallāj achieved his final goal in his death, as the sacrificial martyr who bears witness to divine unity, the eternal flame that consumes everyone who seeks to embrace it. The Urdu poet Mirzā Asadullāh Ghālib of Delhi (d. 1869) described that witness in a couplet whose words inspired those who later suffered in the struggle for Indian independence: "The secret that is hidden in the breast is not a sermon: you cannot utter it in the pulpit, but on the gallows."[78]

The horrific fate of Hallāj was designed to be a cautionary example to anyone with similar ambitions to realize intimate unity with the One God without the mediation of established institutions or the regulation of traditional authorities. But why would a Muslim harbor such extreme religious aspirations? Why seek to be sacrificed for the love of God when one can be submitted to the law of God in the course of a natural life? Why are Sufis, to use their favorite analogy, drawn like moths to the candle?

In partial answer (complete explanation of human motivation is an illusion), the Sufi spiritual quest begins with two āyāt in the Qur'an. First, "We created man. We know the promptings of his soul, and are closer to him than his jugular vein" (50.16). Allāh is the vital power of existence and should, therefore, be remembered with each breath one takes, with each throb of one's pulse. Since God is the source of every being, it follows that God does not *exist* as a separate being. What *ex-ists* does so by virtue of "standing out" from being in general and "standing apart" from other beings in particular. But God cannot "stand apart" because God is in as well as beyond every being; that is why God's transcendent reality cannot be exhausted by the totality of beings. We have seen similar theological reasoning in the mystical traditions of Judaism and Christianity. What it means for Sufis is that a human being cannot be "associated" with God, not only because of God's incomparability, but also because God is not a being that can be thought of in comparison to other beings.

Uniting with God, therefore, cannot take place within the conventional world. Whether that union is called *event* or *experience*—both words with complex and troubled histories in the study of religion— one must "stand out" (the meaning of *ecstasy*) from oneself as a separate being to become one with God. That point brings us to the second Quranic verse that inspires the Sufi quest: "All that lives on earth is doomed to die [*fānin*]. But the face of your Lord will abide forever, in all its majesty and glory" (55.27). From this passage the Sufi master Abū l-Qasīm al-Junayd (d. 910) developed the teaching that the goal of meditation and prayer is fanā' or annihilation. In his book on the subject, Junayd positions the human being between two voids: nothingness from which God creates everything and extinction of self through mystical practice. He writes of God, "He annihilated my construction just as he constructed me originally in the condition of my annihilation."[79] The master explains this statement in cryptic terms that require the translator to resort to innovative typography: "He EX-isted their created nature in a sense other than their existence-in-themselves, a sense that no one can know but he and no one can find but he." One possible reading is that God drew every creature out of the origin of all being in divine reality and caused each one to "stand out" as an existent individual. But their true origin, the divine One to which they are destined to return, is unknowable by the finite mind. Thus, when mystics enter the divine presence it is only as (and the play on words can be rendered in English only roughly) "ecstatic existence."

Junayd insists that mystical experience entails struggle and loss for "the select of the select" because "they have been effaced from every trace and every signification that they find in themselves or that they witness of their own." When the ecstatic moment passes, the veil once again lowers over their true nature. As a result, "They choke on their own selves . . . and they come back to the categories of discursive reason. Grief settles in upon them." Why? Because no sooner does the Sufi begin to witness, to express in language what ecstatic existence is, than it disappears. Junayd notes that when the Sufi "is brought into presence and witnessing, veiling unfolds his presence, and all traces are obliterated in his act of bearing witness." That is the paradox: The servant of God is called to witness to divine unity, but language is an instrument of discrimination and division. As soon as the Sufi begins to speak, the union with God dissolves. In fanā' there is no subject to speak; in the world there is no object to be spoken of. In the gap between there is no certainty, only the yearning to recover the presence of God and "awaiting his command—the command of Allāh be done." Junayd here echoes others in religions of Abraham who offer themselves in self-sacrifice to God with the words, "not my will, but Thine be done."

Nearly all mystics recognize that one cannot remain indefinitely in ecstatic trance. To manifest the love and justice of God, one must resume activity in the world of duration and communal responsibilities. For most Sufis the very return to ordinary activities is a spiritual resurrection. Islamic tradition teaches that God creates the state of the world anew in each passing moment, thus the mystic's reappearance in society is further evidence of divine grace, even though it is re-entry into a world of pain. As Denny comments, "When one is united with God, one is absent from the world and the self. But then the Sufi returns to his or her normal self and the mundane world and in returning experiences great sadness and suffering."[80] The Sufi sacrifice is twofold: The hidden core of the self is extinguished in the divine presence, and the visible individual who returns to the world is given in service to others. As a contemporary shaykh reminds his readers, "Now Allāh says through the Prophet Muhammad that those who are loved most by Allāh are those who serve the creatures of Allāh."[81]

The dialectic of suffering and ecstasy, service and rapture, that marks the Sufi way of self-sacrifice was dramatically illustrated in the life and writings of the best-known Sufi in the West, Jalāl al-Dīn Rūmī (1207–1273), who aroused opposition in part because of his admiration for Hallāj. Writing three centuries after Hallāj's sacrifice for the truth of fanā', Rūmī defended the martyr-mystic's scandalous assertion, "I am Absolute Truth," by calling it less presumptuous than saying one is a servant of God. "The man who says 'I am the slave of God' affirms two existences, his own and God's, but he that says 'I am God' has made himself non-existent and has given himself up."[82] In his poetry Rūmī imagines the natural world testifying to its oneness with the Creator by uttering the words of Hallāj and another Sufi who declared himself the presence of divine majesty: "The ground cries out, *I Am Truth* and *Glory is Here*, breaks open, and a camel is born out of it."[83] If the earth, without mind or spirit, is so imbued with divine presence that it bursts forth with creative power, so much more the mystic who realizes "emptiness" as a state of total surrender of will to God.

In that condition, the "Absolute works with nothing. . . . Try and be a sheet of paper with nothing on it. Be a spot of ground where nothing is growing, where something might be planted, a seed, possibly, from the Absolute" (15). For Rūmī, God was divine friend and lover in whose embrace he was both extinguished and energized. In the preface to the second book of his voluminous collection of couplets called the *Mathnawī*, Rūmī asserts that "God loves you" is "the only possible sentence. The subject becomes the object so totally that it can't be turned around. Who will the 'you' pronoun stand for, if you say, 'You love God'?" (274). In this sense of complete absorption in the divine lover, Rūmī can say, "The way is full of genuine sacrifice."

When consciousness is reduced to pure receptivity, the individual gives up all interest in personal desire and agency and forfeits any investment in the future. "They say there's no future for us. They're right. Which is fine with us" (2). "The moment is all there is" (86). Freedom from concern about what comes next is so extraordinary that Rūmī regarded it as a divine quality: "Forget the future. I'd worship someone who could do that. On the way you may want to look back, or not, but if you can say *There's nothing ahead*, there will be nothing there" (205). "*In the future, in the distance*, those are illusions. Taste the *here* and the *now* of God" (242). In these statements Rūmī teaches that self-sacrifice makes one as free from the limits of time and anxiety about productive achievements as God is. As Bataille remarked, in sacrificing to the deity, one casts the gift as into a furnace so that "in sacrifice the offering is rescued from all utility."[84] As Rūmī puts it, "The only real customer is God" (46). God is not anguished by fear of the future; but humans are bound by time in both directions. Guilt ties us to the past that we cannot change and worry makes us obsess about a future we cannot determine. Rūmī lays both burdens on the altar of sacrifice where divine love reduces them to ashes.

The prominence of the imagery of burnt offering in Rūmī's poetry is remarkable. "Last year, I gazed at the fire," he writes in one couplet, "This year I'm burnt kabob" (7). He calls it a "miracle-sign" that "you sacrifice belongings, sleep, health, your head, that you often sit down in a fire like aloes wood" (11), both fragrant and healing. Working the familiar image of a candle becoming entirely flame—"In that annihilating moment it has no shadow"—Rūmī invites us to look at the guttering stub "as someone who is finally safe from virtue and vice, the pride and the shame we claim from those" (23). "What is it to know something of God? Burn inside that presence. Burn up" (62). Again, "I am scrap wood thrown in your fire, and quickly reduced to smoke. I saw you and became empty." But the sacrifice has the paradoxical effect of both obliterating existence and creating more existence by enlarging the capacity of the Sufi to enrich the world by becoming translucent to divine light. Just as "the only way to measure a lover is by the grandeur of the beloved," so Rūmī advises, "Judge a moth by the beauty of its candle" (266).

In his work oddly titled *Fīhi mā fīhi* (Barks translates, *In It What's in It*, and comments it may indicate the same content as in the *Mathnawī* or "it may be the kind of hands-thrown-up gesture it sounds like"), Rūmī expands on the image. "Reason is like a moth, and the Beloved is like a candle. Though the moth cast itself into the flame and burn and be destroyed, yet the true moth is such that it cannot exist without the candle, much as it may suffer from the pain of its immolation."[85] The lover of God cannot escape sacrificial fire, any more than a cotton ball placed next to a candle in bright sunlight. The light of the candle blends with that of the sun, just as "that candlelight you can't find is what's left of a dervish" (173).

Even when Rūmī uses erotic allusions, the cost of devotion is total. "I would love to kiss you," the poet sings to God and receives the answer, *"The price of kissing is your life"* (37). The place of the divine is the abattoir of sacrifice:

> In the slaughterhouse of love, they kill
> only the best, none of the weak or deformed.
> Don't run away from this dying.
> Whoever's not killed for love is dead meat. (270)

When every attempt to resist the divine allure is overcome, "when you hear *Checkmate*," then you "can finally say, with Hallaj's voice, *I trust you to kill me*" (177). While Rūmī was not a world-denying ascetic (he was married twice and had two children), his religious poetry is filled with recurrent references to death as the closest analogy to mystical ecstasy. In one poem he imagines a lover telling his beloved how much he loved her, "how faithful he had been, how self-sacrificing." She replies, "You've done the outward acts, but you haven't died. You must die." He fell back, "opened like a rose that drops to the ground and died laughing"; it was his "gift to the eternal" (212). Sufis celebrate the anniversary of Rūmī's death on December 17 as his "wedding night," when his union with God was consummated.

If the mystical experience is self-annihilation, is it simply a nihilistic plunge into eternal silence and darkness: a lonely, if ecstatic, spiritual suicide? On the contrary, for Rūmī, the loss of ego in the divine presence is joyful liberation reflected in human love and companionship.

For one thing, the intensity of union with God is not a permanent state of mind. As Bataille observed, if one surrenders unreservedly to immanence (undifferentiated merging with the sacred), then one "would fall short of humanity." For another, it was precisely in human relations that Rūmī found the divine as manifest—and most clearly in his close friend, a wandering dervish named Shams. They engaged in such intense extended conversations that Rūmī's family and friends resented the dervish's influence on the one they called Maulana or "master." They believed Shams compromised Rūmī's urban sophistication and scholarly interests. One night, Shams was called outdoors and never seen again, apparently assassinated with the collusion of Rūmī's youngest son. The devastating loss drove Rūmī to even deeper mystical experience, but not without an appreciation for companions and the footprints they leave for others to follow. "Rushes and reeds must be woven to be useful as a mat. If they weren't interlaced, the wind would blow them away. Like that, God paired up creatures, and gave them friendship" (247).

Mystical quest for union with God may be assisted by teachers and friends, but finally the one who longs to die to self in the divine presence must do so alone, without direction or even orientation. For in that sacrificial moment, all sense of place is gone. Just as the chain of time dissolves into the knife edge of the present *now*, so the expanse of space collapses into the knife point of a single *here*. "Inside the Kaaba it doesn't matter which direction you point your prayer rug!. . . . The love-religion has no code or doctrine. Only God" (167). As theoretical physicist Stephen Hawking said when someone asked what is north of the North Pole, "That is a meaningless question," so for the mystic located at the center of reality there is no point of reference for ritual or thought or language as the instrument of analysis that turns even God into a discrete object to be explained. By contrast, "a gnostic says little, but inside he is full of mysteries, and crowded with voices" (162). "Theologians mumble, rumble-dumble, necessity and free will, while lover and beloved pull themselves into each other" (180). But is it all quiet satisfaction and ecstatic fulfillment? What about the *risk* of self-erasure? What of those moments when the divine lover is silent, when no reciprocity is evident? Rūmī tells the story of a man who was calling on the name of God in the night, when a cynic asked him whether he had ever received a response. The man was taken aback, quit praying, and fell asleep. He dreamed that the figure of Khidr, the guide of souls, asked him why he stopped praying. "Because I've never heard anything back," the man replied. Khidr said, "This longing you express *is* the return message." "The grief you cry out from," Rūmī adds, "draws you toward union" (155). The yearning for the absent Friend, intensified by the self-denying discipline of prayer or fasting or poverty, is the awareness of distance from the transcendent and thus the pain of unrequited love. That very pain, however, is the sign that the sacrifice is genuine—offered without strings attached, plunging like the moth into the incinerating flame of the candle.

One of the most impressive examples of non-attached devotion to God was the Basra Sufi, Rabiʿa al-ʿAdawīyya (d. 801). She was said to have run through the streets of the city, carrying a torch and a bucket of water. When asked what her action meant, she replied, "I am going to burn paradise and douse hell-fire, so that both veils may be lifted from those on the quest and they will become sincere of purpose. God's servants will learn to see him without hope for reward or fear of punishment."[86] In her own devotions, she offered this prayer: "O Lord, if I worship you out of fear of hell, burn me in hell. If I worship you in the hope of paradise, forbid it to me. And if I worship you for your own sake, do not deprive me of your eternal beauty."[87] Her long hours of prayer were legendary and her ascetic self-denial demanding, yet she insisted that her sacrifice was given without interest in reward. She meditated on flames of self-immolation. She once urged another Sufi master, "Like wax, give light to the world as you yourself burn"—a lesson she illustrated one evening when, lacking a lantern by which to continue a conversation, she blew on her fingertips and they blazed with light until the dawn. Rabiʿa is an unalloyed instance of sacrifice as disinterested self-giving. She regards future pleasures of paradise as temptations luring her to compromise her love of God alone.

It is not that Sufis are unconcerned about immortality, but that they understand the Quranic promise of eternal life in a non-mythological way, that is, as a symbol of the experience of spiritual union with God. Sufi practice seeks to quiet and discipline the interests of body and mind in order to awaken the spirit to the consciousness of eternal divine reality within. The point is that immortality cannot be achieved in the material world nor in the realm of history because the world of space and time necessarily involves rising and falling, being born and dying.

In any such world of change and sequence it is not possible to achieve a condition of eternal and immutable perfection. With this insight we arrive at the heart of the Sufi critique of Islamic views of Paradise—and the radical character of sacrifice as devotional ideal.

The problem with all literal views of the afterlife begins with their form as glorified versions of this life. In Paradise I will appear at an ideal age, in full strength, beauty and wit, engaged in pursuits that gave me the most satisfaction in my life on earth, and I will persist in those pursuits and experiences eternally. But what makes any experience enjoyable or satisfying is that it has a definite duration: a period of anticipation, full enjoyment of the experience itself, a time of gradually fading, lingering happiness, and a process of integrating the event into the memory of my previous experiences, and then moving on to other events. If the process did not have a definite end, there could be no satisfaction in the experience; no possibility of other, different experiences coming into consciousness; and no basis for the rise of fresh anticipation. That is why obsession is such a tragedy. To the extent that one cannot let go of an idea or a person or a fear, one cannot continue to develop as a human being. It is a precise metaphysical truth that all good things must come to an end. If they did not, they would become unbearable and inhuman. For this reason, most notions of heaven are dreadful.

No experience in history (actual or potential) could be made eternal without entrapping one forever in a single set of events or activities: fixed endlessly in one place, like the saints transfixed in Dante's portrayal of paradise. Such a vision endorses the Gnostic claim that what is immortal is the spirit that loses its individuality completely in direct contemplation of God. There is no need for embodiment in a state of beatific vision. For if the body changes, it cannot be immortal and, if it does not change, it is dead. Therefore, there can be no immortality in embodied form. It follows that either there is no immortality or immortality belongs to the spirit alone and, therefore, can be experienced *now* through disciplined spiritual practices. It is the Sufi conviction that such release from the limits of individual embodiment is possible and constitutes immediate intuition of the religious truth mediated to the mind by the verbal confession that there is no reality but God.

In this respect, the Sufi ideal of self-annihilation in the love of God and in the service of others stands as a profound critique of conventional views of sacrifice to secure particular benefits. As one contemporary scholar comments, "Modern Islamic movements frequently urge adherents to strive for martyrdom when pursuing a political cause legitimized by religious ideology. Martyrdom is viewed as the highest form of personal sacrifice (*tadhīyah*)."[88] By the standard set by Rabi'a and Rūmī, however, Muslims who sacrifice themselves and others to secure power in this world or delights in Paradise are calculating agents of self-interest. Until they apply the "sword of *lā*" to their own egos and pride, they are not worthy to recite the rest of the shahādah. Along with Sarah's scream, the flame of Rabi'a burns as witness to the danger of sacrificing concrete lives for the sake of abstract constructions of human ambition. Such sacrifice fails to testify to the transcendence of God by becoming merely another strategy in an economy of exchange. From this reading of the Sufi perspective, current Islamic movements conducting jihād through acts of terrorism, including suicide bombing and execution of captives as ritual sacrificial victims, are acting in profoundly bad faith.

Sacrifice in Contemporary Martyrdom Operations

The most sensational practice of sacrifice in the contemporary world is carried out by members of various Islamic movements, called generically jihādists. The term serves many purposes: to associate their activities with jihād understood as "holy war," to link their violence with Islam in general, to portray them as fanatical or irrational, to identify their efforts to resist Western powers as cultural jealousy, and to charge them with crimes of terrorism. Clearly, these purposes are not neutral; rather, the discourse in which jihādist is a primary category is polemical and ideological. Indeed, every term is loaded in the current conversation about "Islamicists," "fundamentalists," "restorationists," or "traditionalists"—to mention only some of the ways they are characterized in the media and in scholarly discussion. It is not my intention to argue which, if any, of these designations is fair or accurate. We shall focus on the function of sacrifice as a religious ideal in the rhetoric and conduct of those who claim to be fighting to defend themselves against oppression or to establish political and economic independence. We will have space to consider only two questions: Do jihādists who kill themselves in the process of killing others perform, or regard themselves as performing, self-sacrifice? Do jihādists who kill captives perform, or regard them-selves as performing, ritual sacrifice?

Before we get to those questions, however, we consider a few background reflections on terrorism and jihād. By definition, terrorism is the use of violence to intimidate civilian population in order to achieve political aims. It is a strategy first employed by governments and later adopted by resistance movements. The term "Reign of Terror" was coined during the French Revolution and later extended to describe efforts to intimidate citizens by secret police and other state authorities. Terror is also employed by guerilla forces who lack adequate weapons to wage conventional war and so engage in unpredictable acts of murder, rape, and destruction. Their acts are called "terrorist," but they often use the term to describe the governments they oppose. That is, the term *terrorism* is employed primarily as a rhetorical device to distinguish good, redemptive violence (ours) from evil, destructive violence (theirs). In this discourse, "we" sacrifice for greater good; "they" die and kill in vain rage. Such distinctions do not necessarily constitute a moral difference.

Terrorist attacks by Muslims began in the tenth century when a militant arm of Ismaili Shiites attacked both their Abbasid rulers as apostates who had betrayed the founding ideals of Islam and also Christian Crusaders as unbelievers fighting against Islam. Their goal was to establish the Fatimid caliphate centered in Cairo as the supreme power in the Islamic world.[89] They used the tactic of hit and run attacks on chosen targets, with the violence designed to make everyone feel insecure and more willing to grant political demands. That is terrorism in a nutshell. As a political strategy it is the gamble that a government or society will regard the threat of indiscriminate violence so high a price that they will make concessions to the terrorists rather than live under such a threat. While the initial response of governments is usually to declare firmly, "We do not negotiate with terrorists," no society can live in perpetual fear of violence that is unrelenting, unpredictable, and imaginative in eluding detection. Inevitably, either terrorists must be ruthlessly eliminated or political change must occur that removes their motivation. What that change will be, of course, is relative to specific historical and cultural conditions. In the meanwhile, the sacrifices of terrorists and of their victims continue.

The purpose of terrorism is coldly calculated: not mindless destruction, but intentional cruelty with maximum injury. Victims of terror in the past were selected for their significance as figures of authority and were dispatched "up close and personal" by the thrust of a dagger. But in our age of "improvised explosive devices" terrorist attacks are less discriminate—and thus more effective in creating insecurity among populations in general. Central to terrorist strategy now is the random choice of victims, without consideration of individual guilt, age, or vulnerability. To perform terrorist acts requires an emotional detachment that is itself terrifying. It does not require physical distance, as in aerial bombing or drone attacks; suicide bombers walk into the very midst of their victims. What is required is a view of others as expendable in the service of political or social transformation.

When members of *Boko Haram*, whose name indicates their condemnation of Western education, storm a school in Nigeria and kidnap the girls to use and sell as sex slaves, how do these men look into the tear-filled eyes of children without flinching? When the jihādists of the Islamic State movement lead their Christian captives to a beach, force them to kneel in the sand as if in prayer, and slit their throats, how do the hands holding those knives not shake? When suicide bombers coordinate their detonations so that those who rush to the scene of the first explosion to help become victims of the second, what do they feel as they plan carnage on themselves and unknown others? How can human agents impose such violence on others with such *apparent* lack of sympathy? The adjective is necessary because we cannot know what the actors feel, only how their actions appear to us.

And clearly they intend to capture our gaze. The videos of throat-gashing, beheadings, and shootings posted by members of the Islamic State present staged events for public viewing to inspire their friends and to horrify their enemies.[90] The Egyptian Christians were dressed in orange jumpsuits as if adorned like sacrificial animals, and their executioners carried large knives and swords. The killers recited from the Qur'an and offered prayers over their victims. Then they shed their blood on the ground and disposed of the bodies. In most of these scenes, they proceed with calm deliberation, allowing no distraction and no reservation, for they are making propaganda pieces that showcase their utter confidence in the cause of establishing an Islamic caliphate. But they are also, in the process, demonstrating faith in transcendent reality that demands the forfeiture of natural impulses and human loyalties as the cost of salvation.

Determined terrorists exemplify the power of ideology to overcome ordinary human responses of sympathy, compassion, and respect. This description applies, of course, to adults capable of self-determination. According to a UNICEF report, jihādists of Boko Haram equip children with explosives and send them out to detonate in strategic locations, in some cases triggering the bomb without the child's knowledge.[91] Swallowing the moral outrage most humans feel rising in their throats at such stories, it must be acknowledged that the tactic is effective. Children are not as suspect as adults and thus are able to approach their victims more closely and easily. The ploy is even more convincing if the child is ignorant of the fate awaiting him or her. In the second *intifada* or "uprising" in Palestinian territories, jihādists employed women as "dealers of death" in martyrdom operations for similar pragmatic reasons.[92]

As appalling as these acts are, however, they are not qualitatively different from the other instances of sacrifice we have cited in this book: dismembering children and beheading adults are offerings of concrete lives, with all their vitality and promise, for the sake of an abstract ideal. Members of different jihādist groups pursue different visions and offer their self-sacrifices or the deaths of others for different versions of "Islam" as they appropriate and interpret different elements of their tradition.[93] The point, and it bears repeating, is that there is no single form of jihādist Islam. The library of books on the subject that has appeared since September 11, 2001, testifies to the breadth and variety of these movements. Nevertheless, there is a common theme running through the rhetoric of sacrifice employed by nearly all of them, namely, that believers are obliged to give their lives in defense of the ideal represented by Medina, the city of the Prophet.

Muhammad's ideal vision was of a society in which the unity of personal and public life under the Qur'an would perfectly mirror the divine unity. Many influential leaders of militant movements over the centuries have stressed that one can be a true Muslim only under the regulation of an Islamic state (for Sunnis that means a society ruled by *sharī'ah* or divine law; for Shiites it means a society led by an inspired representative of the Hidden Imām). While Medina is the paradigm of religious and political order for jihādist groups, however, the ideal is constructed differently by each one through "a chain of memory" that grounds jihād in an authoritative past and promises links to a radically new future conceived as utopia.[94] In her comparative study of Christian and Islamic martyrs, scholar of religious ethics, Shannon Dunn, notes that each sacrificed herself for a "trans-historical ideal": the kingdom of God and the Islamic ummah. "Martyrs play a role in bringing the ideal community nearer to its realization on earth."[95] That ideal community, as Benedict Anderson famously argued, is "imagined." In the case of the paradigm of Medina, what is imagined is an abstract possibility that requires sacrifices for its fulfillment.

Islamic politics often involves struggle over the authority to interpret religious symbolism. In our present context, the contest is over which political order is the authentic replica of Medina. Since the reformer Ahmad ibn Taymiyyhah (1268–1328) appealed to Medina as the critical standard by which he denounced Mongol rulers as apostates, other activists have also cited Medina to oppose autocratic regimes and sectarian movements. The leader of the Muslim Brotherhood, Sayyid Qutb (1906–1966), accused the government of Gamal Abdel Nasser (1918–1970) in Egypt as equivalent to pre-Islamic society in the "time of ignorance" (al-jāhilīyah) and called for its defeat, as Muhammad destroyed the idols of Mecca. Qutb insisted that Muslims must also imitate Muhammad in withdrawal from Egyptian culture (hijrah) and struggle (jihād) to overthrow its government. Nasser jailed him for ten years and finally had him hanged in prison. Qutb is still read throughout the Islamic world and his version of the paradigm of Medina continues to inspire jihādist groups.[96] Qutb's vision of the unity of politics and religion under sharī'ah was absolutist: "Islam stands for the unity of worship and work, of faith and life, of spiritual and material realities, of economic and spiritual values, of the present world and the world to come."[97] He also spoke freely of the necessity of sacrifice to realize the utopian vision of an Islamic state, arguing that "religious war was the only form of killing that was morally sanctioned."[98] Members of the Brotherhood respect his death as an exemplary martyrdom, the model many of them followed during the decades of autocratic rule by Hosni Mubarak and the subsequent political turmoil in Egypt.

Qutb's fervor for an imagined ideal of Medina was matched by scholar and political leader Sayyid Abu-l-A'lā al-Mawdūdī (1903–1979), architect of the Islamic resurgence and founder of the Islamic Society (*Jamaat i-Islami*) in Pakistan. He migrated to Pakistan after the division from India and forcefully urged the government to establish the new nation as an Islamic state that displayed divine tawhīd by integrating sharī'ah into every aspect of society—and blamed the leaders when they failed to implement his ideal. Under martial law, Mawdūdī was condemned to death and refused to petition for mercy, declaring he would rather die than seek clemency from unjust rulers. He faced execution with absolute faith, saying that if Allāh had not set his time, "they cannot send me to the gallows even if they hang themselves upside down in trying to do so." Public admiration for Mawdūdī led the government to commute his sentence and later dismiss it. Mawdūdī taught that belief in the unity of God would inspire courage by taking away the fear of death from the one striving for the cause of God and confirming that "his life and his property and everything else really belong to God." As a result, "This supreme sacrifice of life devolves on all Muslims."[99]

Qutb and Mawdūdī represent two versions of the ideal of Medina; but as Denny points out, "There is no prescribed form of Muslim government, either in the Qur'an or the Sunna."[100] The goal of militant jihād, then, is an imagined community, the product of a few hints in the authoritative textual tradition elaborated by interpretive ingenuity adapted to particular political contexts. The historical construction of the original ummah in Medina presents a complex example of a charismatic leader forming a community on the basis of a new religious viewpoint in the midst of a very hostile environment. While Muhammad did not shrink from killing those he perceived as threats to his project, he preferred to settle most disputes by negotiation, consultation, and mediation. Muhammad counseled his followers to accept every offer of peace and to limit their combat to other warriors. He directed believers to make peace when disputes arose among them; but if either party commits aggression, they are to be fought against "till they submit to God's judgement" (Qur'an 49.9). That Muslims over the centuries have found such ambivalent direction in need of more specific interpretation is hardly surprising.[101]

What sorts of acts constitute aggression? Under what conditions is jihād righteous? These are questions that require the formulation of "just war" theory, including warrants for going to war (*jus ad bellum*) and the rules for conducting war (*jus in bello*), as well as more recent concerns about how to insure that conditions will be better at the conclusion of the war than at the outset (*jus post bellum*). The Qur'an and ahadīth provide elements for a theory of just jihād.[102] First, war must be only for purposes of defense: "Fight for the sake of God those that fight against you, but do not attack them first. God does not love the aggressors" (Qur'an 2.190). Second, there should be no attacks on noncombatants and no forced conversions (Qur'an 2.256). Finally, warriors are addressed directly and instructed to "not with your own hands cast yourself into destruction" (Qur'an 2.195), advice that could mean either do not persist against overwhelming force when you and your comrades face inevitable death or do not commit suicide—or both.

John Esposito comments that Palestinian "suicide bombers" do not see their deaths as suicide, but as "self-sacrifice for the cause of Palestinian freedom."[103] In Dunn's study of one Palestinian bomber, she notes that "martyrdom can communicate the existence of an alternate social reality, as it is often a symbolic realization of an ideal."[104] As in other cases of sacrifice, martyrdom operations forfeit concrete lives in the hope of fulfilling an imagined ideal. In that respect, suicide bombers offer themselves and their victims as sacrifices to advance the "cause of God" on earth, particularly in resistance to aggression. In his comments on the London bombings of July 7, 2005, the second-in-command of al-Qaeda, Ayman al-Zawahiri, addressed the "Crusader coalition," warning that failure to stop "your aggression against the Muslims" will result in devastating reciprocal violence. He warned, "You have made rivers of blood in our countries, so we blew up volcanoes of rage in your countries. . . . You will not be saved unless you withdraw from our land, stop stealing our oil and our resources, and cease your support of the corrupt rulers." Here al-Zawahiri cites just causes for going to war derived from the Qur'an and Islamic history.[105]

The anthropologist Talal Asad, however, criticizes the interpretation of martyrdom operations in Palestine as sacrifices in the sense of gifts to the nation. Asad counters that "in the Islamic tradition, sacrifice involving the slaughter of an animal (*dhabīha*) is made in response to a divine command (e.g., on the annual pilgrimage), or as thanks to the deity (e.g., on returning safely from a journey or recovering from a serious illness), or as a sign of repentance (called *kaffāra*) for particular transgressions. None of these criteria apply to the suicide bomber." Further, "the Arabic for 'gift,' *hadiyya*, is never used to describe sacrifice." Asad argues that designating the deaths of suicide bombers as sacrifices is to lapse into the "orientalist" error of assuming that Christian usage of religious terms is normative. The meaning of sacrifice in Islam should not be confused with "the Christian concept of Christ's supreme gift of himself."[106]

Such confusion would be regrettable since sacrifice in Islam, as we have seen, does not serve to satisfy divine justice or secure divine mercy, as in Israelite offerings for atonement, nor are Islamic sacrifices necessary to appease divine wrath or evoke divine love, as in various Christian interpretations of Jesus's self-giving. Nevertheless, Islamic tradition does regard martyrdom as submission to the will of God, following the example of Ismāʿīl's surrender to sacrifice. In addition, accepting death to further the "cause of God" constitutes an exchange of concrete good for abstract ideal that is a common feature of religious sacrifice.

More helpful to this study is Asad's suggestion that the horror observers feel at the carnage left by suicide bombers is due to "the violent appearance of something that is normally disregarded in secular modernity: the limitless pursuit of freedom, the illusion of an uncoerced interiority that can withstand the force of institutional disciplines."[107] That violent gesture of aspiration to transcend limits set by social order and so realize personal sovereignty demonstrates what Bataille called the total abandon of sacrifice. No more than martyrs in Jewish and Christian history, however, can Muslim suicide bombers control the outcome of their actions. They must accept the risk that their sacrifice may not achieve whatever it is they intend to accomplish by it. It is this element of their death-dealing that is most often expressed in religious terms of divine will (*"God knows best"*) and of transcendence (*"God is greater!"*). In the decisive moment, the specific motive for killing oneself and others becomes irrelevant for, no matter what one intends, success cannot be guaranteed. That is the conditionality of all sacrifice.

Also at that moment one rejects all other determination of one's value (by systems of economic exchange) and values ("institutional disciplines") except one's own will. But suppose that radical individual freedom is not just a theoretical construct in defiance of social forces that shape our subjectivity, what Asad regards as an "illusion." Suppose that self-sacrifice is precisely an exercise of "uncoerced interiority" in which the moment of liberation corresponds to the instant of death—and other instrumental motives are secondary to that goal. Sacrifice is the decisive moment of self-definition, final and irrevocable.

Now these reflections only apply, of course, to those who choose their fates and not to their dupes or victims. That brings us to the second question: Should those killed by suicide bombers be regarded as sacrificial victims? In stark contrast to Asad, the political scientist Melissa Finn argues that we should employ *sacrifice* as the chief analytical term in the study of "martyrdom operations." She believes that sacrificial terms provide a more appropriate context for understanding "suicide bombers," including insight into their subjectivity, the "slaughter" of their victims, and the ideology that drives them. Her example is the organization founded by Osama bin Laden, called al-Qaeda, which uses sacrifice prominently in its discourse.[108] She points out that in his final instructions to the attackers of September 11, 2001, Muhammad 'Atta "used *dhabh* (slaughtering/sacrificing an animal) instead of *qatala* (to kill)" when directing the hijackers to use knives to slit the throats of resisting passengers on the airliners. His advice was a succinct quotation from a hadīth about being merciful in ritual killing: "Sharpen your blade and relieve your *dhabh* [animal of slaughter]."[109]

His precise selection of terms had two effects: to identify the hijackers with Ibrāhīm and his utter surrender to God's call to sacrifice his son, and to place the killings in the ritual context of animal sacrifice during hajj.[110] While the purpose of flying passenger jets into large buildings was to cause indiscriminate mass death, within the planes the killing was to be accomplished in the more intimate manner of ritual slaughter, the blade severing the jugular vein in a single fatal gash while holding the head of the victim in the crook of one's arm. While there is no evidence that the hijackers killed any passengers in that way, 'Atta used sacrificial imagery to identify the jihādists as witnesses to divine justice and to their victims' collective responsibility for what they regarded as the evils of global finance and American military policy.

The one who kills and dies as a martyr bears witness by shedding both blood and light. Finn notes that the term *tadhiya* is used for sacrifice that "makes visible" both injustice and the martyr's act of resisting it, as well as the intention to radiate divine light in a world of darkness.

206 | SACRIFICE IN ISLAMIC TRADITION

Finn also derives from the etymology of tadhiya an affirmation of "the very act-ness of sacrifice," the decisive rupture of complacency or hesitation by the movement to transforming act.[111] Viewing martyrdom operations through the interpretive lens of sacrifice allows us to understand the complexity of jihādist performance. They offer others as sacrifices and, at the same moment, become sacrifices themselves—and the whole event promotes the "cause of God." By this momentous act they witness to their surrender to divine will in "a courageous step to refuse affect, instinct and ego the power of control over one's life decisions."[112] Here again we find the familiar pattern: Sacrifice as a religious ideal requires the suppression of emotional sympathy, bodily desires, and self-interest in order to establish a relation with transcendence.

The central virtue in Islam is surrender to divine will, and in the Qur'an the story of Ibrāhīm's sacrifice represents every actor—father, son, and mother—as pious submitters to God's call for sacrifice. Yet we have noted signs of resistance to his act in glosses on the story in the interpretive tradition; in Quranic principles of compassion, tolerance, and restraint; and in positive relations between the Creator and creatures in which God supports and enhances the beings he brought forth out of nothing and the natural world in which he set them. In that tradition, God's cause is the flourishing of everyone and everything he makes, to promote the increase of their love and beauty. The Qur'an teaches that "doing what is beautiful" (*ihsan*) is one of the attributes of God and should be the highest aspiration of the human soul: "Do what is beautiful. God loves those who do what is beautiful" (2.195).[113] As the esteemed scholar Seyyed Nasr comments in his reflection on *The Heart of Islam*, the "goal of human life is to beautify the soul through goodness and virtue and to make it worthy of offering to God Who is *the* Beautiful."[114] From this perspective, the struggle (jihād) to bring one's selfish will under the discipline of compassion and mercy is the sacrifice that truly reflects divine character.

Conclusion

Sacrifice permeates the ethical, theological, devotional, and ritual discourses of religions of Abraham. The practice of sacrifice follows the example set by the patriarch's near sacrifice of his son, offered in obedience to divine command with faith in divine wisdom and abandonment of personal desire and natural obligation. To render this formative event in the most general terms, sacrifice requires forfeiting concrete human goods for abstract (that is, imagined) transcendent benefit. The examples in this book could be replaced with others, but the main points of analysis and comparison would remain similar. Further, the basic exchange of religious sacrifice carries its moral danger, recognized and registered by dissenting voices, beginning with Sarah's scream, continuing through the tears of Perpetua's father, and carried defiantly in the flame of Rabi'a. These are only symbols of profound misgivings about sacrifice as the means of relating to the divine—misgivings that are expressed directly in dissenting interpretations and indirectly by reading primary texts against themselves.

Protest against animal sacrifice arises in Hebrew prophets and rabbis following the destruction of Jerusalem were required to substitute for it prayer, good works, and Torah study as means of pleasing God. Christians declared the death of Christ as the final sacrifice, but still remember the event in community and represent it in ritual as the ongoing basis of salvation. Islam continues ritual animal sacrifice, but interprets its meaning as expression of gratitude to God and exercise of charity on behalf of the Muslim community. Each of these religions of Abraham has appropriated the "deep symbol" of sacrifice in its own way, but all have elevated it as a religious and moral ideal.

Therein lies the problem. Sacrifice as the means of relating to the sacred often runs afoul of ethical principles, first and foremost the obligation to refrain from killing other human beings who do not pose an imminent danger to one's own life. That principle would seem to be clear enough to forbid killing those who challenge one's ideas or beliefs or fantasies. Once the category of sacrifice is introduced, however, things get murky. Now opponents threaten not just the physical survival of a religious community but the success of its ideological project and thus its spiritual well-being, indeed its eternal salvation. Only their deaths will purify the world of their unbelief and demonstrate the believers' fidelity to divine will. Call the action "conquest of Canaan" or "Crusades for the Holy Land" or "Jihād in God's cause," by one stroke sacrifice cleanses and sanctifies, judges and redeems. Its usefulness as the justifying rationale for violence in religious conflicts and political contests is invaluable. For that very reason, sacrifice in defense of abstractions is as dangerous as sacrifice in service of concrete other creatures is admirable. At the least, sacrifice as self-giving for the welfare of fellow human beings does not have the bloody history that sacrifice for an abstract transcendent perfection does.

The point can be made by reflecting one last time on the story we have followed through this book: Abraham's near sacrifice of his son in obedience to divine direction. We have seen how each tradition wrestles with the theological and moral problems raised by this account. In that struggle Jews, Christians, and Muslims seek to reconcile the strained tension between their commitments to Abraham as exemplar of religious faith and their recognition that his intention was morally dubious. On any scale of humane moral judgment, child sacrifice ranks as a monstrous act. Slaughter of a helpless and innocent human being seems to constitute the very definition of what is immoral, what transgresses the boundary of human decency and falls below the minimal expectation for a civilized person. Yet children die every day as sacrifices to religious, political, and economic systems. Some are denied medical treatment as proof of their parents' faith or as casualties of their government's corruption; others are pressed into service to kill and to die for causes they have no understanding of or interest in; many starve because fields were torched or crops failed and animals stolen. In major cities of the world, children beg and steal and sell their bodies to survive as feral beings.

Children are the fragile tissue connecting humanity to its own future; in them alone can the promise of the future be redeemed. To fail to protect them, to bind them to altars of religious and political and economic abstractions—in short, to sacrifice them for utopian programs—remains a great moral failure. That failure is compounded when there is no guarantee that the sacrifice of children will achieve the glittering ideals offered by those systems: the favor of God or world peace or the triumph of global capitalism. Perhaps religious faith requires the ultimate test of giving up one's child because only sacrifice of the future confirms faith in the present. Religions often insist that their members invest all their energy and attention and devotion in the moment, taking "no thought for the morrow" as a sign of their trust in transcendent guidance and provision. Further, to gain freedom from anxiety about the future and its impending consequences is an alluring aspect of sacrifice. Unconditional renunciation, as Bataille noted, produces ecstatic release. It is not hard to imagine Abraham in mystical transport with the knife in mid-air.

But his hand must be stayed. For his sake, as father and trustee of his son's future; for his son's sake, as victim of his father's ambition; for the sake of God, whose moral character would dissolve in the blood of an innocent child. For the sake of Jews, whose origin would be stained by primordial murder; for the sake of Christians, whose exemplar of faith would be a child-killer; for the sake of Muslims, whose praise of the Compassionate One would stick in their throats. And his hand was stayed. That is the one indisputable point in the sacred texts of all three religions, and it is there that all interpretation should begin: The child was spared.

The positive value of sacrifice as a *moral* ideal is that it encourages individuals to forfeit personal interests for the common good. But sacrifice as a *religious* ideal serves utopian visions for humanity that may not be shared by others and may even be opposed by them. Then conflict is inevitable, conflict that sacrifice both perpetuates and sanctifies. That is the way sacrifice as religious ideal contributes to the problem of religious violence. Sadly, religions of Abraham have violent histories—a fact that stands in stark contrast to their central teachings. They emphasize love, compassion, forgiveness, mercy, and humility. Why then do societies and traditions based on those teachings often promote hatred, cruelty, revenge, and arrogance? That is the question Charles Kimball, scholar of religions in the Mideast, addressed in two books: *When Religion Becomes Evil* and, if that title were not scary enough, *When Religion Becomes Lethal*. Kimball argues that it is possible to spot religious movements that are headed toward violence by "five warning signs," including claims to absolute truth, blind obedience, belief that the end justifies the means, and declaring holy war.[1]

This book identifies another warning sign: *call to sacrifice*. When religious leaders begin urging followers to sacrifice to demonstrate their faith, even to give up their lives and take the lives of others in its defense, we are on the road to catastrophe. How is it possible for humans to kill each other with no regard for their common humanity? Sacrifice is implicated in such violence because it demands that believers cast aside natural affections and human sympathies to confirm their faith and advance their sacred cause, no matter the cost.

My hope is that religions of Abraham can reimagine the ideal of sacrifice as offered in the service of our fellow creatures, rather than to defend and sanction abstract visions of divine will and transcendent perfection. With that hope, confidence for a more harmonious and caring human community in which our children and grandchildren can flourish may be sustained.

NOTES

PREFACE AND ACKNOWLEDGMENTS

1 Paul K. Conkin provides a condensed version of the story in *American Originals*, 117–124. The classic study of the larger topic is Festinger, Riecken, and Schachter, *When Prophecy Fails*.

INTRODUCTION

1 Kolodiejchuk, *Come Be My Light*—, 75, 331.
2 "Cooperation and Commune Longevity: A Test of Costly Signaling Theory," *Cross-Cultural Research* 37:2 (2003), 211–239. I am indebted to Professor Zachary Simpson for this reference.
3 Weddle, *Miracles*, 7.
4 Bakhos, *The Family of Abraham*, 2–10.
5 Levenson, *Inheriting Abraham*, 173–214.
6 Žižek, *Violence*, 162.
7 Calasso, *Ardor*, 42.
8 For an excellent case study of the way sacrificial giving can empower those who are negotiating challenges of migration and dislocation, see Premawardhana, "Transformational Tithing," 85–109.

CHAPTER 1: COMMON FEATURES OF SACRIFICE

1 This view is expressed in the famous passage from *The Republic* in which Plato likens our knowledge to shadows cast on the side of a cave. In order to understand things as they really are, we must emerge from the cave into the light of the intelligible forms united in the absolute ideal or Form of the Good.
2 Kołakowski, *Metaphysical Horror*, 39.
3 Schrag, "Transcendence and Transversality," 204–218.
4 Nietzsche, *Twilight of the Idols*, 43, 45.
5 Nietzsche, *The Anti-Christ*, 131. For more recent moral outrage against religious sacrifice, particularly in the form of sexual repression, see the work of the late Christopher Hitchens, *god is not Great*.
6 Bataille, *Inner Experience*, 137.
7 Mauss, *The Gift*, 17.
8 Pascal, *Pensées*, # 233, 80–83.
9 Hocking, "The Logic of Pascal's Wager," 186–192.

10 Kierkegaard devoted an entire work to interpreting this story as the model of faith in *Fear and Trembling*.

11 The authors of a recent text on ritual distinguish "ritual" as a way of framing actions in terms of their social consequences from "sincerity" as a frame for interpreting actions in terms of the intention and interests of the actors. They trace the contemporary concern with subjectivity and authenticity to the Protestant Reformation and contrast it strongly with "the formalism, reiteration, and externally dictated obligations of ritual." They note that it is "our own sincerity—as a form of framing experience and action—that leads us to frame ritual actions in sincere terms" (Seligman, Weller, Puett, and Simon, *Ritual and Its Consequences*, 4–9). Their distinction helps us see the inadequacy of reading sacrificial narratives exclusively in the frame of sincerity.

12 Available online at www.usahajjmission.com. This site is sponsored by the USA Haj Mission, an organization that makes travel arrangements for pilgrims.

13 Grimes, *Ritual Criticism*, 109–205. Grimes draws his initial categories from J. L. Austin's theory of performative language which formulates two broad categories in which speech-acts fail to work, namely, "misfires" and "abuses." Grimes supplements these categories to construct a list of nine ways that rituals can become ineffectual.

14 Grimes, "Infelicitous Performances and Ritual Criticism," 113: "In a 'flop' all the procedures may be done correctly but the rite fails to resonate. It does not generate the proper tone, ethos, or atmosphere."

15 Firth, *Religion*, 93–94.

16 Hüsken, *When Rituals Go Wrong*, 350.

17 Bataille, *Inner Experience*, 153.

18 Smith, "The Domestication of Sacrifice" in *Relating Religion*, 152. This essay was originally published in Hamerton-Kelly, *Violent Origins*. In the later version cited here, Smith emphasizes the artificiality of the sacrificial animal as a human construction.

19 Of course, the theory breaks down in the face of great disparity of wealth between individuals: The millionaire's tithe may reduce the number of homes he owns, while giving up a tenth of one's earnings from a minimum-wage job can mean the difference between buying food or medicine.

20 Mauss, *The Gift*, 20.

21 Smith, *Imagining Religion*, 4.

22 McClymond, *Beyond Sacred Violence*, 26.

23 McClymond, *Beyond Sacred Violence*, 34.

24 "I appeal to you, brothers and sisters, to present your bodies as a living sacrifice, holy and acceptable to God, which is your reasonable service" (Romans 12:1). The theologian Sarah Coakley expands on this phrase to argue for "the new notion of *evolutionary* sacrifice [as] a principle of divine reason" in her 2009 inaugural lecture at the University of Cambridge, *Sacrifice Regained*, 25.

25 Whitehead, *Religion in the Making*, 17.

CHAPTER 2: THEORIES OF SACRIFICE

1 Smith, *HarperCollins Dictionary of Religion*, 948.

2 For a historical overview of sacrificial practices and theories of their origin, see Joseph Henninger's entry on "sacrifice" in the first edition of the *Encyclopedia of Religion* (1987), reprinted with a supplementary essay by David Carrasco in the second edition, edited by Lindsay Jones (Detroit: Thomson Gale, 2005), 7997–8010.

3 Thomas Tweed observes that the term theory is related to itinerary: "Theories are simultaneously proposals for a journey, representations of a journey, and the journey itself" (*Crossing and Dwelling*, 9). It follows that no theory can be an all-encompassing explanation from a stationary and universal viewpoint. As Tweed notes, theories are "*sightings* from sites. They are positioned representations of a changing terrain by an itinerant cartographer" (13). Nevertheless, "to say we cannot have a God's-eye view, and to acknowledge blind spots, is not to say we can see nothing at all" (28). It is in that mixed spirit of modesty and confidence that we proceed to venture along the paths traced by theoretical wanderings.

4 For selections of primary sources, see Carter, *Understanding Religious Sacrifice*. For commentary on leading theorists of sacrifice, see Keenan, *Question of Sacrifice*. For an extensive list of major works on sacrifice in the modern period from a wide range of scholarly disciplines, see Bibliographical References in Meszaros and Zachhuber, *Sacrifice and Modern Thought*, 240–270.

5 Keenan, *Question of Sacrifice*, 2.

6 James W. Watts, "The Rhetoric of Sacrifice," in Eberhart, *Ritual and Metaphor*, 9.

7 Watts in Eberhart, *Ritual and Metaphor*, 11.

8 Durkheim, *Elementary Forms of Religious Life,*, 165, 250.

9 Durkheim, *Elementary Forms of Religious Life*, 254.

10 *The Epic of Gilgamesh*, 100–102. This story, found in Tablet XI, predates the account of Noah and the Flood in Genesis 6 and provides a source for the story in the Bible, although many details are changed significantly, including the feature I am emphasizing here, namely, the divine need for humans to offer sacrifices. While Noah also presents a burnt offering upon exiting the ark, the Bible presents the sacrifice as a gesture of thanks to God for surviving the flood.

11 Durkheim, *Elementary Forms of Religious Life*, 256–258.

12 Mauss, *The Gift*, 33.

13 Mauss, *The Gift*, 78.

14 Ivan Strenski argues that Mauss sought to replace the Roman Catholic idea of sacrifice as total "giving *up of* self," based on the example of Jesus's crucifixion, with a more limited ideal of "giving *of* self." Mauss and his fellow author, Henri Hubert, promoted this prudent form of sacrifice as a means of protecting citizens from unconditional demands of the modern nation-state (Strenski, *Contesting Sacrifice*).

15 Milbank, "Stories of Sacrifice, 30.

16 Durkheim, *Elementary Forms of Religious Life*, 253, 255, 287.
17 Durkheim, *Elementary Forms of Religious Life*, 157–158.
18 Durkheim, *Elementary Forms of Religious Life*, 163–164.
19 Smith, *To Take Place*, 3–13.
20 Durkheim, *Elementary Forms of Religious Life*, 257.
21 Durkheim, *Elementary Forms of Religious Life*, 319.
22 Taylor, *About Religion*, 52.
23 Taylor, *About Religion*, 57.
24 Girard, *Sacrifice*, 62.
25 Girard, *Violence and the Sacred*, 68–88. Girard extends the interpretation of the myth of Oedipus as a "persecution text" to the claim that "all myths must have their roots in real acts of violence against real victims" in *The Scapegoat*, 24–44.
26 Freud, *The Future of an Illusion*, 69. Freud detailed his account of the primal murder in *Moses and Monotheism* (1939).
27 Girard, *Sacrifice*, 74.
28 Girard, *Sacrifice*, 39–40.
29 See Bailie, *Violence Unveiled*. Bailie is a Roman Catholic writer who promotes Girard's views online at the Cornerstone Forum.
30 Richard Kearney also questions the "radical discontinuity between biblical and non-biblical cultures" that Girard assumes by asking whether it is not possible to read the myth of Oedipus, along with other "Greek narratives of victimization," as "accounts of the sacrifice of innocent scapegoats where the audience is encouraged to side with the scapegoats" ("Myths and Scapegoats," 9–10).
31 Jay, *Throughout Your Generations*, 40.
32 Jay, *Throughout Your Generations*, 39.
33 Jay, *Throughout Your Generations*, 102.
34 Jay, *Throughout Your Generations*, 132.
35 Jantzen, *Becoming Divine*. She projected a six-volume work on *Death and the Displacement of Beauty in Western Philosophy*, but lived long enough to complete only the first book, *Foundations of Violence* (2004).
36 Bataille, *Theory of Religion*, 49. This essay was published posthumously in French in 1973, but appears in Bataille's *Collected Works* in volume 7 with correspondence from 1947–48, placing its composition at the time when memories of massive destruction in Europe during World War II, the continuing threat of Fascism, and ghastly horrors of the Holocaust were still fresh.
37 Bataille, *Theory of Religion*, 52.
38 Bataille, *Accursed Share*, 28.
39 Bataille, *Accursed Share*, 46.
40 Lewis, *Ritual Sacrifice*, 83–84. For an authoritative overview, see Carrasco, *City of Sacrifice*.
41 Bataille, *Accursed Share*, 49.
42 Bataille, *Accursed Share*, 59, 58.

43 Kathryn McClymond emphasizes that killing is only the preliminary condition for vegetal and liquid offerings, where manipulation of the ritual objects constitutes the sacrificial event. In these forms of sacrifice, "killing does not always occur and certainly is often not the focal point of sacrificial activity." She concludes that violence should not serve as the basis for a theory of sacrifice (*Beyond Sacred Violence*, 89). Bataille, however, understands violence in a broader sense than destruction of life.

44 Bataille, *Theory of Religion*, 43–44, 49.

45 Bataille, *Theory of Religion*, 87.

46 Bataille, *Erotism*, 126.

47 Bataille, *Erotism*, 23.

48 Bataille, *Inner Experience*, 9.

49 Bataille, *Inner Experience*, 13.

50 Bataille, *Erotism*, 184, 236.

51 Bataille, *Inner Experience*, 88, 22, 120.

52 Bataille, *Inner Experience*, 151.

CHAPTER 3: SACRIFICE IN JEWISH TRADITION

1 Stroumsa, *End of Sacrifice*, 4.

2 Halbertal, *On Sacrifice*, 77–78.

3 The description of the story is derived from the use of the verb ʿ*qd*, to bind, in Genesis 22:9 (Van Seters, *Abraham in History*, 227, n. 3).

4 The text here and throughout the book, unless otherwise indicated, is from the New Revised Standard Version (1989), in the edition sponsored by the international Society of Biblical Literature. The version sponsored by the Jewish Publication Society reads, "your son, your favored one, Isaac, whom you love," thereby interrupting the word order which builds to the final disclosure of the son's name (Berlin and Brettler, *Jewish Study Bible*, 42). The JPS translation, however, closely parallels the Septuagint: "your son, the beloved." The NRSV retains both senses of "only" and "favored." Neither adjective decisively identifies the son.

5 Levenson, *Inheriting Abraham*, 83–84.

6 Many commentators interpret the Akedah that way, from Alexandrian philosopher Philo (20 BCE–50 CE), known for his allegorical interpretation of Torah, to contemporary biblical scholars. Among the latter, John Day argues that some Israelites sacrificed children to Molech, a West Canaanite deity, along with worship of Yahweh, and that Genesis 22 should "be seen as directed against the offering of human sacrifices to Yahweh" (Day, *Molech*, 85).

7 Levinas, *Proper Names*, 77.

8 Meeks, *HarperCollins Study Bible*, 32.

9 Levenson, *Death and Resurrection of Beloved Son*, 17.

10 Levenson notes that "Jeremiah's attacks on child sacrifice are aimed not only at the practice itself, but also at the tradition that YHWH desires it" (*Death and Resurrection of Beloved Son*, 5). Jacob Milgrom argues that the Hebrew verb for

"give" (*nātan*) in Exodus 22:29 does not mean to sacrifice, but "donate," as Hannah "giving" her child Samuel to service in the temple (Milgrom, "Were the Firstborn Sacrificed to YHWH?" 51).

11 Levenson makes this point the criterion of adequacy for any interpretation of the Akedah: "Abraham will have his multitudes of descendants only because he was willing to sacrifice the one who is destined to beget them. Any construal of the text that minimizes that willingness misses the point" (*Death and Resurrection of Beloved Son*, 13).

12 Zornberg, *Murmuring Deep*, 176. The passage cited is *Bereshit Rabbah* 55:4.

13 Zornberg, *Murmuring Deep*, 184.

14 Zornberg, *Murmuring Deep*, 197.

15 Zornberg, *Murmuring Deep*, 178.

16 In *The Gift of Death*, Derrida writes, "I cannot respond to the call, the request, the obligation or even the love of another without sacrificing the other other, the other others. *Every other (one) is every (bit) other*; everyone else is completely or wholly other" (69).

17 Derrida, *Gift of Death*, 71.

18 Derrida, *Gift of Death*, 71.

19 Sanders, "Kierkegaardian Reading," 179–180.

20 Buber, *Eclipse of God*, 118–120.

21 Derrida, *Gift of Death*, 76. Heleen Zorgdrager notes that "Sarah is, symbolically speaking sacrificed as the mother of this child" ("The Sacrifice of Abraham" in Baumgarten, *Sacrifice in Religious Experience*, 195–196).

22 Zornberg cites this rabbinic commentary: "Isaac then returned to his mother and she said to him, 'Where have you been, my son?' He answered, 'My father . . . took me to the top of one mountain, built an altar and laid it out, and arranged the wood, and bound me on top of the altar, and took the knife to slaughter me.' She said, 'Were it not for the angel, you would already be slaughtered?' He said, 'Yes.' At that, she screamed six times, corresponding to the six shofar notes. She had not finished doing this when she died" (*Va-yikra Rabbah* 20:2).

23 Zornberg, *Beginning of Desire*, 127–128.

24 Levenson, *Inheriting Abraham*, 108.

25 Levenson, *Inheriting Abraham*, 112.

26 That risk is clear in one paraphrase of the story Florentino Garcia Martínez cites from *Targum Neophyti* 1, in which Isaac urges, "Father, tie me well lest I kick you and your sacrifice be rendered useless" ("The Sacrifice of Isaac in 4Q225" in Noort and Tigchelaar, *Sacrifice of Isaac*, 54).

27 Zornberg, *Murmuring Deep*, 176.

28 There is scholarly debate over whether the rituals were actually performed as they are ideally described in these texts. Even if they were so conducted, they may represent an ideal rather than express lived reality. Jonathan Z. Smith concludes that ritual "is a means of performing the way things ought to be in conscious tension to the way things are" ("The Bare Facts of Ritual," in *Imagining Religion*, 63). Our

focus is not on how regulations were enacted, but on how they were interpreted and applied as incentives for obedience to divine commands, "the way things ought to be."

29 Regina M. Schwartz attributes Cain's violent rage to "sibling rivalry" in competition for the favor of a God who is monotheistic "not only because he demands allegiance to himself alone but because he confers his favor on one alone" (*Curse of Cain*, 3). At least, it is clear that in this story, forms of sacrifice served to distinguish between the one chosen and the one rejected.

30 Ilana Pardes set the model for reading biblical texts "against themselves"—or at least against the interpretive traditions they engender—in her remarkable book *Countertraditions in the Bible*.

31 Halbertal, *On Sacrifice*, 8–10, 18.

32 The variety of animal sacrifices in ancient Israel was astounding. There were four types, each with multiple subtypes: burnt offerings (*olah*) of fourteen varieties, peace offerings of four kinds, sin offerings for both individual and communal offenses, and guilt offerings for six categories of transgression. Each sacrifice required different animals and was accompanied by a libation of wine and a meal-offering. Also, the priests offered nine varieties of grain and loaves on specified occasions, burned incense on a special altar twice a day, and conducted different sacrifices on Sabbaths and holy days. It is no wonder that such a complex schedule of sacrifices caused a high level of anxiety about the possibility of ritual failure. See entry on "offerings and sacrifices" in Wigoder, *New Encyclopedia of Judaism*, 672.

33 See Exodus 28. In rabbinic tradition, each of the eight garments of the high priest "atone for particular sins that Israel commits" (Jacob Neusner, "Sacrifice and Temple in Rabbinic Judaism," in Neusner et al., *Encyclopedia of Judaism*, III:1292).

34 Neusner, *Talmud of Babylonia*, V: *Yoma* 5:1, IV.3.E, 195.

35 Neusner, *Talmud of Babylonia*, IV: *Bavli Tractate Pesahim*, VI–VII.

36 Neusner, *Encyclopedia of Judaism*, III: 1297.

37 Smith, *To Take Place*, 103.

38 McClymond, "Don't Cry Over Spilled Blood," in Knust and Varhelyi, *Ancient Mediterranean Sacrifice*, 248.

39 Steinberg, *Celebrating the Jewish Year*, 27, 30–31.

40 *Pirke Avot*, 5:9, cited by Wout Jac. Van Bekkum in "The Aqedah and its interpretations in Midrash and Piyyut" (Noort and Tigchelaar, *Sacrifice of Isaac*, 89).

41 Steinberg, *Celebrating the Jewish Year*, 57–58.

42 This reference is found in *Tosefta*, a collection of teachings from 300 CE at *Rosh Hashanah* 1:13. Cited by Reuven Hammer in Steinberg, *Celebrating the Jewish Year*, 50.

43 *Mishneh Torah*, Laws of Repentance 1:3, 2:1, 9, 10. Cited in Steinberg, *Celebrating the Jewish Year*, 78.

44 James W. Watts points out that the semantic range of the Hebrew *kipper* extends from "wipe off or purify" to "pay or compensate." The English term "atone" comes

closest to covering the range, "though it also carries theological connotations that may not be implied by the Hebrew verb." Because *kipper* occurs most often in the source document for the Pentateuch that scholars call P for priestly source, Watts argues that its rhetorical effect is to confirm the essential role of the priesthood in mediating Israel's relation to God (*Ritual and Rhetoric*, 136).

45 Grimm, *From Feasting to Fasting*, 25.

46 See the insightful analysis of this shift in interpretation by Halbertal in *On Sacrifice*, 41–47.

47 Stroumsa, *End of Sacrifice*, 25.

48 Stroumsa, *End of Sacrifice*, 48.

49 Stroumsa, *End of Sacrifice*, 57–62.

50 Neusner, *First-Century Judaism in Crisis*, cited on 169.

51 In addition to Hosea 6:6, see Micah 6:6–8; Amos 5:21–24; Isaiah 66:2b–3.

52 Neusner, *Between Time and Eternity*, 34.

53 Neusner, *First-Century Judaism in Crisis*, 67.

54 Cited in Neusner, *First-Century Judaism in Crisis*, 83–84. Michael Satlow demonstrates how the rabbis substituted Torah study for sacrifice in "'And on the Earth You Shall Sleep,'" 204–225.

55 Neusner, *First-Century Judaism in Crisis*, 132, 178.

56 Stroumsa, *End of Sacrifice*, 69–70.

57 Neusner, *First-Century Judaism in Crisis*, 169.

58 Silber, "Echoes of Sacrifice," 304.

59 Heschel, *Man's Quest for God*, 69–71.

60 Heschel, *Man's Quest for God*, 137.

61 Heschel, *Man's Quest for God*, 131, 148, 151.

62 Wills, "Ascetic Theology Before Asceticism?," 902–925.

63 The cycle of "suffering servant songs" appears in Isaiah 40–53 and is from a later hand than the earlier chapters. Scholars refer to the author as Deutero-Isaiah, writing at the time of Cyrus's defeat of Babylon (539 BCE).

64 Green, *Guide to the Zohar*, 20.

65 Gershom G. Scholem, *On the Kabbalah*, 35.

66 Green, *Guide to the Zohar*, 39.

67 Green, *Guide to the Zohar*, 49.

68 Scholem, *On the Kabbalah*, 110–111.

69 Scholem, *Major Trends in Jewish Mysticism*, 260–261.

70 Scholem, *On the Kabbalah*, 113.

71 Scholem, *On the Kabbalah*, 116.

72 Green, *Guide to the Zohar*, 140.

73 Scholem, *Major Trends in Jewish Mysticism*, 274.

74 Zohar 1:119b.

75 Green, *Guide to the Zohar*, 120.

76 Buber, *Tales of the Hasidim*, 23.

77 Buber, *Tales of the Hasidim*, 168, 166.

78 Rosenberg, *Dreams of Being Eaten Alive.*

79 Ginsburg, *"I am asleep yet my heart is awake,"* 23.

80 Matt, *Essential Kabbalah*, 71–72.

81 Scholem, *Major Trends in Jewish Mysticism*, 123.

82 The Temple Institute maintains an informative website at www.templeinstitute. org.

83 The purification ritual for Israelites contaminated by contact with a corpse required the sacrifice of a red heifer and is detailed in Numbers 19. For centuries after the destruction of the temple, ashes of a red heifer were preserved but have been long lost. Contemporary groups continue experimental breeding to produce a cow of the requisite color.

84 Nahshoni, "Rabbi Calls for Sacrifice on Temple Mount," available online at www. templeinstitute.org.

85 "The Red Heifer," available online at www.templeinstitute.org.

86 Eliade, *The Sacred and the Profane*, chapter 1.

87 Bokser, "Ritualizing the Seder," 443, 445.

88 Smith, *To Take Place*, 117.

89 Such suffering is what Marilyn McCord Adams calls "horrendous evil" which robs the victim of any confidence in the meaning of life (*Horrendous Evils*).

90 Morgan, *Beyond Auschwitz*, 146, 151.

91 Cohen, *Tremendum.*

92 Otto, *The Idea of the Holy*, 4.

93 Otto, *The Idea of the Holy*, 19.

94 Smith, *Imagining Religion*, 102–120.

95 Wiesel, *Night*, 33, 34.

96 Wiesel, *Night*, introduction by Elie Wiesel, xi.

97 Rubenstein, *After Auschwitz*, 240.

98 Rubenstein, *After Auschwitz*, 128.

99 Fackenheim, *God's Presence in History*, 70–71. Joseph Marcus notes, however, that during the Crusades Jewish parents did know what they were doing when they killed their children to prevent them from being baptized. Poems, called "Akedahs," celebrated their sacrifices, comparing them to Abraham (Landman, *Universal Jewish Encyclopedia*, 1: 144).

100 Fackenheim, *Jewish Return into History*, 23–24. This passage is posted online by The 614th Commandment Society at www.the614thcs.com. The Society is dedicated to promoting the practice of Judaism among younger generations of post-Holocaust Jews.

101 Fackenheim, *To Mend the World*, 14.

102 Fackenheim, *To Mend the World*, 312.

103 Firestone, "Holy War in Modern Judaism?," 974.

104 Milman, "The Sacrifice of Isaac and Its Subversive Variations," 69.

105 Feldman, "Nation and Sacrifice: the Akedah and Zionist Ideology," adapted from Feldman, *Glory and Agony.*

106 Milman, "The Sacrifice of Isaac and Its Subversive Variations," 80.

107 See review by Lucille Marshall, available online at www.lucystarer.wordpress.com.

CHAPTER 4: SACRIFICE IN CHRISTIAN TRADITION

1 Watts, *Ritual and Rhetoric in Leviticus*, 192.

2 The term belongs to Edward Farley, who defines deep symbols as "the values by which a community understands itself, from which it takes its aims, and to which it appeals as canons of cultural criticism" (*Deep Symbols*, 3).

3 Paul records a sharp encounter with Peter on just these points in Galatians 2.

4 Eisenbaum, *Paul Was Not a Christian*, 238.

5 Apuleius, *The Golden Ass* (*Metamorphoses*), a work from late second century CE, in Barrett, *New Testament Background*, 128, 129.

6 Prudentius, *Peristephanon*, written in late fourth century, in Barrett, *New Testament Background*, 126.

7 The popular account of the cult of Dionysius is based largely on the play by Euripides, *Bacchae* (407 BCE). See comments by Smith, *Imagining Religion*, 112–115.

8 Knust and Varhelyi, *Ancient Mediterranean Sacrifice*, 16. The essays in this volume demonstrate that not all sacrifice involved violence, or even killing, and that its many purposes included negotiating political power within the Roman Empire.

9 Stendahl, *Paul Among Jews and Gentiles*, 23–40.

10 Paul signed his dictated letter to the Galatians in "large letters," suggesting limited eyesight (Galatians 6:11).

11 Perkins, *The Suffering Self*, 7, 190, 40.

12 Helmut Koester was one of the first biblical scholars to point out that the literary genre of "gospel" implies an understanding of Christ's nature and mission that centers on his death and resurrection. New Testament Gospels represent Jesus as crucified and risen Lord and thus became "the true criterion of faith" for early Christians ("One Jesus and Four Primitive Gospels," 203–247).

13 Ehrman, *The New Testament*, 11.

14 Pagels, *Beyond Belief*, 24.

15 For an insightful account of the process, see Gamble, *The New Testament Canon*. He demonstrates that by the end of the second century most lists of authoritative Christian writings included the four Gospels and a collection of Paul's letters. Gamble rightly cautions, however, that once the canon was established, the interests and purposes of individual writers were minimized to construct a unified apostolic tradition set over against views then regarded as "heterodox" (75). But he also notes that the Gospels and Paul's letters "had been valued so long and used so widely that their orthodoxy could only be taken for granted" (70).

16 Gamble, *The New Testament Canon*, 39.

17 While Christian tradition attributed this writing to the apostle Paul, and on that basis it was included in the New Testament canon, the unknown author states he was of a later generation (Hebrews 2:3). Further, the sophisticated Greek style and elaborate typology drawn from Jewish sacrificial practices are not characteristic of Paul.

18 Pfitzner, *Hebrews*, 137.

19 For a critical discussion of the variety of views attributed to Gnostics, see King, *What Is Gnosticism?*.

20 *The Gospel of the Egyptians* in Robinson, *Nag Hammadi Library in English*, 217.

21 Rousseau, "The Desert Fathers: Antony and Pachomius," 129, 130.

22 *Gospel of Philip*, in Robinson, *Nag Hammadi Library*, 48.

23 *The Gospel of Thomas: The Hidden Sayings of Jesus*, 62, translated with introduction by Meyer.

24 Jeffrey J. Kripal offers a provocative interpretation of the contemporary relevance of Gnostic myth in *The Serpent's Gift*.

25 Hyam Maccoby offers a version of the appalling story in *Judas Iscariot and the Myth of Jewish Evil*. For a more recent retelling, see Gubar, *Judas: A Biography*.

26 Kasser, Meyer, and Wurst, *Gospel of Judas*, 43.

27 Kasser et al., *Gospel of Judas*, 27–28.

28 *Gospel According to Philip*, in *Gnostic Scriptures*, 338.

29 John Dart discussed these Gnostic themes in *The Jesus of Heresy and History*, 93–101.

30 *Gnostic Scriptures*, 423.

31 Townsend, "Sacrifice and Race in the *Gospel of Judas*," 171.

32 *Treatise on Resurrection* in *Gnostic Scriptures*, 322. This introduction to a form of Gnostic teaching was likely composed in the fourth century and intended as a spiritual interpretation of orthodox creedal formulae.

33 *Martyrdom of Saint Polycarp*, 150.

34 Stephen Benko, *Pagan Rome and Early Christians*, 4.

35 Candida Moss provides a highly readable discussion of "Why did the Romans dislike Christians?" in *The Myth of Persecution*, 163–187.

36 Athenagorus, *A Plea Regarding Christians*, in Richardson, *Early Christian Fathers*, 306, 311.

37 For an illuminating case study of this process, see Ashley and Sheingron, *Writing Faith*.

38 Imitation, of course, is not reproduction, nor did it mean the same thing in different contexts. For a detailed analysis of various forms of imitation of Christ in accounts of early martyrs, see Moss, *The Other Christs*.

39 *The Passion of the Holy Martyrs Perpetua and Felicitas*. The text is available online at www.earlychristianwritings.com, among the works of Tertullian, even though scholars do not believe Tertullian was the author.

40 Perkins, *The Suffering Self*, 104–106.

41 Lefkowitz, "The Motivations of St. Perpetua's Martyrdom," 417–421.

42 Recla, "*Autothanatos*: The Martyr's Self-Formation," 472–494.

43 Candida R. Moss argues that the criticism of voluntary martyrdom as "unnatural" is an anachronistic insertion of normative notions of "nature" developed in the early modern period, but her own evidence traces the objection back to Thomas Aquinas who in turn drew from Aristotle's notion of a "natural law" against

suicide ("Discourse of Voluntary Martyrdom," 549). One can grant her point as a methodological caution for historians, while continuing to maintain that Perpetua's insistence on martyrdom is represented in the text in tension with her father's appeal to familial sympathy. Modern readers are as free as ancient ones to question Perpetua's choice.

44 Chidester, *Christianity*, 91–108.

45 St. Athanasius, *De Incarnatione Verbi Dei*, sections 19–20, 48–49; section 9, 35.

46 St. Anselm, *Cur Deus Homo*, Book First, chapter XXIII, 232.

47 St. Anselm, *Cur Deus Homo*, Book Second, chapter VI, 245.

48 Abelard, *Historia Calamitatum*, chapter IX. Abelard composed the work around 1133. The translated text is available online through *Christian Classics Ethereal Library*, at www.ccel.org.

49 Aulén, *Christus Victor*, 95.

50 Aulén, *Christus Victor*, 96.

51 Abelard, *Collationes*, section 58, 71.

52 Thomas à Kempis, *The Imitation of Christ*, Book II, VII, 1. Subsequent citations will be enclosed in parentheses in the text.

53 Ullmann, "Life of Thomas à Kempis," 43.

54 Grimm, *From Feasting to Fasting*, 161.

55 St. Teresa of Avila, *Life of St. Teresa of Jesus*, chapter XXIX, 17, 13.

56 Kolodiejchuk, *Come Be My Light*, 346.

57 St. Teresa of Avila, *The Way of Perfection*, chapter 26, italics added.

58 Flynn, "Spiritual Uses of Pain in Spanish Mysticism," 273.

59 Dionysius, *The Mystical Theology*, chapter 1, in *Pseudo-Dionysius*, 135–137.

60 Dionysius, *The Mystical Theology*, chapter 5, in *Pseudo-Dionysius*, 141.

61 Bataille, *Erotism*, 239.

62 St. Augustine, *City of God*, X, 5, 309.

63 St. Augustine, *City of God*, X, 6, 310.

64 St. Augustine, *City of God*, X, 20, 325.

65 St. Thomas Aquinas, *Summa Theologica*, Part 2, Second Part, Questions 85–86, available online at www.ccel.org.

66 St. Thomas Aquinas, *Summa Theologica*, Part 3, Question 73, Article 4.

67 St. Thomas Aquinas, *Summa Theologica*, Part 3, Question 75, Article 4. The term had already been accepted by the Fourth Lateran Council in 1215 to declare the presence of Christ's body and blood under the species of bread and wine.

68 Calvin, *Institutes of the Christian Religion*, Book IV, Chapter xvii. Subsequent citations will be enclosed in parentheses in the text.

69 St. Thomas Aquinas, *Summa Theologica*, Part 3, Question 48, Article 3.

70 "Disputation on the Power and Efficacy of Indulgences," Thesis 50 in *Works of Martin Luther*, edited by Adolph Spaeth, et al. (Philadelphia: Holman, 1915), available online at www.iclnet.org.

71 Luther, *Lectures on the Epistle to the Hebrews* (1517–1518) in *Early Theological Works*, 126.

72 Luther, *Disputation against Scholastic Theology* (1517), in *Early Theological Works*, 272–273.

73 An account of the history and deliberations of the Council can be found in *New Catholic Encyclopedia*, available online at www.newadvent.org.

74 Council of Trent, Session XXII, canon 1.

75 Homily delivered at the Cathedral of the Most Precious Blood of Our Lord Jesus Christ in Westminster, England, on September 18, 2010, available online at www. w2.vatican.va.

76 What has not changed is the insistence that priests be male in order to act in Christ's stead. Nancy Jay pointed out that two receptions of Vatican II had opposite outcomes for the ordination of women to the priesthood. Theologian Hans Küng concluded that the Mass is not a sacrifice; therefore, there is no ground for excluding women from its celebration. The defender of the Tridentine Latin Mass, French Archbishop Marcel Lefebvre (1905–1991), took the position that the sacrifice of the Mass can be performed only by ordained men who transmit through their succession the "apostolic seed" (Jay, *Throughout Your Generations*, 118–127).

77 Homily, July 3, 2013, reprinted in *Pope Francis: His Essential Wisdom*, 55. Second quotation is from Vatican press conference on March 16, 2013 (17).

78 Inaugural Mass, March 19, 2013 (*Pope Francis*, 18); World Youth Day, July 26, 2013 (23).

79 Lenten letter, February 22, 2012; Address at homeless shelter, May 21, 2013 (*Pope Francis*, 30).

80 Gary Dorrien traces the career of Bushnell in detail in his magisterial survey, *American Liberal Theology*, volume I, 111–178.

81 This address was published with two others under the title *God in Christ* (1849). The citation is from the reprint edition, 190–192. Subsequent citations will be enclosed in parentheses in the text.

82 Bushnell, "The Power of God in Self-Sacrifice," in *Sermons for the New Life*, 353–355.

83 Bushnell, *The Vicarious Sacrifice*, Part II, Chapter III, available online at www.ccel.org.

84 Bushnell, "The Personal Love and Lead of Christ," in *Sermons for the New Life*, 136.

85 Bushnell, "The Efficiency of the Passive Virtues," in *Sermons for the New Life*, 407.

86 Dorrien, *American Liberal Theology*, volume I, 171–172. The quotation is from *Forgiveness and Law* (1874).

87 Faust, *This Republic of Suffering*, 190–191.

88 From a paper on "[Reinhold] Niebuhr's ethical dualism" (1952), cited by Dorrien, *American Liberal Theology*, volume II, 152. Rufus Burrow, Jr., in *God and Human Dignity* provides an insightful account of King's religious education, including the influence of the personalist theology of Edgar Sheffield Brightman on his faith in the persuasive power of sacrificial suffering.

89 King, Jr., *Strength to Love*, 56.

90 King, Jr., *Strength to Love*, 56.

91 Cone, *Cross and Lynching Tree*, 79.

92 Cited by Cone, *Cross and Lynching Tree*, 110. The visual parallel is disturbingly clear in the exhibit of lynching photos, *Without Sanctuary*, available online at www.withoutsanctuary.org.

93 Cited by Bakhos, *The Family of Abraham*, 203.

94 Kant, *Religion Within the Limits of Reason Alone*, 175.

CHAPTER 5: SACRIFICE IN ISLAMIC TRADITION

1 Unless otherwise indicated, English versions of the Qur'an are by N. J. Dawood, *The Koran with Parallel Arabic Text*, original edition 1956 (London: Penguin Books, 1995).

2 Details are available online at www.saudiembassy.net.

3 One slaughterhouse is open for pilgrims who wish to perform their own sacrifices. The Kingdom of Saudi Arabia recently established the Project of Utilization of Sacrificial Animals that manages purchase and processing of animals; see the website, available online at www.isdb.org. For a standard historical account of pilgrimage rituals see Peters, *The Hajj*.

4 With more than two million pilgrims visiting Mecca each year, the hajj can still constitute a risky test of endurance and even survival. The ritual locations are tightly packed, and a tragic stampede in 2015 killed nearly 2,500 people (*New York Times*, December 10, 2015).

5 Compare Isaiah 44 where the prophet ridicules idol worshippers for carving their gods out of the same wood they burn to bake their bread and warm their backsides.

6 Cragg, *Readings in the Qur'an*, 120. The story is also told in Qur'an 21.51–73, where Ibrāhīm interrogates the largest idol to demonstrate its impotent and inanimate character, recalling a similar story about Joash, father of Gideon, in the Hebrew Bible (Judges 6:31).

7 F. Leemhuis notes that "in the discipline of Koranic commentary, the issue was discussed for many centuries, without a clear general winner for the honour of being the sacrificial son" ("Ibrāhīm's sacrifice of his son in the early post-Koranic tradition," Noort and Tigchelaar, *Sacrifice of Isaac*, 136).

8 This version and the others discussed in this paragraph are cited by Ådna, *Muhammad and the Formation of Sacrifice*, 134–146. Some passages in this chapter are adapted from my review of the book in *Journal of Quranic Studies* 18:3 (2016).

9 Said, *Orientalism*. Said argued that the representation of Arab culture and religion by Western scholars produced a discourse of exotic "otherness" that emphasizes passivity on the part of colonized peoples in contrast to the agency of imperial power.

10 These indications are "always carefully couched in filial piety but are also delicately, paradoxically, scripted so that Isaac can take a position inside, but also more than slightly outside, the narrative of prescribed obedience unto death." Sherwood refers to "The Sacrifice of Isaac" by the Italian painter Caravaggio (1571–1610) as a visual sign of the instinctual terror of the son, the recoil of his body at the prospect of becoming a sacrifice to his father's dream ("Binding-Unbinding," 821–861).

11 This version is from Yusuf al-Bahrānī (1695–1772), a commentator on the Qur'an, cited by Firestone in "Merit, Mimesis, and Martyrdom," 107.

12 Combs-Schilling, *Sacred Performances*, 233–244.

13 Bakhos, *The Family of Abraham*, 210.

14 Cited in Ruthven, *Islam in the World*, 49.

15 Bukarhi, *Hadith*, volume 4, book 52, number 68. This authoritative collection of traditional stories about Muhammad and his Companions was compiled in the ninth century.

16 Armstrong, *Muhammad*, 203–210.

17 Ruthven, *Islam in the World*, 54–56.

18 Esposito, *Islam: The Straight Path*, 15.

19 Denny, *Introduction to Islam*, 77.

20 Bukarhi, *Hadith*, volume 4, book 52, number 210.

21 Ådna, *Muhammad and Formation of Sacrifice*, 234.

22 Rappaport, *Ritual and Religion*, 119. Rappaport proposed a universal "natural religion," uniting nature and culture through the self-guided evolution of humans as "that part of the world through which the world as a whole can think about itself." Ådna shows little interest in Rappaport's larger humanistic project, but appropriates his functional theory of ritual.

23 Ådna, *Muhammad and Formation of Sacrifice*, 238.

24 Powers, "Interiors, Intentions," 425–459.

25 Ishāq, *Life of Muhammad*.

26 Ådna, *Muhammad and Formation of Sacrifice*, 223.

27 Ådna, *Muhammad and Formation of Sacrifice*, 18.

28 Ådna, *Muhammad and Formation of Sacrifice*, 224.

29 Bukhari, *Hadīth*, volume 1, book 8, number 386.

30 Ådna, *Muhammad and Formation of Sacrifice*, 219.

31 Ådna, *Muhammad and Formation of Sacrifice*, 250.

32 Bukhari, *Hadīth*, volume 7, book 68, number 454.

33 Denny, *Introduction to Islam*, 124–125.

34 Bukhari, *Hadīth*, volume 2, book 24, number 515.

35 Bukhari, *Hadīth*, volume 1, book 8, number 468.

36 Bukhari, *Hadīth*, volume 2, book 24, number 567.

37 Bukhari, *Hadīth*, volume 2, book 24, number 517.

38 Ådna, *Muhammad and Formation of Sacrifice*, 83.

39 Yocum, "Notes on an Easter Ramadan," 201–230.

40 Bukhari, *Hadīth*, volume 3, book 31, number 128.

41 Bukhari, *Hadīth*, volume 3, book 31, number 125.

42 Bukhari, *Hadīth*, volume 3, book 31, number 120.

43 While this distinction between two kinds of jihad is often cited, the story does not appear in any of the six classic collections of *ahadīth*. In the Qur'an jihād refers to defending the Islamic community against its enemies by arms.

44 Bukhari, *Hadīth*, volume 4, book 52, number 50.

45 There is a similar linkage between meanings of the Greek *martyria* as "martyr" and "witness" in Christian tradition. Jewish tradition also regards martyrdom as a form of witness, as in the story of the seven sons of a Jewish mother, tortured to death for refusing to violate Torah by eating the flesh of swine (2 Maccabees 7).

46 Bukhari, *Hadīth*, volume 4, book 52, number 54.

47 Dale F. Eickelman and James Piscatori provide a nuanced analysis of contemporary negotiations over Islamic symbols and institutions in *Muslim Politics*. See also Esposito, *Unholy War*.

48 Denny, *Introduction to Islam*, 83.

49 Finn, *Al-Qaeda and Sacrifice*, 55.

50 Schubel, *Religious Performance in Contemporary Islam*, 77, 113.

51 Heinz Halm provides detailed accounts of Ashura rituals during their formative period when scripted plays were introduced in *Shi'a Islam*, 63–85.

52 Schubel, *Religious Performance in Contemporary Islam*, 146–150.

53 Schubel, *Religious Performance in Contemporary Islam*, 155.

54 Halm, *Shi'a Islam*, 16.

55 Ayoub, "The Problem of Suffering in Islam," 289. See also his authoritative *Redemptive Suffering in Islam*.

56 Firestone, "Merit, Mimesis, and Martyrdom," 110.

57 Khuri, *Imams and Emirs*, 108. Karen Armstrong notes that, as Muhammad's ward, the teenaged ʿAlī had served the meal and declared his loyalty to the Prophet, evoking this designation (*Muhammad: A Biography*, 105).

58 This hadīth is dated 10 AH (632 CE), the same year Muhammad died, and seems his final word on the subject.

59 The formal statement was that "the gate of *ijtihād* (reasoning) is closed." *Ijtihād* means "making an effort" and is related to jihād or "strenuous effort." One who makes such effort to understand and apply the Qur'an is called a *mujtahid*. While this pronouncement established a conservative approach to Islamic law, Malise Ruthven notes that innovative interpretation continued in Sunni legal tradition, although often represented as "imitation" of the views of past jurists (*Islam in the World*, 142–144).

60 A website sponsored by a Sunni organization for the purpose of informing American converts to Islam includes a section on the "evil and blasphemous beliefs of Shiism," while disavowing violence against individual Shiites; available online at www.discoveringislam.org.

61 Khuri, *Imams and Emirs*, 127–128.

62 Halm, *Shi'a Islam*, 28–30. The medieval compiler of Shiite *ahadīth*, Shaikh Ibn Babuya al-Saduq (d. 991), offered a statement of Twelver devotion in *A Shiite Creed*: "We believe that the Proof of Allah is in His earth and His vicegerent among His slaves in this age of ours is the Upholder of the laws of God, the Expected One, Muhammad ibn al-Hasan al-'Askari. He it is . . . who will fill the earth with justice and equity just as it is now full of oppression and wrong. . . . He is the rightly-guided Mahdi about whom the Prophet gave information that when he appears,

Jesus, son of Mary, will descend upon the earth and pray behind him"; available online at www.al-islam.org.

63 Halm, *Shi'a Islam*, 150.

64 Juergensmeyer, *Terror in the Mind of God*, 170–171.

65 Schimmel, *Mystical Dimensions of Islam*, 14.

66 Hoffman, "Eating and Fasting for God," 469. This essay is a rich source of stories about extreme fasting by early Sufis and the more moderate practice among modern Sufis, who value the virtue of hospitality.

67 Schimmel, *Mystical Dimensions of Islam*, 324–325. Videos of the ceremony are available on YouTube.

68 Lings, *What is Sufism?*.

69 In five case studies of Islamic saints, Scott Kugle highlights their integration of mind and body in *Sufis and Saints' Bodies*. While appreciative of Kugle's conclusion that "Sufism contains crucial resources in the struggle of conscientious Muslims to assert basic human dignity, human values, and humanitarian rights" (292), I find the language of incorporeality to be indispensable in mystic discourse to convey fully the sacrifice of self.

70 Schimmel, *Rumi's World*, 111.

71 Friedlander, *Ninety-Nine Names of Allah*, 16–18.

72 Schuon, *Sufism*, 12.

73 Schimmel, *Mystical Dimensions of Islam*, 68.

74 Armstrong, *History of God*, 228.

75 Schimmel, *Mystical Dimensions of Islam*, 71.

76 Ruthven, *Islam in the World*, 228–230.

77 Schimmel notes the claim that "in rare moments of ecstasy, the uncreated spirit may be united with the created human spirit" is parallel to the Christian mystery of the union without identity between the human and divine "natures" of Christ, although she thinks Hallāj's theory is too complicated and innovative to attribute it to any Christian influence (*Mystical Dimensions of Islam*, 72).

78 Cited in Schimmel, *Mystical Dimensions of Islam*, 76.

79 Al-Junayd, *Kitāb al- Fanā'* (*Book of Fanā'*), in *Early Islamic Mysticism*, 260–265.

80 Denny, *Introduction to Islam*, 233.

81 Haeri, *Elements of Sufism*, 26.

82 Cited by Denny, *Introduction to Islam*, 238.

83 Rūmī, *The Essential Rumi*, translated by Coleman Barks (New York: HarperSanFrancisco, 1995), 39. Subsequent references will be enclosed within parentheses in the text.

84 Bataille, *Theory of Religion*, 49.

85 Cited by Schimmel in *Rumi's World*, 89.

86 *Early Islamic Mysticism*, 151.

87 Recorded by the Sufi writer and poet Farīdu d-Dīn 'Attār (d. 1230) in his *Memorial of the Friends of God*, in *Early Islamic Mysticism*, 169. Other material in this paragraph comes from the same source.

88 Ebrahim Moosa, "Sacrifice," in Esposito, *Oxford Encyclopedia of the Islamic World*, volume 5, 2.

89 Esposito, *Unholy War*, 43. See also Fred M. Donner's account of "The Ismaili Challenge" in *Oxford History of Islam*, 44–49.

90 Professor of Religion David Frankfurter noted at the 2016 Rocky Mountain–Great Plains regional meeting of the American Academy of Religion that we are both repulsed by and drawn to depictions of horrific acts; and the critical question is how much guilt *we* should experience for our fascination. For a discussion of dramatic performances of sacrificial themes in twentieth-century Europe, see Fischer-Lichte, *Theatre, Sacrifice, Ritual*. Jon Pahl provides an examination of literary and cinematic imagery of violent sacrifice in American culture in *Empire of Sacrifice*.

91 Reported by *Al-Jazeera* (April 12, 2016), available online at www.aljazeera.com.

92 Dunn, "The Female Martyr and the Politics of Death, 217.

93 John Esposito sketches appropriations of Islamic themes for militant forms of jihād in *Unholy War*, 41–61.

94 Hervieu-Léger, *Religion as a Chain of Memory*, 143–149.

95 Dunn, "The Female Martyr," 214.

96 See article on Qutb by Paul Berman, "Al Qaeda's Philosopher."

97 Qutb, *Social Justice in Islam*, 46.

98 Cited in Juergensmeyer, *Terror in the Mind of God*, 82.

99 Mawdūdī, *Towards Understanding Islam*, 100.

100 Denny, *Introduction to Islam*, 208.

101 Asma Afsaruddin traces the early interpretive tradition of jihād, showing that its militant meaning became dominant among legal scholars, in *Striving in the Path of God*. She also explores the dissenting interpretation of legal experts who advocated for the greater moral excellence of exercising patience and avoiding violence.

102 For a detailed examination of parallels with Western just war theory, see Kelsay, *Arguing the Just War in Islam*.

103 Esposito, *Unholy War*, 99.

104 Dunn, "The Female Martyr," 216.

105 Cited in Kelsay, *Arguing the Just War in Islam*, 156–157.

106 Asad, *On Suicide Bombing*, 43–44.

107 Asad, *On Suicide Bombing*, 91.

108 Finn, *Al-Qaeda and Sacrifice*, 13.

109 The hadīth is cited in Murata and Chittick, *The Vision of Islam*, 273. The text of Muhammad 'Atta's final instructions to the hijackers is reproduced in Lincoln, *Holy Terrors*, 93–98. It is significant that 'Atta urged, "Remember the battle of the prophet . . . against the infidels, as he went on building the Islamic state." Their own deaths were on behalf of Osama bin Laden's version of that ideal.

110 Finn, *Al-Qaeda and Sacrifice*, 48, 60–61.

111 Finn, *Al-Qaeda and Sacrifice*, 55.

112 Finn, *Al-Qaeda and Sacrifice*, 71.

113 This translation is by Murata and Chittick in their section on *Ihsan* as the dimension of intentionality in the Islamic worldview (*The Vision of Islam*, 267–317).

114 Nasr, *The Heart of Islam*, 235–236.

CONCLUSION

  1 Kimball, *When Religion Becomes Evil*; Kimball, *When Religion Becomes Lethal*.

BIBLIOGRAPHY

Abelard, Peter. *Collationes*. Translated by John Marenbon and Giovanni Orlandi. Oxford: Clarendon Press, 2001.

Adams, Marilyn McCord. *Horrendous Evils and the Goodness of God*. Ithaca: Cornell University Press, 1999.

Ådna, Gerd Marie. *Muhammad and the Formation of Sacrifice*. Frankfurt: Peter Lang GmbH, 2014.

Afsaruddin, Asma. *Striving in the Path of God: Jihad and Martyrdom in Islamic Thought*. New York: Oxford University Press, 2013.

St. Anselm. *Cur Deus Homo* in *Saint Anselm: Basic Writings*. Translated by S. N. Deane. Boston: Open Court, 1962.

Armstrong, Karen. *A History of God: The 4000-Year Quest of Judaism, Christianity and Islam*. New York: Alfred A. Knopf, 1994.

———. *Muhammad: A Biography of the Prophet*. New York: HarperSanFrancisco, 1992.

Asad, Talal. *On Suicide Bombing*. New York: Columbia University Press, 2007.

Ashley, Kathleen and Pamela Sheingron. *Writing Faith: Text, Sign, and History in the Miracles of Sainte Foy*. Chicago: University of Chicago Press, 1999.

St. Athanasius. *De Incarnatione Verbi Dei (On the Incarnation of the Word)*. Translated by a Religious of C.S.M.V. London: A. R. Mowbray, 1953.

'Attār, Farīdu d-Dīn. *Memorial of the Friends of God* in *Early Islamic Mysticism*.

St. Augustine. *The City of God*. Translated by Marcus Dods et al. New York: Modern Library, 1950.

Aulén, Gustaf. *Christus Victor: An Historical Study of the Three Main Types of the Idea of the Atonement*. Translated by A. G. Hebert. New York: Macmillan, 1969.

Ayoub, Mahmoud. *Redemptive Suffering in Islam: A Study of the Devotional Aspects of 'Ashura' in Twelver Shiism*. The Hague: Mouton, 1978.

———"The Problem of Suffering in Islam." *Journal of Dharma* 2:3 (1977).

Bailie, Gil. *Violence Unveiled: Humanity at the Crossroads*. New York: Crossroads, 2001.

Bakhos, Carol. *The Family of Abraham: Jewish, Christian, and Muslim Interpretations*. Cambridge, MA: Harvard University Press, 2014.

Barrett, C. K., editor. *The New Testament Background*. San Francisco: HarperCollins, 1989.

Bataille, Georges. *Theory of Religion*. Translated by Robert Hurley. New York: Zone Books, 1992.

———. *The Accursed Share: An Essay on General Economy*. Volume 1: *Consumption*. Translated by Robert Hurley. New York: Zone Books, 1991.

————. *Inner Experience*. Translated by Leslie Ann Boldt. Albany: SUNY Press, 1988.

————. *Erotism: Death and Sensuality* (1957). Translated by Mary Dalwood. San Francisco: City Lights Books, 1986.

Baumgarten, Martin, editor. *Sacrifice in Religious Experience*. Leiden: Brill, 2002.

Benko, Stephen. *Pagan Rome and Early Christians*. Bloomington: Indiana University Press, 1984.

Berlin, Adele and Marc Zvi Brettler, editors. *The Jewish Study Bible: Jewish Publication Society Tanakh Translation*. Second edition. New York: Oxford University Press, 2014.

Berman, Paul. "Al Qaeda's Philosopher." *New York Times Magazine*, March 22, 2003.

Bokser, Baruch K. "Ritualizing the Seder." *Journal of the American Academy of Religion* 56:3 (1988).

Buber, Martin. *Eclipse of God*. New York: Harper Torchbook, 1957.

Buber, Martin, editor. *Tales of the Hasidim: The Later Masters*. New York: Schocken Books, 1948.

Bukarhi, Muhammad. *Hadith*. www.sahih-bukhari.com.

Burrow, Rufus, Jr. *God and Human Dignity: The Personalism, Theology, and Ethics of Martin Luther King, Jr.* Notre Dame: University of Notre Dame Press, 2006.

Bushnell, Horace. *God in Christ* (1849). Reprint edition. New York: AMS Press, 1972.

————. *Sermons for the New Life*. New York: Charles Scribner's Sons, 1903.

————. *The Vicarious Sacrifice, Grounded in Principles of Universal Obligation*. New York: Charles Scribner, 1871.

Calasso, Roberto. *Ardor*. Translated by Richard Dixon. New York: Farrar, Straus and Giroux, 2014.

Calvin, John. *Institutes of the Christian Religion*. Translated by Ford Lewis Battles. Philadelphia: Westminster Press, 1960.

Carrasco, David. *City of Sacrifice: The Aztec Empire and the Role of Violence in Civilization*. Boston: Beacon Press, 1999.

Carter, Jeffrey, editor. *Understanding Religious Sacrifice: A Reader*. New York: Continuum, 2003.

Chidester, David. *Christianity: A Global History*. New York: HarperSanFrancisco, 2000.

Coakley, Sarah. *Sacrifice Regained: Reconsidering the Rationality of Religious Belief*. Cambridge: Cambridge University Press, 2012.

Cohen, Arthur. *The Tremendum: A Theological Interpretation of the Holocaust*. New York: Crossroads, 1981.

Combs-Schilling, M. E. *Sacred Performances: Islam, Sexuality, and Sacrifice*. New York: Columbia University Press, 1989.

Cone, James H. *The Cross and the Lynching Tree*. Maryknoll, NY: Orbis Books, 2011.

Conkin, Paul K. *American Originals: Homemade Varieties of Christianity*. Chapel Hill: University of North Carolina Press, 1997.

Cragg, Kenneth. *Readings in the Qur'an*. London: Fount Paperbacks, 1995.

Dart, John. *The Jesus of Heresy and History: The Discovery and Meaning of the Nag Hammadi Gnostic Library*. New York: Harper & Row, 1988.

Day, John. *Molech: A God of Human Sacrifice in the Old Testament*. Cambridge: Cambridge University Press, 1989.

Denny, Frederick Mathewson. *An Introduction to Islam*. Second edition. New York: Macmillan, 1994.

Derrida, Jacques. *The Gift of Death & Literature in Secret*. Second edition. Chicago: University of Chicago Press, 2008.

Donner, Fred M. "The Ismaili Challenge" in Esposito, *Oxford History of Islam*, 44–49.

Dorrien, Gary. *The Making of American Liberal Theology: Crisis, Irony, & Postmodernity, 1950–2005*. Philadelphia: Westminster John Knox Press, 2006.

———. *The Making of American Liberal Theology: Imagining Progressive Religion, 1805–1900*. Louisville: Westminster John Knox Press, 2001.

Dunn, Shannon. "The Female Martyr and the Politics of Death: An Examination of the Martyr Discourses of Vibia Perpetua and Wafa Idris." *Journal of the American Academy of Religion* 78:1 (2010).

Durkheim, Émile. *The Elementary Forms of Religious Life* (1912). Translated by Carol Cosman and abridged by Mark S. Cladis. New York: Oxford University Press, 2001.

Early Islamic Mysticism: Sufi, Qur'an, Mi'raj, Poetic and Theological Writings. Translated by Michael A. Sells. New York: Paulist Press, 1996.

Eberhart, Christian A., editor. *Ritual and Metaphor: Sacrifice in the Bible*. Atlanta: Society of Biblical Literature, 2011.

Ehrman, Bart D. *The New Testament: A Historical Introduction to the Early Christian Writings*. New York: Oxford University Press, 1997.

Eickelman, Dale F. and James Piscatori. *Muslim Politics*. Princeton: Princeton University Press, 1996.

Eisenbaum, Pamela. *Paul Was Not a Christian: The Original Message of a Misunderstood Apostle*. New York: HarperOne, 2009.

Eliade, Mircea. *The Sacred and the Profane: The Nature of Religion*. Translated by Willard R. Trask. New York: Harcourt Brace Jovanovich, 1959.

The Epic of Gilgamesh. Translated by Maureen Gallery Kovacs. Stanford: Stanford University Press, 1989.

Esposito, John L., editor-in-chief. *The Oxford Encyclopedia of the Islamic World*. New York: Oxford University Press, 2009.

Esposito, John L., editor. *The Oxford History of Islam*. New York: Oxford University Press, 1999.

Esposito, John L. *Unholy War: Terror in the Name of Islam*. New York: Oxford, 2002.

———. *Islam: The Straight Path*. Third edition. New York: Oxford University Press, 1998.

Fackenheim, Emil L. *To Mend the World: Foundations of Post-Holocaust Thought*. New York: Schocken Books, 1982.

———. *The Jewish Return into History: Reflections in the Age of Auschwitz and a New Jerusalem*. New York: Schocken Books, 1978.

———. *God's Presence in History: Jewish Affirmations and Philosophical Reflections*. New York: Harper Torchbooks, 1970.

Farley, Edward. *Deep Symbols: Their Postmodern Effacement and Reclamation*. Valley Forge, PA: Trinity Press International, 1996.

Faust, Drew Gilpin. *This Republic of Suffering: Death and the American Civil War*. New York: Vintage Books, 2008.

Feldman, Yael S. *Glory and Agony: Isaac's Sacrifice and National Narrative*. Stanford: Stanford University Press, 2010.

Festinger, Leon, Henry Riecken, and Stanley Schachter. *When Prophecy Fails*. Minneapolis: University of Minnesota Press, 1956.

Finn, Melissa. *Al-Qaeda and Sacrifice: Martyrdom, War and Politics*. London: Pluto Press, 2012.

Firestone, Reuven. "Holy War in Modern Judaism? 'Mitzvah War' and the Problem of the 'Three Vows.'" *Journal of the American Academy of Religion* 74:4 (2006).

———. "Merit, Mimesis, and Martyrdom: Aspects of Shi'ite Meta-historical Exegesis on Abraham's Sacrifice in Light of Jewish, Christian, and Sunni Muslim Tradition." *Journal of the American Academy of Religion* 66:1 (1998).

Firth, Raymond. *Religion: A Humanist Interpretation*. New York: Routledge, 1996.

Fischer-Lichte, Erika. *Theatre, Sacrifice, Ritual: Exploring Forms of Political Theatre*. New York: Routledge, 2005.

Flynn, Maureen. "The Spiritual Uses of Pain in Spanish Mysticism." *Journal of the American Academy of Religion* 64:2 (1996).

Pope Francis. *Pope Francis: His Essential Wisdom*. Edited by Carol Kelly-Gangi. New York: Fall River Press, 2014.

Freud, Sigmund. *The Future of an Illusion* (1927). Translated by W. D. Robson-Scott. Garden City, NY: Anchor Books, 1964.

Friedlander, Shems. *Ninety-Nine Names of Allah*. San Francisco: HarperCollins, 1993.

Gamble, Harry Y. *The New Testament Canon: Its Making and Meaning*. Philadelphia: Fortress Press, 1985.

Ginsburg, Yitzchak. *"I am asleep yet my heart is awake": a Chassidic discourse*. Rechovot, Israel: Gal Einai Institute, 1996.

Girard, René. *Sacrifice*. Translated by Matthew Pattillo and David Dawson. East Lansing: Michigan State University Press, 2011.

———. *The Scapegoat*. Translated by Yvonne Freccero. Baltimore: Johns Hopkins University Press, 1986.

———. *Violence and the Sacred*. Translated by Patrick Gregory. Baltimore: Johns Hopkins University Press, 1977.

The Gnostic Scriptures: Ancient Wisdom for a New Age. Translated by Bentley Layton. New York: Doubleday, 1987.

The Gospel of Thomas: The Hidden Sayings of Jesus. Translated with introduction by Marvin Meyer. New York: HarperSanFrancisco, 1992.

Green, Arthur. *A Guide to the Zohar*. Stanford: Stanford University Press, 2004.

Grimes, Ronald L. *Ritual Criticism: Case Studies in Its Practice, Essays on Its Theory*. Columbia: University of South Carolina Press, 1990.

———. "Infelicitous Performances and Ritual Criticism." *Semeia* 43 (1988).

Grimm, Veronika E. *From Feasting to Fasting, the Evolution of a Sin: Attitudes to Food in Late Antiquity.* New York: Routledge, 1996.

Gubar, Susan. *Judas: A Biography.* New York: Norton, 2009.

Haeri, Shaykh Fadhlalla. *The Elements of Sufism.* New York: Elements Books, 1990.

Halbertal, Moshe. *On Sacrifice.* Princeton: Princeton University Press, 2012.

Halm, Heinz. *Shi'a Islam: From Religion to Revolution.* Translated by Allison Brown. Princeton: Markus Wiener Publishers, 1997.

Hamerton-Kelly, Robert G., editor. *Violent Origins: Walter Burkert, René Girard, and Jonathan Z. Smith on Ritual Killing and Cultural Formation.* Stanford: Stanford University Press, 1987.

Hervieu-Léger, Danièle. *Religion as a Chain of Memory.* Translated by Simon Lee. New Brunswick, NJ: Rutgers University Press, 2000.

Heschel, Abraham Joshua. *Man's Quest for God: Studies in Prayer and Symbolism.* New York: Charles Scribner's Sons, 1954.

Hitchens, Christopher. *god is not Great: How Religion Poisons Everything.* New York: Twelve, Hachette Book Group USA, 2007.

Hocking, Ian. "The Logic of Pascal's Wager." *American Philosophical Quarterly* 9:2 (1972).

Hoffman, Valerie J. "Eating and Fasting for God in Sufi Tradition." *Journal of the American Academy of Religion* 63:3 (1995).

Hüsken, Ute, editor. *When Rituals Go Wrong: Mistakes, Failure, and the Dynamics of Ritual.* Leiden: Brill, 2007.

Ibn Ishāq. *The Life of Muhammad: A Translation* [from Ibn Hishām's adaptation] *of Ishāq's Sirat rasul Allāh* by A. Guillaume. New York: Oxford University Press, 1967.

Jantzen, Grace M. *Becoming Divine: Towards a Feminist Philosophy of Religion.* Bloomington: Indiana University Press, 1999.

Jay, Nancy. *Throughout Your Generations Forever: Sacrifice, Religion, and Paternity.* Chicago: University of Chicago Press, 1992.

Jones, Lindsay, editor. *Encyclopedia of Religion.* Second edition. Detroit: Thomson Gale, 2005.

Juergensmeyer, Mark. *Terror in the Mind of God: The Global Rise of Religious Violence.* Berkeley: University of California Press, 2001.

Kant, Immanuel. *Religion Within the Limits of Reason Alone* (1794). Translated by T. M. Green and H. H. Hudson. New York: Harper Torchbooks, 1960.

Kasser, Rodolphe, Marvin Meyer, and Gregor Wurst, editors. *The Gospel of Judas from Codex Tchacos.* Washington, DC: National Geographic Society, 2006.

Kearney, Richard. "Myths and Scapegoats: The Case of René Girard." *Theory, Culture & Society: Explorations in Critical Social Science* 12 (1995).

Keenan, Dennis King. *The Question of Sacrifice.* Bloomington: Indiana University Press, 2005.

Kelsay, John. *Arguing the Just War in Islam.* Cambridge, MA: Harvard University Press, 2007.

Khuri, Fuad I. *Imams and Emirs: State, Religion and Sects in Islam/* London: Saqi Books, 1990.

Kierkegaard, Søren. *Fear and Trembling* (1843). Translated by Alastair Hannay. New York: Penguin, 1986.

Kimball, Charles. *When Religion Becomes Lethal: The Explosive Mix of Politics and Religion in Judaism, Christianity, and Islam.* San Francisco: Jossey-Bass, 2011.

———. *When Religion Becomes Evil: Five Warning Signs.* New York: HarperOne, 2008.

King, Karen L. *What Is Gnosticism?* Cambridge, MA: Belknap Press, 2005.

King, Martin Luther, Jr. *Strength to Love* (1963). Philadelphia: Fortress Press, 1981.

Knust, Jennifer Wright and Zsuzsanna Varhelyi, editors. *Ancient Mediterranean Sacrifice.* New York: Oxford University Press, 2011.

Koester, Helmut. "One Jesus and Four Primitive Gospels." *Harvard Theological Review* 61:2 (1968).

Kołakowski, Leszek. *Metaphysical Horror* (1988). Revised edition. Chicago: University of Chicago Press, 2001.

Kolodiejchuk, Brian, editor. *Mother Teresa: Come Be My Light—The Private Writings of the Saint of Calcutta.* New York: Random House, 2007.

The Koran. Translated by N. J. Dawood. New York: Penguin Books, 1997.

Kripal, Jeffrey J. *The Serpent's Gift: Gnostic Reflections on the Study of Religion.* Chicago: University of Chicago Press, 2007.

Kugle, Scott. *Sufis and Saints' Bodies: Mysticism, Corporeality, and Sacred Power in Islam.* Chapel Hill: University of North Carolina Press, 2007.

Landman, Isaac, editor. *The Universal Jewish Encyclopedia.* New York: Universal Jewish Encyclopedia, 1939–1943.

Leemhuis, F. "Ibrāhīm's sacrifice of his son in the early post-Koranic tradition" in Noort and Tigchelaar, *Sacrifice of Isaac.*

Lefkowitz, Mary R. "The Motivations of St. Perpetua's Martyrdom." *Journal of the American Academy of Religion* 44:3 (1976).

Levenson, Jon D. *Inheriting Abraham: The Legacy of the Patriarch in Judaism, Christianity, and Islam.* Princeton: Princeton University Press, 2012.

———. *The Death and Resurrection of the Beloved Son: The Transformation of Child Sacrifice in Judaism and Christianity.* New Haven: Yale University Press, 1993.

Levinas, Emanuel. *Proper Names.* Translated by Michael B. Smith. Stanford: Stanford University Press.

Lewis, Brenda Ralph. *Ritual Sacrifice: An Illustrated History.* Sparkford, UK: Sutton Publishing, 2001.

Lincoln, Bruce. *Holy Terrors: Thinking about Religion after September 11.* Chicago: University of Chicago Press, 2003.

Lings, Martin. *What is Sufism?* Berkeley: University of California Press, 1975.

Luther, Martin. *Luther: Early Theological Works.* Translated by James Atkinson. Philadelphia: Westminster Press, 1962.

———. "Disputation on the Power and Efficacy of Indulgences" in *Works of Martin Luther,* edited by Adolph Spaeth et al. Philadelphia: Holman, 1915.

Maccoby, Hyam. *Judas Iscariot and the Myth of Jewish Evil.* New York: Free Press, 1992.

Martínez, Florentino Garcia. "The Sacrifice of Isaac in 4Q225" in Noort and Tigchelaar, *Sacrifice of Isaac.*

The Martyrdom of Saint Polycarp. Translated by Massey Hamilton Shepherd, Jr. in *Early Christian Fathers*, edited by Cyril C. Richardson. Philadelphia: Westminster Press, 1953.

Matt, Daniel C., translator and editor. *The Essential Kabbalah: The Heart of Jewish Mysticism* New York: QPB, 1995.

Mauss, Marcel. *The Gift: The Form and Reason for Exchange in Archaic Societies* (1950). Translated by W. D. Halls. New York: W. W. Norton, 2000.

Mawdūdī, Sayyid Abul A'lā. *Towards Understanding Islam.* Leicestershire, UK: Islamic Foundation, 1982.

McClymond, Kathryn. *Beyond Sacred Violence: A Comparative Study of Sacrifice.* Baltimore: Johns Hopkins University Press, 2008.

Meeks, Wayne A., general editor. *The HarperCollins Study Bible.* New York: Harper-Collins, 1993.

Meszaros, Julia and Johannes Zachhuber, editors. *Sacrifice and Modern Thought.* Oxford: Oxford University Press, 2013.

Milbank, John. "Stories of Sacrifice: From Wellhausen to Girard." *Theory, Culture & Society: Explorations in Critical Social Science* 12 (1995).

Milgrom, Jacob. "Were the Firstborn Sacrificed to YHWH? To Molek? Popular Practice or Divine Command?" in Baumgarten, *Sacrifice in Religious Experience.*

Milman, Yoseph. "The Sacrifice of Isaac and Its Subversive Variations in Contemporary Hebrew Protest Poetry." *Religion & Literature* 23:2 (1991).

Moosa, Ebrahim. "Sacrifice" in *Oxford Encyclopedia of the Islamic World.*

Morgan, Michael L. *Beyond Auschwitz: Post-Holocaust Jewish Thought in America.* New York: Oxford University Press, 2001.

Moss, Candida R. *The Myth of Persecution: How Early Christians Invented a Story of Martyrdom.* New York: HarperCollins, 2013.

———. "The Discourse of Voluntary Martyrdom: Ancient and Modern." *Church History* 81:3 (2012).

———. *The Other Christs: Imitating Jesus in Ancient Christian Ideologies of Martyrdom.* New York: Oxford University Press, 2010.

Murata, Sachiko and William C. Chittick. *The Vision of Islam.* New York: Paragon House, 1994.

Nahshoni, Kobi. "Rabbi Calls for Sacrifice on Temple Mount." *Ynet*, April 5, 2011.

Nasr, Seyyed Hossein. *The Heart of Islam: Enduring Values for Humanity.* New York: HarperSanFrancisco, 2002.

Neusner, Jacob. *The Talmud of Babylonia: An Academic Commentary.* Atlanta: Scholar's Press, 1994.

———. *Between Time and Eternity: The Essentials of Judaism.* Belmont, CA: Wadsworth, 1975.

———. *First-Century Judaism in Crisis: Yohanan ben Zakkai and the Renaissance of Torah.* Nashville: Abingdon Press, 1975.

Neusner, Jacob, Alan J. Avery-Peck, and William Scott Green, editors. *The Encyclopedia of Judaism*. New York: Continuum, 1999.

Nietzsche, Frederick. *Twilight of the Idols* (1889). Translated by R. J. Hollingdale. Baltimore: Penguin Books, 1974.

———. *The Anti-Christ* (1895). Translated by R. J. Hollingdale. Baltimore: Penguin Books, 1974.

Noort, Edward and Eibert Tigchelaar, editors. *The Sacrifice of Isaac: The Aqedah (Genesis 22) and Its Interpretations*. Leiden: Brill, 2002.

Otto, Rudolf. *The Idea of the Holy: An Inquiry into the Non-rational Factor in the Idea of the Divine and Its Relation to the Rational*. Translated by John W. Harvey. London: Oxford University Press, 1924.

Pagels, Elaine. *Beyond Belief: The Secret Gospel of Thomas*. New York: Random House, 2003.

Pahl, Jon. *Empire of Sacrifice: The Religious Origins of American Violence*. New York: New York University Press, 2010.

Pascal, Blaise. *Pensées*. Translated by W. F. Trotter. New York: Modern Library, 1941.

Pardes, Ilana. *Countertraditions in the Bible: A Feminist Approach*. Cambridge, MA: Harvard University Press, 1993.

Perkins, Judith. *The Suffering Self: Pain and Narrative Representation in the Early Christian Era*. New York: Routledge, 1995.

Peters, F. E. *The Hajj*. Princeton: Princeton University Press, 1994.

Pfitzner, Victor C. *Hebrews* in *Abingdon New Testament Commentaries*, edited by Victor Paul Furnish. Nashville: Abingdon Press, 1997.

Powers, Paul R. "Interiors, Intentions, and the 'Spirituality' of Islamic Ritual Practice." *Journal of the American Academy of Religion* 72:2 (2004).

Premawardhana, Devaka. "Transformational Tithing: Sacrifice and Reciprocity in a Neo-Pentecostal Church." *Nova Religio: The Journal of Alternative and Emergent Religions* 15:4 (2012).

Pseudo-Dionysius: The Complete Works. Translated by Colm Luibheid. New York: Paulist Press, 1987.

Qutb, Sayyid. *Social Justice in Islam*. Translated by John B. Hardie. Oneonta, NY: Islamic Publications International, 1953.

Rappaport, Roy A. *Ritual and Religion in the Making of Humanity*. New York: Cambridge University Press, 1999.

Recla, Matthew. "*Autothanatos*: The Martyr's Self-Formation." *Journal of the American Academy of Religion* 82:2 (2014).

Robinson, James M., General Editor. *The Nag Hammadi Library in English*. Revised edition. New York: Harper & Row, 1988.

Rosenberg, David. *Dreams of Being Eaten Alive: The Literary Core of the Kabbalah*. New York: Harmony Books, 2000.

Rousseau, Philip. "The Desert Fathers: Antony and Pachomius" in *The Study of Spirituality*, edited by Cheslyn Jones et al. New York: Oxford University Press, 1986.

Rubenstein, Richard. *After Auschwitz: Radical Theology and Contemporary Judaism.* Indianapolis: Bobbs-Merrill, 1966.

Rūmī, Jalāl al-Dīn. *The Essential Rumi.* Translated by Coleman Barks. New York: HarperSanFrancisco, 1995.

Ruthven, Malise. *Islam in the World.* Second edition. New York: Oxford University Press, 2000.

Said, Edward. *Orientalism.* New York: Random House, 1978.

Sanders, Andy F. "Kierkegaardian Reading of the Sacrifice of Isaac" in Baumgarten, *Sacrifice in Religious Experience.*

Satlow, Michael. "'And on the Earth You Shall Sleep': *Talmud Torah* and Rabbinic Asceticism." *Journal of Religion* 83:2 (2003).

Schimmel, Annemarie. *Rumi's World: The Life and Work of the Great Sufi Poet.* Boston: Shambhala, 2001.

———. *Mystical Dimensions of Islam.* Chapel Hill: University of North Carolina, 1975.

Scholem, Gershom. *Major Trends in Jewish Mysticism* (1961). New York: Schocken Books, 1995.

———. *On the Kabbalah and Its Symbolism.* Translated by Ralph Manheim. New York: Schocken Books, 1969.

Schrag, Craig O. "Transcendence and Transversality" in *Transcendence and Beyond: A Postmodern Inquiry,* edited by John Caputo and Michael J. Scanlon. Bloomington: Indiana University Press, 2007.

Schubel, Vernon James. *Religious Performance in Contemporary Islam: Shiʻi Devotional Rituals in South Asia.* Columbia: University of South Carolina Press, 1993.

Schuon, Frithjof. *Sufism: Veil and Quintessence.* Bloomington, IN: World Wisdom Books, 1981.

Schwartz, Regina M. *The Curse of Cain: The Violent Legacy of Monotheism.* Chicago: University of Chicago Press, 1997.

Seligman, Adam B., Robert P. Weller, Michael J. Puett, and Bennett Simon. *Ritual and Its Consequences: An Essay on the Limits of Sincerity.* New York: Oxford University Press, 2008.

Sherwood, Yvonne. "Binding-Unbinding: Divided Responses of Judaism, Christianity, and Islam to the 'Sacrifice' of Abraham's Beloved Son." *Journal of the American Academy of Religion* 72:4 (2004).

Silber, Ilana F. "Echoes of Sacrifice? Repertoires of Giving in the Great Religions," in Baumgarten, *Sacrifice in Religious Experience.*

Smith, Jonathan Z. *Relating Religion: Essays in the Study of Religion.* Chicago: University of Chicago Press, 2004.

Smith, Jonathan Z., editor. *HarperCollins Dictionary of Religion.* New York: HarperCollins, 1995.

———. *To Take Place: Toward Theory in Ritual.* Chicago: University of Chicago Press, 1987.

———. *Imagining Religion: From Babylon to Jonestown.* Chicago: University of Chicago Press, 1982.

Sosis, Richard, and Eric Bressler. "Cooperation and Commune Longevity: A Test of Costly Signaling Theory." *Cross-Cultural Research* 37:2 (2003).

Steinberg, Paul. *Celebrating the Jewish Year: The Fall Holidays.* Edited by Janet Greenstein Potter. Philadelphia: Jewish Publication Society, 2007.

Stendahl, Krister. *Paul Among Jews and Gentiles.* Philadelphia: Fortress Press, 1976.

Strenski, Ivan. *Contesting Sacrifice: Religion, Nationalism, and Social Thought in France.* Chicago: University of Chicago Press, 2002.

Stroumsa, Guy G. *End of Sacrifice: Religious Transformations in Late Antiquity.* Translated by Susan Emanuel. Chicago: University of Chicago Press, 2009.

Taylor, Mark C. *About Religion: Economies of Faith in Virtual Cultures.* Chicago: University of Chicago Press, 1999.

St. Teresa of Avila. *The Way of Perfection.* Translated and edited by E. Allison Peers. New York: Image Books, 1964.

———. *Life of St. Teresa of Jesus, of the Order of Our Lady of Carmel.* Translated by David Lewis. New York: Benziger Bros., 1904.

Thomas à Kempis. *The Imitation of Christ.* Translated by John Payne. Boston: Gould and Lincoln, 1856.

St. Thomas Aquinas. *Summa Theologica.* Translated by Fathers of the English Dominican Province. Benziger Bros., 1947.

Townsend, Philippa. "Sacrifice and Race in the *Gospel of Judas,*" in *Judasevangelium und Codex Tchacos,* edited by Enno Edzard Popkes and Gregor Wurst. Mohr Siebeck, 2012.

Tweed, Thomas A. *Crossing and Dwelling: A Theory of Religion.* Cambridge, MA: Harvard University Press, 2006.

Ullmann, C. "Life of Thomas à Kempis," in *Thomas à Kempis's Imitation of Christ.* Boston: Gould and Lincoln, 1863.

Van Seters, John. *Abraham in History and Interpretation.* New Haven: Yale University Press, 1975.

von Stuckrad, Kocku, editor. *The Brill Dictionary of Religion.* Leiden: Brill, 2007.

Watts, James W. *Ritual and Rhetoric in Leviticus: From Sacrifice to Scripture.* New York: Cambridge University Press, 2007.

Weddle, David L. *Miracles: Wonder and Meaning in World Religions.* New York: New York University Press, 2010.

Whitehead, Alfred North. *Religion in the Making* (1926). Cleveland: Meridian Books, 1960.

Wiesel, Elie. *Night.* Translated by Marion Wiesel from French edition of 1958. New York: Hill and Wang, 2006.

Wigoder, Geoffrey, editor-in-chief. *The New Encyclopedia of Judaism.* New York: New York University Press, 2002.

Wills, Lawrence M. "Ascetic Theology Before Asceticism? Jewish Narratives and the Decentering of the Self." *Journal of the American Academy of Religion* 74:4 (2006).

Yocum, Glenn. "Notes on an Easter Ramadan." *Journal of the American Academy of Religion* 60:2 (1992).

Žižek, Slavoj. *Violence: Six Sideways Reflections.* London: Profile Books, 2009.

The Zohar. Translated by Daniel C. Matt. Pritzker Edition. Stanford: Stanford University Press, 2004.

Zorgdrager, Heleen. "The Sacrifice of Abraham as a (Temporary) Resolution of a Descent Conflict? A Gender-motivated Reading of Genesis 22" in Baumgarten, *Sacrifice in Religious Experience.*

Zornberg, Avivah Gottlieb. *The Murmuring Deep: Reflections on the Biblical Unconscious.* New York: Schocken Books, 2009.

———. *The Beginning of Desire: Reflections on Genesis.* New York: Doubleday, 1995.

INDEX

Abelard, Peter: atonement theory of, 131–132, 146, 147

Abraham, 11, 13, 15; as Christian "father of faith," 4, 102–103; as Islamic prophet, 4, 156–164; as Jewish patriarch, 4–5. *See also* Akedah

"Abrahamic religions," controversy about, 5–6

Adams, Marilyn McCord: "horrendous evil," 219n89

Ådna, Gerd Marie: analysis of Islamic ritual sacrifice by, 167–170

Afsaruddin, Asma, 228n101

Akedah (binding), 48–59, 96, 208–209; interpretation of in Zohar, 81; interpretations of, by Derrida, 54–56; by Jay, 37–38; by Kant, 154; by Kierkegaard, 15, 53–54, 58; by Zornberg, 52–53; Jewish ritual appropriation of, 64–66; moral criticism of, 57–58, 64; as prototype of sacrifice of Christ, 111, 123, 142; Shiite interpretation of, 181; as site of Temple, 85; as Zionist ideal and poetic critique, 98–99

'Alī: first Shiite Imam, 178–179, 181–183, successor (caliph) of Muhammad, 175–177, 182

Amicahai, Yehuda, 98–99

Anderson, Benedict: "imagined community," 201, 202

Anselm: atonement theory of, 128–129

Aquinas, Thomas, 137, 142, 144; Eucharistic theology of, 140–141

Ariel, Yisrael: founder of Temple Institute, 85–86

Aristotle, 21, 140, 221n43

Armstrong, Karen, 165, 226n57

Asad, Talal, 203–205

'Ashūrā: ritual enactment of martyrdom of Husayn, 178–181

Athanasius, 115; defense of sacrificial theology by, 127–128

Athenagorus: defense of Christian faith by, 121–122

'Atta, Muhammad: sacrificial discourse of, 205, 228n109

Augustine: Eucharistic theology of, 139–140

Aulén, Gustaf, 131

Ayoub, Mahmoud, 180–181

Azazel (goat demon), 64, 67

Bakhos, Carol, 5, 163

Barks, Coleman, 193

Bataille, Georges: sacrifice as "accursed share," 40–45, 60; in mystic experience, 83, 138, 186, 192, 194, 209; in release from self-interest, 135, 186, 204

Berkovitz, Will, 66

Bokser, Baruch, 88

Buber, Martin, 73, 82; critique of sacrifice by, 55–56, 58, 99

Bushnell, Horace: atonement theory of, 147–150

Cain, 59–61, 117, 217n29

Calvin, John: Eucharistic theology of, 141–142

meaning of by Hallāj, 188; sacrificial rituals of Muhammad during, 167–170
Halbertal, Moshe, 47, 61
al-Hallāj (Husayn ibn Mansūr), 187–188
Halm, Heinz, 180
Hawking, Stephen, 194
Hervieu-Léger, Danièle: religion as "chain of memory," 201
Heschel, Abraham Joshua, 72, 82
Hitler, Adolph, 90, 96, 97
Holocaust (burnt offering), 72; as metaphor, 3, 26; as Nazi genocide, 72–73, 89–91, 93–98

Ibrāhīm (Abraham): call to sacrifice as test of, 156–160; miraculous rescue from fire of, 157, 180; in Shiite tradition, 181
Imams: in Shiʿa Islam, 181–184
Incarnation of Christ: as sacrifice, 105–106
Irenaeus: critic of Gnostic writings, 115, 119; disciple of Polycarp, 122, 124
Ismāʿīl (Ishmael): prophet of Islam, 157; son of the sacrifice, 158–160

Jantzen, Grace, 39, 162
Jay, Nancy: sacrifice as marker of patriarchy, 37–39, 120, 223n76
Jesus, 5, 11, 12, 16, 103; Gnostic view of, 115–120; incarnation of, 105–106, 128–129; as model, 120, 122–125, 133, 135, 146–149, 152, 213n14; in New Testament Gospels, 110–111; as ransom to Devil, 130; real presence of in Mass, 2, 139; role in Islam, 163–164, 176, 204; sacrificial death of, 9, 26, 36, 100–102, 107, 109, 121, 127, 131, 144–145; wounds of, 146
Jihād, 173–175; just conditions of, 202–203; mystical criticism of, 197; polemical use of, 197; as sacrifice of self and others, 203–206; in Shiite tradition, 184; and terrorism, 198–200
al-Junayd, Abū l-Qasīm, 189–190

Kaʿbah, 158, 164, 166
Kabbalah, 76–85, 87, 90; cosmic vision of, 109; rejection by Wiesel, 94
Kant, Immanuel, 92, 154
Kearney, Richard, 214n30
Keegan, Dennis: "sacrifice of sacrifice," 25
Khārijites (seceders): as models for Islamic reformers, 177
Khuri, Fuad, 182, 183
Kierkegaard, Søren, 15, 53, 58, 160; Fear and Trembling, 163
Kimball, Charles, 209–210
King, Martin Luther, Jr.: moral authority of sacrificial love, 150–153
Koester, Helmut, 220n12
Kołakowski, Leszek: "metaphysical horror," 10
Kripal, Jeffrey J., 221n24
Kugle, Scott, 227n69

Laiter, Shaul: director of Ascent, 84
Lefkowitz, Mary, 126
Levenson, Jon D., 5, 48, 51, 57–58
Levinas, Emmanuel, 50, 57
Levy, Barry, 84
Lincoln, Abraham, 149
Lings, Martin, 185
Luria, Isaac, 78–81, 83, 93; death as ascent of, 84
Luther, Martin, 103; denial of Mass as sacrifice by, 143–144

Magdalene, Mary, 3, 117
Maimonides, Moses, 67, 77
Martyrdom: in Christianity, 120–127; in Judaism, 226n45; in Shiʿa Islam, 175–185; in Sunni Islam, 174, 204
Mauss, Marcel, 13; sacrifice as gift exchange, 20–21, 29
al-Mawdūdī, Sayyid Abu-l-Aʿlā, 202
McClymond, Kathryn, 23, 63–64, 215n43

ABOUT THE AUTHOR

David L. Weddle is Professor Emeritus of Religion at Colorado College, where he taught courses in philosophy of religion, ethics, comparative religious studies, and American religions. He is the author of *Miracles: Wonder and Meaning in World Religions* (NYU Press, 2010) and holds lifetime honorary membership in the American Academy of Religion.